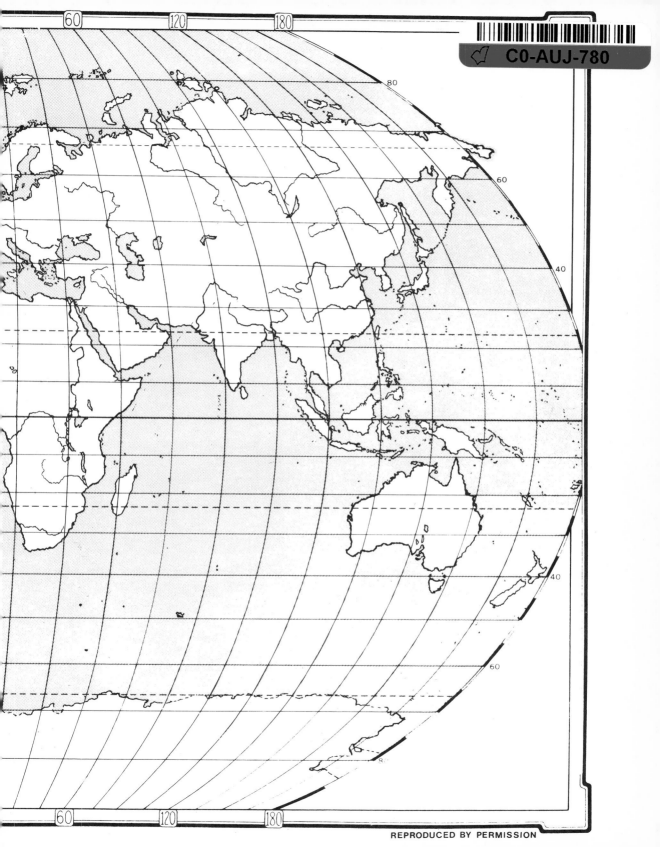

C0-AUJ-780

REPRODUCED BY PERMISSION

BOARD OF TRUSTEES

Ernest Brooks, Jr.
Chairman
William H. Whyte, Jr.
Vice Chairman
T. F. Bradshaw
John A. Bross
Louise B. Cullman
Maitland A. Edey
Charles H. W. Foster
David M. Gates
Charles Grace
D. Robert Graham
Nixon Griffis
Philip G. Hammer
Walter E. Hoadley
William T. Lake
Richard D. Lamm
Melvin B. Lane
Lord Llewelyn-Davies
Cruz Matos
David Hunter McAlpin
Tom McCall
Eugene Odum
Richard B. Ogilvie
James W. Rouse
William D. Ruckelshaus
Anne P. Sidamon-Eristoff
George H. Taber
Barbara Ward (Baroness Jackson)
Pete Wilson

William K. Reilly
President

The Conservation Foundation is a non-profit research and communication organization dedicated to encouraging human conduct to sustain and enrich life on earth. Since its founding in 1948, it has attempted to provide intellectual leadership in the cause of wise management of the earth's resources. It is now focusing increasing attention on one of the critical issues of the day—how to use wisely that most basic resource, the land itself.

IN THE WAKE
OF THE TOURIST

IN THE WAKE
OF THE TOURIST

Managing Special Places in Eight Countries

by Fred P. Bosselman

THE CONSERVATION FOUNDATION
WASHINGTON, D.C.

0819394

In the Wake of the Tourist: Managing Special Places in Eight Countries is a product of the International Comparative Land-Use Project, established by The Conservation Foundation in 1974, with principal support from the German Marshall Fund of the United States, and additional assistance from the Ford Foundation, the Rockefeller Foundation, and others.

IN THE WAKE OF THE TOURIST
Managing Special Places in Eight Countries

Copyright © 1978 by The Conservation Foundation

Library of Congress Catalog Card Number: 78-65196

International Standard Book Number: 0-89164-051-7

All rights reserved. No part of this book may be reproduced in any form without the permission of The Conservation Foundation.

Jacket and book design by Sally A. Janin.

Maps by Deborah Carole.

Printed in the United States of America.

The Conservation Foundation
1717 Massachusetts Avenue, N.W.
Washington, D.C. 20036

ACKNOWLEDGMENTS

So many people have worked on this project it would be impossible to describe all of them and their contributions with appropriate superlatives. Therefore, my most sincere thanks to Pamela Baldwin, John Banta, Karen Bryan, David Callies, Paul DeStefano, Richard Ducker, Bill Duddleson, Chris Duerksen, John Gissberg, Gwen Harley, Sally Janin, Jerry Kline, George Lefcoe, Paula Loveland, Jacqueline Merikangus, Phyllis Myers, Jack Noble, Abraham Rabinovitch, Richard Roddewig, John Rosenberg, Shelly Rothschild, Dave Sleeper, Lewis Smith, Mary Stoik, Claudia Wilson, and Phoebe Wiley.

For their patience during the unconscionable amount of time I spent working on this project, I am most grateful to my wife, Kay, my children, Judy, Carol, and Mark, and all of my law partners.

Bill Reilly's support and consultation was invaluable throughout the project. And despite his impatience with my quotes from Gertrude Stein, Bob McCoy is an editor is an editor is an editor.

Finally, the evolution of my thinking during the course of this project was undoubtedly influenced by my good friends, the citizens of Sanibel, Florida.

Fred Bosselman
Evanston, Illinois
September 1978

CONTENTS

081939Ⴘ 53347

III PLANNING

IV MEDIATING

V PLACEMAKING

Introduction

by William K. Reilly

Fred Bosselman is the Johnny Appleseed of American land-use reformers. For 20 years he has crisscrossed the country providing advice to states and local governments about planning laws. As associate reporter of the Model Land Development Code of the American Law Institute, he has drafted an original, comprehensive model statute that formulates a new relationship between states and their localities in guiding and managing urban growth. The Bosselman stamp is on the Land and Water Management Act of the state of Florida, a law that adopts the principal elements of the ALI Model Code.

Not long after Bosselman had advised Florida on the drafting of its pioneering land-use law, I had occasion to ride in a car with him from Sarasota Airport to Sanibel Island. On the road to Port Charlotte, we passed through a long stretch of particularly tedious clutter, of fast-food stands, motels, drive-in banks, restaurants, gas stations, and car showrooms, all surrounded by asphalt lots. I asked, "When will we get to Florida?" He looked out the window and said, "In 10 years all of Florida could look like this, if people don't wake up." To be sure, the state's new land-use law would help protect some of its major, still pristine places. And that law would equip the state to control its largest new developments. But in the mind of its originator, this land-use reform could not be expected to conserve much of the state's open space against the economic forces and land owner expectations that were so evident along the road outside Sarasota. Nor could that law guarantee the survival of Florida's special character. Could any set of laws or plans help Florida conserve its special qualities?

This is the sort of question we had in mind when we conceived the International Comparative Land-Use Project, of which this book is a product. The project grew out of a dissatisfaction with land-use management in the United States and a desire to learn from the experience of other nations. The countryside in much of Europe is pastoral and beautiful, even near the larger cities. Crowded little countries have managed to create the deeply satisfying impression of space, order, and harmony by separating clearly their areas of bustle and stimulation and human vitality from their farms, woodlands, and meadows. How have they done it? What has it cost them? How have they resisted the settlement pressures

13

created by widespread automobile ownership? How do they plan and regulate land? Can the experience of countries similar in so many ways to the United States, with private property, free-market economies, relatively affluent people, high rates of housing construction, illuminate American problems and offer leads toward solutions?

We prepared a proposal to the German Marshall Fund of the United States, an American foundation established in 1972 by the Federal Republic of Germany as a memorial to the Marshall Plan. The Fund's grant to the International Comparative Land-Use Project was among its first and largest gifts, for which we are deeply grateful.

The proposal contemplated a project in eight countries: Australia, France, the Federal Republic of Germany, Israel, Japan, Mexico, the Netherlands, and the United Kingdom. Preliminary visits were made to the European countries and Israel by Professor George Lefcoe of the University of Southern California Law School. A research agenda was prepared, and eight staff members engaged, who reflected a variety of professional backgrounds, including law, planning, economics, ecology, and natural resources.

The eight researchers were dispatched to the project countries, to serve as resident staff for a year in most cases, and for more than two years in Japan. A coordinator, John Banta, oversaw the day-to-day administration of the project. In addition to Bosselman and Lefcoe, the senior staff included David Callies, now professor of law at the University of Hawaii, Jack Noble, vice president of The Conservation Foundation, and me as project director. Resident staff prepared detailed reports according to a set of task requirements prepared by the senior staff. Twice during the project everyone assembled, once in Washington and once in London. The project contemplated publication of four major books and a film. To date, 31 articles, four books, including this one, and a film have been completed and released. Two additional books, by Professor Lefcoe and me, are yet to come.

In the Wake of the Tourist: Managing Special Places in Eight Countries looks at what happens in places that attract tourists—at what makes these areas special, and how they have been affected by the impact of tourism. Tourism development will unquestionably continue, because more and more people want to enjoy the opportunities it provides. As Bosselman recognizes, however, tourists can destroy what attracts them, the very qualities that make a place special.

This dilemma is not unique to tourism, of course. Expanding cities may transform the countryside far more radically than some second homes and campgrounds. Yet one must welcome Bosselman's choice of tourism as the vehicle for exploring the development dilemma. For the places that tourists visit tend to be—certainly, all those discussed in this book are—especially attractive, and thus especially likely to be recognized as worthy of conservationists' concern. And since tourism itself depends on the continuing attractiveness of such areas, they are especially appropriate places to search for conservation methods.

One must also welcome the creative way in which the author has culled the overseas experience. He has not limited himself to the technician's search for imitable techniques, methodologies, and rules. Nor does he preach to us that other countries have all the answers. Rather, he examines the foreign experience, exploring both its similarities to and differences from our own, in search of general guidance and insight into American problems and their solution.

There was a time, as recently as a decade or two ago, when the United States seemed to have land-use problems that other countries had somehow avoided. American planners were often apologetic about their inability to provide the sort of orderly growth that Britain or the Netherlands or Scandinavia took for granted. Now, although other countries sometimes manage their land in ways that Americans must admire, the picture is less clear. Throughout the world the automobile is making nonsense of settlement patterns established 50 or more years ago. Not only the automobile, but air travel is increasing access to remote mountains and seashores, removing the best defense these areas have had, their very inaccessibility. The demands of affluence—for resorts and vacation homes as for single-family houses with gardens—are not easily denied. And some resulting problems described in this book—high-rise buildings disrupting the urban skyline, condominium construction altering the coast, summer homes transforming pastoral landscapes—do not respect national boundaries. Now, more than ever, looking abroad can help us to understand ourselves.

The approach of each nation to its land-use problems is, of course, shaped by its geography, history, and culture. Overseas land-use techniques, therefore, cannot simply be imported into the United States. Even so, foreign experience can help Americans to propose or evaluate innovative responses to their own problems.

Consider the experience of France and Mexico, as described in this book, with MIACA and FONATUR, powerful public agencies established to promote development. The coastal tourism projects of these agencies differed in an important respect from what one might have anticipated from purely private development. The agencies had vastly more power and scope to realize their intentions: their projects covered substantial areas and were grand in scale and comprehensive in execution. Had the agencies not been created, development would likely have been small-scale, piecemeal, accommodating many fewer people. (In fact, in the case of Cancún, on the coast of Yucatan, relative inaccessibility and lack of infrastructure might have precluded private development for some years.) Because the scale of their operation was so large, MIACA and FONATUR were able to conduct extensive planning and environmental studies. Nevertheless, MIACA initially proved vulnerable to market forces and compromised its policy against construction on beach dunes. In Cancún, a beautiful lagoon has been altered by extensive development, risking deterioration in the health and beauty of the waters, plants, and aquatic life. Nothing about these problems is peculiarly attributable to the public character of the developments, save the size of them. Nevertheless, it is instructive that the best intentions, substantial financing, great power, and careful planning did not immunize these developments against the market forces and economic pressures that afflict the private sector.

Bosselman also describes the frustrations of Dutch and British planners in trying to prevent the piecemeal development of the countryside of Zeeland and Devon. Even powerful and sophisticated systems for guiding urban growth are having difficulty casting fine enough nets to catch the odd new house here, the small camping settlement there, the little restaurant, the few new shops that cumulatively are altering the character of rural areas in contravention of government policy. That is not very encouraging to those concerned with land use in small towns and rural areas to which Americans are relocating in unprecedented numbers. But it is a useful reminder to those who would "solve" these problems by giving more power to planners.

As Bosselman repeatedly warns, even the most sophisticated methods of planning and controlling land cannot protect a public that does not know what it wants. He stresses the importance of public-participation methods. But what if citizens can't agree on what they want? What if many agree only on what they *don't* want (sprawl, for example, or blocked access to the coast) without providing guidance on what they *do* want instead? Countless American communities are wrestling with this problem. This book has something important to say to them.

Perhaps the abiding lesson of the book is that we should define what is unique, special, or most valued about a place and seek positively to conserve and enhance those qualities. This has not been the way of American urban policies, which have focused on slums, crime, and decay—in short, on what's worst rather than what's best. Nor has it been the way of traditional American land-use controls, with their emphasis on what is sanitary, if not exciting, safe, if not beautiful.

Communities across America, however, are now turning more of their attention to conserving what they value. People have begun to recognize urban areas as a focus for revitalization strategies in a number of American cities. And rural as well as urban communities are increasingly tailoring their plans and regulations to the uniqueness of nature and history rather than trying to force each area into a common mold of R-1 zones and streets designed for garbage trucks.

With the perspective of conservation, one does not ask what's wrong or what might go wrong. Instead, one asks what's working, what do people value, what will it take to enlist public and private cooperation in conserving and improving what's there already. The principal advantage of having, or believing that you have, a place that is special is that planning can begin from an agreed-upon point of reference. Consensus, always elusive in land-use planning, is more attainable when special qualities have been commonly recognized.

The special places discussed in this book are experiencing profound changes, from Ayers Rock in Australia to the island of Sylt in Germany, from Aquitaine to the slopes of Mt. Fuji. In the face of this change, Bosselman exhorts tourists to be more sensitive to the places they visit, more demanding of sensitive planning and more alert to the consequences of their actions. Although the one-time visitor may have only limited influence, the tourism developer has both the opportunity and the responsibility to enhance the special qualities of the place in which he works. The planner who guides and monitors his work shares that opportunity and responsibility. All can profit from the examples of the places that built on their dunes and lost their beaches, that overbuilt and lost their character, that forgot what made them special and became ordinary.

From countless such places the world over, people have withdrawn. Eventually, the tourist does judge and act. And, fortunately for the future of planning in special places, the interests of tourists—and thus of tourism developers—can

further sound planning, conservation, and a high standard of environmental
protection. This is what has permitted Fred Bosselman to confront staggering
changes and nevertheless write a hopeful, even optimistic book.

Washington, D.C.
September 1978

Prologue
Jerusalem—The Tourists' Gifts

Before King David and his followers conquered Jerusalem 3,000 years ago—they surprised and overpowered its defenders by emerging from a water tunnel—the small village had seemed invulnerable. Built atop a series of hills and ridges, and surrounded by deep ravines, it lay secluded and unrenowned in the arid mountains. Today, the city is renowned and vulnerable not only to enemies, but to would-be friends.

Jerusalem contains the greatest variety of religiously significant buildings found anywhere in the world. For some, the city appears "full of horrible tourist churches and monuments raised by every sect and every religion, the symbol of diversity and spiritual falsehood."[1] For many people, however, the diversity of the city's religious heritage is the essence of Jerusalem's greatness.

Sacred to three major religions and dozens of religious sects, Jerusalem contains, within a stone's throw of one another, the Western Wall, the Church of the Holy Sepulchre, and the Muslim holy precinct where "a prayer is worth ten thousand prayers." It is the city where, in the centuries following David's conquest, Solomon built his temple, Jesus preached and died, and Muhammad made his miraculous night visit and ascended to heaven. Churches, mosques, and temples proliferate in bewildering variety. The narrow, twisting streets are a meeting place for pilgrims of many faiths.

The pilgrim's first view of the Jerusalem skyline is one of the most dominant images in travel literature. Even Mark Twain felt the impact:

> We toiled up one more hill, and every pilgrim and every sinner swung his hat on high! Jerusalem! Perched on its eternal hills, white and domed and solid, massed together and hooped with high gray walls, the venerable city gleamed in the sun.[2]

Buildings throughout the city are marked by differences in style, but unified by color and texture. A description of the anatomy of Jerusalem must invariably emphasize the solid massiveness of its stone, the native rock which attracted early settlers to the site.[3] This "stony metropolis of stones," as Herman Melville

---

Field research for this chapter was conducted by Abraham Rabinovitch and Shelly Rothschild.

View of Jerusalem from the top of the Plaza Hotel. (Photo by author.)

called it, seemed almost part of the earth itself—more a creation of God than of man:

> Overlooked, the houses sloped from him—
> Terraced or domed, unchimnied, gray,
> All stone—a moor of roofs. No play
> Of life; no smoke went up, no sound
> Except low hum, and that half drowned.[4]

Jerusalem's oldest buildings—the great blocks of the Western Wall, ramparts of the Turks and Crusaders, even the uncovered sections of David's original city—were all constructed of the same earth-colored rock. Later, ordinances required that it be used for the street frontage of every house. Thus, the strolling visitor will find the city relatively uniform in color, and in height as well. Most of the residences face inward on courtyards, creating a "back door" atmosphere.[5]

Only from a distance can one perceive Jerusalem as a whole—its skyline a unique combination of mosques, churches, and temples, ruins from Crusader times, and myriad low buildings, uniformly sandy in color. Most of the buildings have the "economical and repetitive forms" that characteristically give Mediterranean architecture the appearance of having been "developed organically," not created by individual men.[6] Providing accents to this repetition are the domes and towers of the religious institutions. The combination has long given Jerusalem an aura of permanence.

Incorrigible Pilgrims

In recent years, Jerusalem's skyline has been broken by high-rise hotels, each designed to give tourists a panoramic view. The visitor ends up seeing Jerusalem seeing Jerusalem, the view becoming increasingly mundane with each new hotel.

Is tourism a destructive activity? That question arises many times in this book. The reputation of tourism has suffered, in part, because tourist facilities often create adverse changes. While tourism may also bring economic benefits and foster cultural attractions, the unwelcome changes are frequent enough to tarnish tourism's name.

This book examines how tourism development changes places, and how people try to control those changes. Also considered are ways of thinking about places that will help ensure that tourism development enhances, rather than destroys, the qualities the tourist seeks.

Tourism is an important part of modern life. Residents of developed countries, their wants for material goods abating, are opting for more leisure time and more travel. Once a luxury for the rich, tourism is now commonplace among all but the very poor. In developing countries, too, people have begun to turn to tourism once their basic needs are satisfied.

The tarnished reputation of tourism is not new: "The incorrigible pilgrims have come in with their pockets full of specimens broken from the ruins," wrote Mark Twain in *Innocents Abroad*. "Heaven protect the Sepulchre when this tribe invades Jerusalem."[7] The following chapters discuss, in part, how tourism has contributed to fouling the waters of Fuji's lakes and Zeeland's canals, bringing noise and litter to the quiet streets of Bayswater, eroding the dunes of Aquitaine, destroying herons and turtles in Cancún, defiling Australian aborigine shrines, filling the streets of Westerland with carbon monoxide, and disrupting the peace and quiet of old Amsterdam.

The world offers many examples for those who inveigh against tourism as a malign force. In their book *The Golden Hordes*, Louis Turner and John Ash call tourism a new form of colonialism in which "the rich of the world fan out through the poorer countries looking for areas to colonize which are pleasanter than their existing homes."[8] In *The Image*, Daniel Boorstin has accused tourists of destroying the authenticity of the cultures they visit.[9]

It is easy to understand the pessimism expressed by the noted British economist E. J. Mishan. The basic human motivation, he says, is greed: "Greed pulses through our psyche as naturally as blood through our veins."[10] Given this motivation, Mishan suggests that the more people are made aware of tourism's potential for destruction, the more each individual will rush to get to an attractive spot before it's too late. The individual tourist will recognize "that any personal sacrifice he makes will have no practical effect in reducing mass tourism. . . . If anything, there is an incentive for him to travel the sooner, and the more frequently, before the potential tourist haunt in question is irredeemably ruined."[11]

But tourism can also create benefits for the place being visited. Insofar as the tourist seeks the beautiful, the exciting, or the authentic, the economic benefits he brings may provide the incentive to create and maintain these qualities.

Tourism has provided a major source of support for the arts and other cultural activities, and contributed substantially to the preservation of historical areas. Religious organizations often find in tourism an opportunity to spread their spiritual message, and, in some cases, receive substantial financial assistance from tourists for preservation of religious buildings and sites.

For the natural environment as well, the tourist's desire to learn can be a constructive force. "That thing called nature study," wrote Aldo Leopold, "despite the shiver it brings to the spines of the elect, constitutes the first embryonic groping of the mass-mind toward perception."[12] Scientists may scoff at the simple lover of nature, but the support of such people is an essential factor in preserving natural areas.

Organizations such as the International Union for the Conservation of Nature (IUCN) recognize that tourism can be used to educate more people in the need for natural areas. The educated tourist may support preservation of those types of natural areas where, as IUCN former director Gerardo Budowski puts it, "a symbiotic relationship exists between tourism and conservation," with all the physical, cultural, ethical, and economic benefits that such a relationship affords.[13]

In Israel's Lake Kinneret region (see chapter 10), an attempt is being made to develop just this sort of symbiotic relationship. The hotel boom in Jerusalem, however, took place at a time when the potential hazards of tourism were either unknown or ignored, while its economic benefits were eagerly anticipated.

Welcome to the Holy Land

In the 1950s, the Israelis were among those who recognized that tourism was about to begin a worldwide boom. Israel, born out of a prolonged conflict and maintaining a wartime economy with limited natural resources, had imports amounting to about twice its exports. To improve the balance of trade, an extensive campaign was launched to promote tourism.

At the time, tourism had been touted worldwide as a trouble-free way to achieve what Israel wanted. Tourism, it was argued, brought in spenders who created few demands on the local economy; it depleted few natural resources, created minimal pollution, and required little in the way of special training or education of the local people. Developed and developing countries alike were sold tourism plans as painless therapy for economic problems.

The logic was simple. Tourists' money comes from outside a region and is spent in the region. Therefore, it is similar to an export of goods that brings in foreign currency and helps the balance of payments. Economists also credit tourism with a "multiplier effect" that magnifies the benefits substantially. The multiplier represents the second level of spending of the tourists' money—for example, a taxi driver buying groceries for his family at the local store. When money spent by tourists, enhanced by this multiplier, is balanced against the direct costs of providing the facilities and services necessary to attract tourists, the economists' cost-benefit analyses typically show tourism producing a substantial net benefit.

Israeli economists strongly encouraged tourism development. Before the economic potential of tourism could be achieved, however, certain handicaps had to be overcome.

In the first place, when major promotion of tourism was initially considered, many important religious sites of the Holy Land were located in Jordan—including the Old City of Jerusalem. Travel between the two countries was possible, but only with awkward restrictions.

Moreover, the tension that has pervaded the Middle East since the 1940s, with the possibility of guerrilla attack or even war, has deterred some tourists from visiting Israel (though sympathy with Israel's problems has undoubtedly drawn tourists as well). And it is expensive to get to Israel and to stay there. The country is far from its main tourist suppliers, northern Europe and the United States; until 1976, the government-owned airline, El Al, prohibited competing charter flights, making costs even greater than to other destinations of equal distance. Also, the Israeli workers' relatively high standard of living is reflected in prices for hotels and services.

By reputation at least, the services for tourists in Israel leave much to be desired. Waiters almost pride themselves on their stereotype of being unhelpful and nasty. Some Israelis resent wealthy Jewish visitors who won't risk their lives or economic well-being by making a permanent move.

Finally, traditional tourism in Israel is seasonal, basically concentrated in

The walls of the Old City of Jerusalem. (Photo by author.)

the summer months and during major religious holidays. In winter, hotels are often two-thirds empty. As a result, places full in season have a low annual rate of occupancy, cutting into profits. The hotels lay off employees during the slow months, and have difficulty finding staff because of the fear of job instability.

Most of Israel's traditional tourists come to visit the archaeological, historical, or religious sites, or because they identify with the Zionist cause. While continuing to welcome these tourists, since the late 1950s the Israeli government has tried to attract more of the millions of potential "holiday makers" who choose vacation spots for neither historical nor political reasons.

To increase tourism, the Israeli Ministry of Tourism has encouraged development of "sun and sand" hotels. The government has aided most major projects through low-interest loans, grants, and tax benefits. Since 1958, government loans have supplied some 44.5 percent of the total investment in tourism. Of Israel's hotels built during that period, 90 percent have received such loans, in amounts up to 67 percent of the net investment, at an interest rate of as low as 6.5 percent.[14] In contrast, because of the high rate of inflation, Israeli banks have charged up to 36 percent interest on loans.

Public land often is sold or leased to hotel developers at reduced rates. Grants are given for purchase of Israeli-made equipment (15 percent of value) and infrastructure (10 percent of cost). Income tax, property tax, customs duty, purchase tax, excise levies—all are substantially reduced. The government often builds new roads and sewers to facilitate hotel construction.[15]*

This subsidy program—and a quick victory in the 1967 war—improved the investment atmosphere in Israel. Hotel facilities, subsidized by government incentives and serving a tremendous tourist influx, expanded rapidly between 1967 and 1973. By 1973, when a new war sobered investors, the number of hotel rooms was almost double what it had been in 1967.[18] Tourism had brought in more foreign currency in real terms than any other part of the Israeli economy.[19] In 1972, the Tourism Ministry claimed that the 720,000 tourists increased the purchasing power of Israel's population by 30 percent.[20]

Service industries, like restaurants, shops, taxis, and night clubs, have unquestionably benefited, as have the clothing, jewelry, and handicraft industries. Tourists become acquainted with Israeli brand names (Gottex swim suits, Beged-Or suede clothes) and continue to buy the products on returning home, increasing Israel's exports. Moshe Kol, Minister of Tourism, declared that the tourist dollar had an average added value of 85 percent in 1976.[21]

---

*Israel's subsidy program is by no means unusual. Many developing countries, such as Morocco, Kenya, and Thailand, have worked hard to promote tourism. Hotels, considered a high-risk investment even in stable developed nations, have proved difficult to attract. In untried markets, developers would look for a return in the range of 20 to 25 percent before becoming interested. Thus, a subsidy is often deemed necessary to sweeten the return of 10 percent or so that might otherwise reasonably be anticipated from hotel investment.[16]

In Tunisia, for example, foreign hotel developers have been granted a five-year exemption from the corporate income tax and property tax and a guarantee against an increase in all taxes for 25 years. The government guarantees a bank loan for half the cost of construction and will provide the remainder at favorable rates from government development banks. The developer is promised unlimited rights to take his capital and profits out of the country and to convert the local currency. In addition, the government provides public utilities and other infrastructure without charge. "Short of the Minister of Tourism personally undertaking to change the sheets, it is difficult to imagine more favorable treatment," comments George Young, a British economist, in his book *Tourism: Blessing or Blight?*[17]

Ü219394

Beyond these benefits, the government sees tourism as strengthening Israel's links with Jews around the world, ensuring financial and political support in case of war, and encouraging immigration. Tourists who indicate interest in becoming immigrants are given a low-key, but carefully developed, sales pitch. A survey found that 20 percent of the people visiting Israel were thinking about immigrating.[22]

Tourism also brings outsiders into contact with the issues in dispute in the Middle East.

And, finally, tourism is seen as a potential stimulant to the growth of Israel's underdeveloped areas, reducing the pressure on the overcrowded Mediterranean coast. The development of new areas as tourist centers increases opportunities for investment and employment. For example, in Eilat, a town on the Red Sea developed since 1948, 40 percent of all workers are employed in the tourist industry.[23]

A New Jerusalem

Despite the benefits that tourism has brought to Israel, uncertainty remains about the long-term impact of the government's tourism-development program. In Jerusalem, if the qualities that attract tourists are destroyed, will the immediate benefits of tourism seem insignificant in comparison?

As an attraction, Jerusalem is unmatched. Its physical beauty complements its unique historical and religious significance. Only the most unfeeling visitor can be unmoved by a view of the city's monuments and homes, clustered snugly among the brown hills.

In the opinion of Paul Goldberger, *New York Times* architecture critic, Jerusalem prior to 1967 was "one of the most remarkable cases of city and nature in dialogue with each other." It represented "a very delicate balance, capable of being damaged far more seriously by insensitive building than more resilient urban landscapes such as New York's or Los Angeles'."[24]

In the euphoria following the 1967 war, developers insisted that modern generations had not only the right, but the obligation, to add their own contribution to Jerusalem's architectural history. The city was destined to be transformed into a modern international capital, they argued, and should be designed according to universally valid modern architectural principles. Jerusalem's quaint and pastoral image was thought to be inadequate for its new importance.[25]

The tourism subsidy program produced a network of complex interrelationships between the Ministry of Tourism and private developers. The need to protect the government's investment gave the ministry a vested interest in the success of each hotel development. Consequently, the ministry has often persuaded planning authorities to amend the local plan or waive height, density, or appearance regulations.

For a number of years this philosophy of development held sway. Tall hotels, apartments, and office buildings sprang up throughout Jerusalem. Citizens at first were proud of the new development. Then, as the shape and effect of the buildings became apparent, pride gave way to outrage. The result of the special favors to hotel builders had left its mark on the city.

To most Israelis, probably the most offensive example of new development is the Plaza Hotel. A city hall was originally planned for the site where the hotel

The Plaza Hotel, viewed from the walls of the Old City. (Photo by author.)

stands, but plans were changed and the land sold to a private developer. The site was rather special. The 22-story Plaza is right in the middle of Jerusalem's finest city park. The hotel has been described by Goldberger as a "bloated version of a Miami Beach tower." Jerusalem Mayor Teddy Kollek called the Plaza "the height of ugliness."[26]

It is not alone. The Jerusalem Hilton now dominates the western sections of the city, towering over such earlier architectural landmarks as the Knesset and the Israel Museum, which were designed to blend with the landscape, not dominate it.

Near the walls of the Old City, the Jerusalem Tower hotel resembles the worst of American public housing. El Al received permission to build a hotel on land destined originally for a public park, despite objections that the structure would create traffic congestion and increase noise levels in a quiet residential area.* All of these approvals followed Ministry of Tourism threats that foreign investors would be angered and would not invest in hotel developments unless the city waived all regulations.

Despite controversy, the ministry continues to seek even higher subsidies for more hotel development.[27] It views the shortage of skilled manpower as the only factor hampering a virtually unlimited growth of the tourist industry.[28]

Arthur Kutcher, a Jerusalem city planner who objected to the city's high-rise policies and lost his job, has written as follows of tourism ministry practices:

> Ministerial officials receive word that a foreign investor is in town, who is interested in building a large luxury hotel. The man is invited to lunch, and after they have been assured to their satisfaction that he is actually prepared to build a mammoth luxury hotel just like those in Miami Beach, the officials take the man for a little drive around the city. He is shown four or five of the city's breathtaking panoramic views, all on public open space, and is then asked which he would prefer. He chooses, the deal is sealed, and shortly thereafter the legal planning committees make their mark on the official document. . . . [The government and municipal officials] realize that Jerusalem can probably never rival Manhattan. So they have set their sights a bit lower. Their dream of Jerusalem is a sort of copy of Kansas City.[29]

Mayor Kollek realizes that the city made some terrible mistakes in the 1967-73 period. Today, new development proposals are scrutinized much more closely. But, says Kollek, "I can't see why three- or four-story houses are necessarily more beautiful than eight-story buildings."[30] Jerusalem faces the same demands for clean, economical buildings as any other city. Can it afford to hamper itself by restricting the use of efficient, high-rise construction?

Yet what is the value of a city's image? The picturesque view of Jerusalem seen by tourists a few years ago has vanished. It took only a few high-rise hotels to transform a romantic vista, in which one could dream of prophets, camel trains, and Crusaders, into the prospect of a middle-sized town in a developing country. Was this transformation a necessary part of a program to attract tourists?

What Price Tourism?

There are questions raised by the Israeli experience that have been raised throughout the world, and that will recur in the following chapters. Of particular concern to many is the question of subsidization—in relation to the costs and benefits of tourism, and in relation to planning.

People increasingly wonder whether it is really necessary to grant subsidies, low-interest loans, and tax concessions to attract tourist development. For example, most Caribbean countries offer extensive inducements to foreign hotel developers, typically giving them a 10-year tax holiday with no personal or corporate income tax paid on profits during that period. In addition, hotels are granted substantial, if not complete, exemptions from import duties on materials used in construction and operation. Having studied the use of such incentives in these countries, economist John Bryden concluded that there was "little doubt in

---

*Public pressure, fortunately, has thwarted some particularly offensive developments. The Ministry of Tourism pressured Hebrew University to cede land so that a Hyatt House hotel might be built on Mount Scopus. Despite numerous objections on environmental and aesthetic grounds, and although it violated Jerusalem's town plan, local and district planning authorities approved the hotel. At the national level, however, the proposed hotel was finally disapproved.

53347

The Old City—and new construction. (Illustration by Arthur Kutcher, from The New
Jerusalem: Planning and Politics, published by Thames & Hudson, London, and the
M.I.T. Press, Cambridge, Mass., 1975.)

most people's minds that a substantial proportion of investment in hotels would
have taken place even in the absence of incentives, or at any rate with substantially reduced incentives." He found that the incentives tended to attract
speculative investors who sold out at the end of the tax-holiday period to obtain
large, untaxed capital gains.[31] Other countries have had similar experiences.

Responsible segments of the industry agree that no nation should think of
tourism as a panacea. Nevertheless, in both developed and developing countries,
tourism continues to be sold, as it was in Israel, as a means of improving the
balance of trade. This has produced a substantial backlash, with some critics
arguing that the costs of tourism have been underestimated and the benefits
exaggerated.

The scope of the industry is significant. Throughout the world, more people
are traveling, and they are traveling longer distances. In the United States,
expenditures for tourism (in constant dollars) increased 65 percent between
1960 and 1970, while the share spent on transportation increased at an even
greater rate.[32] The growth of international tourism expenditures has been even
more rapid, doubling between 1968 and 1976.[33] European member countries of

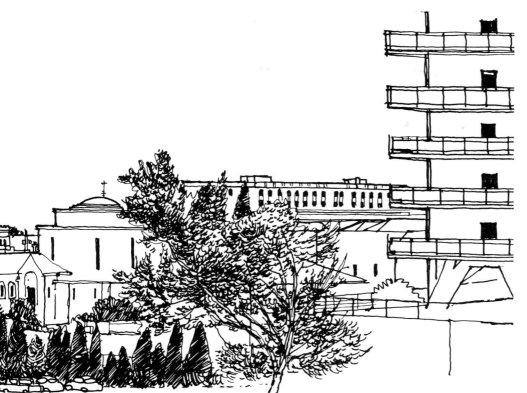

the OECD reported a 239 percent increase in international tourism receipts between 1962 and 1972.[34] By 1976 these countries reported over $25,000,000,000 in receipts for the year from tourists from other countries.[35]

To the tourist, travel is fun. But in the places he visits, tourism is a business—the largest single item in the world's foreign trade, and increasing in importance every year.[36] It should not be surprising, therefore, that many countries cherish a popular tourist attraction in much the same way as they would cherish an oil field or a copper mine: as a valuable national asset. The thought of the billions of dollars tourists spend brings a gleam to the eye of businessmen and governments all over the world. If it's going to be spent, they feel, why not here?

But sorting out the costs and benefits of tourism poses many questions. A Caribbean island must build a jet airport if it is to attract tourists. Should the expense of this airport be treated as a cost of tourism? Or as a lasting benefit to residents of the island who can use the airport? Again, chapter 1 discusses the major Mexican tourist development of Cancún, where sewers have been installed not only for hotels but for an adjacent community that houses the local labor force. Should the expense of these sewers be treated as a cost imposed by tourism or a benefit brought by it?

Aside from problems of allocation, critics argue that benefits from tourism have been exaggerated because promoters usually assume that a large share of the tourist's money will stay where it is first spent. Actually, much of it can go elsewhere. If enough tourists insist on the same things they had at home, and these are not locally available, the dollars brought to a country may have to go out again to pay for imports.

Food is a typical example. Will tourists eat local commodities, or will they insist on the type of imported food to which they are accustomed? After a visit to Majorca, the British conservationist Lord Duncan-Sandys commented: "I was horrified in Palma to see all along the beach great notices advertising 'Tea as Mum Makes It.' "[37] Although veteran travelers might recoil from the thought of eating their native food in foreign countries—of being caught sneaking into a Colonel Sanders in Paris—the tourist industry believes that most tourists want to see exotic sights only in the context of familiar food and surroundings.[38]

Depending on a number of factors, including the extent to which a country has a well-balanced agricultural industry and a highly regarded cuisine, the amount spent on imports will vary greatly. France and Italy, for example,

TV antennas sprout from roofs of old homes. (Photo by Valerie Callies.)

probably import only a small amount of food for tourists; on smaller Caribbean islands, almost 100 percent of the food may be imported.

Critics argue that the rapid growth of package tours has likewise affected economic benefits. Organizers and agents located in the country from which the tour originates may be in a competitive position to drive down prices in the destination country and bargain for an increasingly larger share of a smaller tourist dollar.[39] Hotel operators in the Bayswater area of London (discussed in chapter 7), who cater to package tours from the continent, often complain that tours have been priced so low that they attract people who spend very little money beyond their basic investment.

Two other factors are cited as operating against economic benefits from tourism development—namely, multinational corporations and foreign labor. Critics believe that multinationals divert a large share of tourists' money to the corporation's home territory. Although the extent to which this occurs varies, it is often a point of friction. As to personnel, in many developing nations the experienced hotel administrators come from outside the country, while in countries such as England and northern Europe low-paid labor unattractive to local residents is often undertaken by foreign workers. In one of London's leading hotels, for example, about 75 percent of the staff at one time came from overseas.[40] The presence of foreign workers, whether at the high or low end of the wage scale, is seen by people native to the area as diluting their own economic gains.

Where, then, does the tourist dollar go? Does it make tourism a profitable investment in light of the associated costs? The answer depends on the individual case. Perhaps, as George Young suggests, for Mauritius, isolated in the Indian Ocean, it is only 10 percent of the tourist's dollar that sticks.[41] But for a country that has few other opportunities for economic advancement, 10 percent of something may be better than 100 percent of nothing.

In reality, such computations have little meaning. Serious disadvantages are sometimes found beyond the scope of this kind of traditional economic analysis, and these unquantified disadvantages often have been ignored—as Jerusalem's experience demonstrates.

The Environment of Tourism

The basic problem with most tourist subsidy programs has been a tendency to concentrate on easily quantified values: if 1,000 tourists bring in x dollars, then 2,000 tourists will bring in 2x dollars, and 100,000 tourists will bring in 100x dollars. More subtle qualitative values tend to be submerged under the logic of such simple equations. Even when a government has strong programs for preserving community character and protecting environmental quality, the establishment of numerical goals and quotas can pressure the enforcing agencies to give ground.

Thus, in Jerusalem, tourism officials seeking to achieve numerical goals strong-armed municipal authorities into giving away public parks to hotel developers, who were allowed to destroy the appearance of the city. In retrospect, it seems unlikely that these concessions were necessary to acquire additional hotel rooms in Jerusalem. Many more tourists than now visit the Holy City could be accommodated in smaller hotels that fit the scale of the landscape. It

The Hilton Hotel seen from the construction site of new high-rise apartments. (Photo by author.)

was the random scattering of subsidies and incentives, together with the effective removal of planning controls, that caused the change. And the tourism industry must bear a share of the blame for being unconscious of its impact on the environment.

The industry, to be sure, is very conscious that tourist attractions are subject to depletion. Everyone is familiar with places that have declined as a result of overdevelopment. A 1973 Conservation Foundation study noted:

> . . . despite the demand for various sophisticated facilities which often accompanies it, tourism is basically dependent on unspoilt environment. In most other types of development, some environmental values have to be sacrificed in return for expected benefits, but for tourism the maintenance of these values at a high level is essential. Well-planned tourism can in fact help both to justify and safeguard the quality of the environment.[42]

The tourism developer cannot regard his attention to environmental considerations as a grudging concession to public pressure. He must treat the protection of environmental quality as an "internality"—a cost of doing business that feeds back into the long-range profitability of his hotel, campground, or resort. Different segments of the tourist industry vary greatly in their responsiveness to environmental issues, but most of the industry is well aware that at some point overcrowding and overdevelopment can cause an area to be perceived by tourists as less desirable.

Why doesn't the tourism industry's dependence on maintaining desirable environmental qualities provide a self-regulating mechanism? If it did, government could promote and subsidize tourism, confident the industry itself would see that quality was maintained in order to maximize income.

Unfortunately, a hotel like the Jerusalem Plaza, while an abomination to most residents of that city, is an unknown quantity to the average tourist from New York or Stockholm. That tourist is unlikely to ask his travel agent to select different accommodations unless he is unusually sophisticated. And if the tourism industry should suffer because Jerusalem becomes less desirable, the older, less modern hotels will probably bear the brunt of the loss.

The fact that the tourist industry as a whole may eventually suffer from the excesses of certain developers is unlikely to deter these developers from attempting to maximize immediate gains.[43] Consequently, deficiencies of the market have spurred a search for ways to strengthen control over the development process. Different approaches to this objective will be examined in the following chapters.

In Israel, tourism development should be a matter of high national priority. The Ministry of Tourism, however, still shows little concern for the fact that its policies threaten the very values that make Israel a tourist attraction. Only the vocal objections of Israeli citizens, and the watchful eye of other government ministries, have prevented even greater depredations.

Fortunately, the charm of Jerusalem has not entirely disappeared. Up close, it still has a unique magic, though touched with the knowledge that beauty is fragile. "Jerusalem is still Jerusalem, and God's coming city has no other name," writes Jacques Ellul. "She is ever, by her history, the surety of the promise that a new Jerusalem is coming."[44]

1 BUILDING

Chapter 1
Mexico Reaches for the Moon

Mexican tourism has been symbolized for years by Acapulco. In 1928, when it was linked to Mexico City by a highway, Acapulco became fashionable among adventurers who sought an inexpensive tropical hideaway. In 1940, J. Paul Getty reportedly purchased 900 acres at the now-famous resort at three cents an acre.[1] In those days, after a harrowing drive over rough mountains, a visitor was rewarded at the road's last turn with a view of one of the world's most exquisite natural sites—a beautiful bay facing the winter sun, lush green jungles on steep slopes contrasting sharply with sparkling blue waters.

The Acapulco of today is primarily a post-World War II phenomenon. In the 1950s, it began to attract substantial numbers of both Mexican and foreign tourists. Hotel construction proceeded rapidly in the 1960s and early 1970s, as developers were offered favorable tax treatment, with few rules imposed on new construction. By 1972, a million and a half visitors annually filled the city's 12,000 hotel rooms.[2]

The resident population has grown even faster than the number of visitors, with estimates ranging up to a 20-percent increase per year. People from rural areas have migrated to Acapulco looking for work. Their makeshift residences cover the hills. Now, the once-quiet fishing village has a permanent population of 300,000. Although unemployment is very high, and many people end up hawking rugs and begging pesos, the influx continues.

Unabashed luxury was designed into the Acapulco hotels. The adjacent town just grew. The lean-tos dotting the hills are unserviced by sewers, potable water, electricity, schools, or recreation facilities. Public health is poor. An open canal in the town carries runoff to the bay, while the hotels plan and build their own services. "There is no sense of community here, no sense that what one hotel does affects everybody. This place is private enterprise gone mad," a local businessman has complained.

The Bay of Acapulco, with its stretches of wide beach, is obscured by development. The green hills are pitted with erosion. There are no breathing spaces of greenery. In fact, even gardens and flowers are rare.

Field research for this chapter was conducted by Phyllis Myers and Lewis J. Smith.

Although a 1972 government study of Acapulco anticipated an annual growth rate of tourism of 7.4 to 9 percent, the rate of growth has leveled off.[3] Has the glamour of Acapulco begun to fade? Mexican officials, while loath to admit that publicly, are worried. For the showpiece of international resorts has been a source of national pride as well as a money-making machine. Perhaps Acapulco is a victim of worldwide recession. On the other hand, it may well be that tourists are beginning to be offended by the polluted ocean and the raucous jumble of high-rise hotels and fast-food restaurants.

In the mid-1970s, a Plan Acapulco was developed under the joint administration of several of Mexico's federal ministries. The plan's main emphasis is sewage treatment, but it ranges over many areas and has led to such im-

Acapulco. (Photo courtesy Mexican National Tourist Council.)

provements as a local bus system, new infrastructure, upgrading of the local market, a tourist institute for training hotel workers, and houses for low-income people.

The rapid growth of Acapulco, however, makes the pace of progress seem painfully slow. Putting in services today that should have been put in many years ago is costly and disruptive. And when the status of a tourist center begins to decline, it is usually a one-way process. For some things, like much of the natural environment, it is clearly too late.

Starting from Scratch

Subsidies without planning can produce unfortunate consequences. The city officials of Jerusalem and Acapulco no doubt would agree that, while they are not sorry they attracted tourists, they should have planned more carefully for tourism development.

Enough examples like Jerusalem and Acapulco can be found so that many countries now recognize the dangers inherent in incentives not accompanied by planning. In some places, governments have reacted by withdrawing the incentives and not encouraging tourism. More commonly, however, attempts are made to encourage tourism with more forethought given to the consequences. Some governments, for example, have chosen to develop major new tourist destinations by assigning responsibility for all phases of planning and development to a single agency. Long-term planning and control of extensive space by this kind of authority would seem to offer excellent opportunities for minimizing adverse environmental impacts.

In 1969, Mexico began to concentrate on building large-scale new facilities to siphon off some of the potentially dangerous overgrowth of resorts like Acapulco. After an intensive two-year search, two sites were chosen for development: Cancún, an island off the isolated northeastern part of the Yucatan peninsula, and Ixtapa, 125 miles north of Acapulco on the Pacific Coast.

Financing for these projects was obtained from two international agencies: $21,500,000 for Cancún from the Inter-American Development Bank, and $22,000,000 for Ixtapa from the World Bank. These agencies emphasize the importance of helping the residents of the project area. The funds from the banks, providing half of the projected development costs, were targeted for infrastructure—international jetports, potable water, sewage treatment, roads, telephones, and electricity. At both Ixtapa and Cancún the infrastructure was designed to serve not only the tourist area but also a nearby service city. A World Bank official commented that the agency would not be interested in projects that were simply money-making machines for tourism. "We are only interested because of the broader implications for helping the people."

A New Development Authority

The ambitious efforts to create two new tourist cities raised many eyebrows in a country not historically known for effective planning and regulation of development. But by the mid-1970s Ixtapa and Cancún were in operation. As a result, worldwide attention has been attracted to FONATUR (*Fondo Nacional de Fomento al Turismo*), the Mexican tourism development authority largely re-

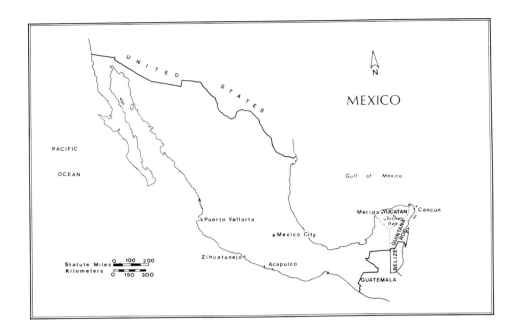

sponsible for the projects. Its success has given FONATUR an aura comparable to that which surrounded the United States space program after the first moon shots. "We took a great risk," says a FONATUR official, but learned that "we can do anything. We have gained a lot of credibility. We've gone to the moon. The next time it will take less time."

FONATUR's powers are broad. It may buy, develop, and sell land—subject, however, to the intricate system of laws designed to preserve the priorities of Mexican nationals and, particularly, small farmers. Beyond that, it depends heavily on its skill in orchestrating the activities of other federal and state agencies. And it has had two important assets. First, there was almost $50,000,000 in international money, an important lever in moving FONATUR priorities to the top of the list. ("We have *cabeza* and *poder*—intelligence and power," explains a FONATUR architect. "We would say, 'We have money for this. You come and do it.'") Second, an intangible but valuable asset, FONATUR had the strong personal support of Luis Echeverria, president of Mexico during the initial development of Cancún and Ixtapa. Intervention by the president's office was sometimes required to obtain cooperation from other powerful government ministries.

Ready financing and strong presidential support enabled FONATUR to undertake development projects speedily. With a skill reminiscent of Robert Moses, Enriquez Savignac, president of FONATUR, overcame many obstacles. The initial project, Cancún, was attracting tourists as early as 1974, and by the winter of 1978 visitors to its *zona turistica* could choose among a dozen hotels averaging about 100 rooms each. With a modern convention center, shops, golf courses, growing numbers of condominiums and vacation homes, and with advertising campaigns in both Europe and North America, Cancún has attracted a steady stream of tourists eager to see Mexico's new pot of gold. Coincidentally, *pot of gold* is the meaning of *cancún* in the language of the Mayan Indians, the original inhabitants of the Yucatan.

Mayan Nugget

When FONATUR selected Cancún for development, the golden qualities were not readily apparent to the 170 impoverished squatters who lived on the island. Nonetheless, Mexican officials saw the Caribbean coast of the Yucatan as an untapped mine.

The climate in this region is hot, but steady sea breezes cool its islands. Extensive periods of dryness sometimes last six months. During some parts of the year, there are torrents of rain. Because the soil in the area is shallow, however, drainage is rapid. The Yucatan coast shares the same ocean and climate as the West Indies, but with a less-turbulent political atmosphere and unique archaeological attractions.

Four major islands lie off the coast of northern Yucatan. Cozumel has had modest amounts of tourist traffic for years, and small numbers of tourists regularly enjoy the rustic simplicity of Isla Mujeres. When FONATUR considered the potential of the area, however, it was clear that the distance from shore of these islands would have made more extensive tourism development difficult. The northernmost island of the four, Contoy, is a national wildlife sanctuary.

Mangrove wetland being filled for development. (Photo by author.)

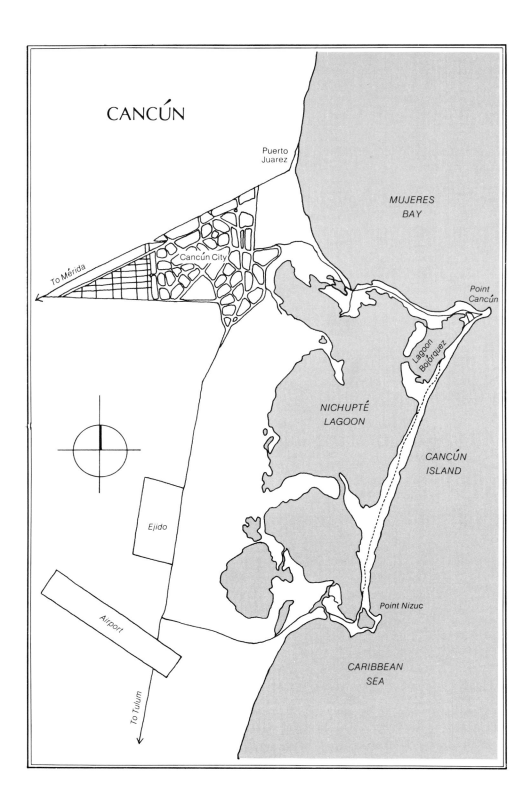

CANCÚN

Puerto
Juarez

MUJERES
BAY

To Mérida

Cancún City

Point
Cancún

Lagoon
Bojórquez

NICHUPTÉ
LAGOON

CANCÚN
ISLAND

Ejido

Point Nizuc

Airport

To Tulum

CARIBBEAN
SEA

The remaining island, Cancún, offered greater development potential. It was separated from the mainland only by a lagoon and extensive saltwater marshes, across which a causeway could easily provide access for vehicles.

A barrier island roughly one-quarter mile wide and 15 miles long, Cancún has a sandstone ridge as its backbone, giving it a stability that has helped it survive the hurricanes of many centuries. Dunes of sparkling white sand separate the ridge from the sea, while on the landward side mangroves cover a broad belt of marshland linking the island with the mainland. Within this marshland are two lagoons, Nichupté and Bojórquez, of substantial size and picturesque beauty.

Cancún is part of the state of Quintana Roo, which encompasses roughly the eastern half of the Yucatan peninsula. Quintana Roo is lightly populated, with narrow roads connecting the Mayan ruins that have long been the main attraction for visitors to the region. The houses are primitive and spaced farther and farther apart as one approaches Cancún from more populous western Yucatan.

To most people, the area appears scruffy, neglected, and ugly. John Stephens, who visited in 1841, called it "a barren strip of land" inhabited by "swarms of moschetoes, which pursued us with the same blood thirsty spirit that animated the Indians along this coast when they pursued the Spaniards."[4]

Where the land has remained undisturbed for many years it supports a dense forest. The sclerophyllous leaves of the trees and shrubs are adapted to a long dry season, giving the forest some resemblance to those in California or Australia. However, not much full-grown forest remains in Quintana Roo. The land has been used for "slash and burn" subsistence agriculture since the time of the early Mayans, who grew their corn in a field for three years, exhausted the thin topsoil, and moved on to burn another forest and begin another field. Behind them, they left grasses and shrubs to begin the centuries-long process of creating a new forest on the eroded land. "Nothing grows well here," says Jorge Gleeson, who managed FONATUR's development of Cancún.

Even what can be grown is no longer profitable. Chicle and hemp, for example, once were boom crops, but in the past two decades have declined on the world market. Fishing, too, is less productive than off other parts of Mexico's coast, leading Gleeson to ask, "What do we do with an area like this?"

Given these handicaps, it is easy to see why FONATUR officials compare the audacity of their decision to develop Cancún with going to the moon. Yet there is striking beauty in this corner of the Caribbean, and Cancún is accessible to affluent travelers in the eastern United States and Europe—only three hours from New York, less than two hours from Houston or Miami. Although the nearby Mayan ruins provide a special lure, the appearance of Cancún itself is the major attraction. The shading of the water, aquamarine blending into indigo, is dazzling; the beach is unrivaled, with 23 miles of pulverized white sand. A great variety of tropical birds and fish inhabit the areas.

Although FONATUR hoped to take advantage of Cancún's natural assets, it saw no need to preserve the natural environment as an entity. "We came to Cancún with an idea of good tourist development: good hot water, a golf course, a convention center," says Gleeson. "We used sound planning and set up stiff regulations on the size and shape of hotels. We knew on the basis of our economic analyses that hotels did not have to be big or look like Miami Beach to

Water skiing in the lagoon; Cancún Caribe Hotel in background. (Photo courtesy Cancún Information Bureau.)

make money. You don't have to ruin the area in order to be financially viable.''

For development purposes, Cancún's environment offered a stability and resiliency that barrier islands often lack. The sandstone ridge provided a solid foundation to protect buildings against storms and shifting sands. And the huge Nichupté lagoon, its fertility enhanced by many square miles of mangroves on the landward side, seemed large enough to withstand the impact of oil and other pollutants that would run off the streets, parking lots, and roofs of the hotel zone.

Sewage was to be piped to a central treatment plant located on the main golf course. After secondary treatment the sewage would be sprayed on the grass at night, providing needed moisture and nutrients. The soil's filtering action presumably would neutralize toxic organisms and prevent eutrophication of the lagoons.

FONATUR is developing 900 of the 7,000 acres it owns at Cancún in a three-phase plan stretching over 25 years. Phase one completed all basic services, such as roads, drainage, water and sewage systems, for an eight-mile strip of the island connected to the mainland by a broad causeway boulevard. A $10,000,000 international jetport and a conference center have been constructed. On the mainland FONATUR has built Cancún City—the "service.city"—with infrastructure designed for an eventual 70,000 inhabitants. It already serves an estimated 25,000 people.

Cancún island itself has been divided into hotel zones and residential zones. The latter will provide approximately 200 homes and condominiums during the first stage. The first-phase hotel zones provide sites for two dozen hotels facing either Bahía Mujeres on the north or the open Caribbean on the east; about half the sites were occupied by the end of 1977. Recreation opportunities include golf (one 18-hole course opened in 1977, with a second planned), tennis, scuba diving, nightclubbing, and shopping. Local boatmen take tourists fishing or to nearby Isla Mujeres for snorkeling.

The initial phase of development, which began in 1970, moved faster than

Camino Real Hotel. (Photo courtesy Cancún Information Bureau.)

expected. The dozen hotels that have opened are drawing well. Few new ones
are under construction, however. The 1976 law limiting the deductibility of
foreign convention expenses from United States income taxes has deterred new
investment. It now seems clear that FONATUR will not meet its 1980 goal of
completing phase two, which is to include an extension of the main boulevard
and the construction of an additional 4,000 hotel rooms. By the completion of
phase three, originally scheduled for the early 1990s, the plan for Cancún
foresees 10,000 hotel rooms.[5]

The master plan incorporates a series of height and bulk limits, density
requirements, and separate zones for different uses. There are regulations on the
percentage of lot that can be developed, on parking spaces, and on setbacks.
These regulations have permitted a wide variety of architectural styles, ranging
from the innovative elegance of the splendidly sited Camino Real hotel, to the
Cancún Caribe, where, despite FONATUR's protests, the developer has succeeded in cramming the worst features of Miami Beach hotels onto one of the
world's most beautiful beaches.

By Mexican law, the *municipio*—or local government—has such responsibilities as issuing construction permits, maintaining the public beaches and
open spaces, hooking up water facilities, and running a police system. There was
no local government in Cancún when development began, so a new *municipio*
—named Benito Juárez after Mexico's great patriot and president of Indian

descent—was established in 1974 to take over these functions. Its jurisdiction encompasses a regional area, but its capital is Cancún City. Everything that happens in the municipality, however, depends on FONATUR, which has produced the master plan and passes on all development proposals.

A Plan Plus a Philosophy

FONATUR's brochures proudly proclaim its commitment to what it calls environmental planning. The Mexican government has recognized that unplanned tourism development—as in Acapulco—is a mixed blessing. On one hand, tourism development has attracted foreign currency, needed to help bridge the widening balance-of-payments gap. It has created jobs, critically important in a nation of rapidly growing population and high unemployment. For the middle-class Mexican, it has provided many investment opportunities because of the laws requiring Mexican ownership of coastal land.* It has also provided many Mexicans with recreational opportunities: almost two-thirds of the tourists visiting Acapulco, for example, are Mexican citizens.

Yet a country that prides itself on its revolutionary tradition is hard put to explain the contrast between the homes of the poor in places like Acapulco and the luxury hotels along the beaches. Moreover, there is an increasing concern that the rapid growth of such areas will eventually destroy the very characteristics that made the areas desirable for development.

Consequently, FONATUR officials have two goals: increased economic yield from tourism, and a higher quality of life for the rural peasantry. More than ever before, these efforts involve land-use planning, policy coordination, control of development, and integrated regional social and economic strategies.

Guillermo Grimm, a FONATUR vice president, sees Cancún as a plan plus a philosophy. "We had a choice of providing funds to improve existing resorts or to start new resorts with integral master plans." By developing new cities, serviced with infrastructure and planned to deter the deterioration and pollution observed in private development, FONATUR hopes to avoid a replication of Acapulco. The infrastructure created by FONATUR is given to the *municipio*, which then levies charges for public services. The charges are higher for the hotels than for the local residents so that tourism can subsidize the town. Grimm says that FONATUR wants to make sure that the children, instead of living in hovels and shanty towns, have access to basic utilities, education, and a better life.

What can be said of the yardsticks by which FONATUR asks that Cancún be measured—increased economic yield and a higher quality of life for the rural peasantry? How much of the new pot of gold will be used for the benefit of the local people?

Most residents of the Yucatan peninsula have little in common with the sophisticated, urbanized citizens of Mexico City or Acapulco. Their Mayan heritage is not the ancient glories of the temples, but the rural desolation that

---

*An officer of a Mexican industrial corporation that purchased a large resort complex, Las Hadas, near Manzanillo, after justifying the acquisition by the traditional financial criteria, added: "And it will be something fun for the company to do. Tourism is fun."[6] Because few businessmen are so candid, little emphasis has been given to this benefit of tourism development—the fact that it offers enjoyable and creative work for developers.

New public housing in Cancún City. (Photo by author.)

remained when the temples crumbled. Until recently, the condition of the peasants had changed little since the 1930s, when Frans Blom observed:

> Today there are more than one million Indians speaking Maya and Maya dialects. . . . They gain their living from their land in the same way as their ancestors did. They still retain a little of the ancient ritual, but the art of building great temples and paved highways and the science of reading the stars and writing Maya characters in books have forever been lost to the Maya people. The Maya has not vanished from the surface of the earth; he still lives in his own country as the humble Indian raising corn on the squares between the magnificent crumbling temples which stand as testimonies of his ruined civilization.[7]

Until the 19th century, the people of Yucatan were a *gente aparte*—separate people—and got arms from nearby British Honduras (now Belize) to help them oppose the Mexicans. Before 1930, many had led a serflike life as peons in a *hacienda*. After President Lazaro Cardenas abolished the hacienda system, they began living in communal *ejidos*, but did not significantly change their life-style. As they had resisted the Spanish conquest, so in many ways they have been reluctant to adopt Mexican values.

In recent years, the Mexican government has built schools and attempted to bring the Mexican way of life to the Yucatan. With loans from FONATUR, the Mexican Institute for Social Security has been teaching construction skills and hotel trades. Schools for adults teach beginning reading and writing during a basic four-month course. Students can train as kitchen aides, bar aides, and domestics, or continue their education in three technical schools: a regional school for agricultural workers, a school for fishing-related trades, and a school of technology.

FONATUR has encouraged hiring workers from the Yucatan peninsula. Some of these natives speak only Mayan, not Spanish. Many had not earned 10 pesos a day before the advent of FONATUR, and afterwards earned 60 or 70. During the earth-moving stage of development a great number of jobs for un-skilled labor were filled by these local people. In a 1975 interview, the mayor of Cancún City, a sociologist by training, pointed out that the workers came from "primitive, tribal life in a disintegrated social state. They are descendants of the Mayans, but they have forgotten the Mayan ways."

As part of their efforts to build a local economy that is interdependent with tourism, FONATUR's regional development planners talk of light industry, food packaging, an ice plant, a fishing center, and a seaport. Through the *secretaria de la reforma agraria*, collective ejidos operate small industries to supply building

Broiler factory. (Photo by author.)

Homes in Puerto Juárez. (Photo by author.)

materials and other commodities. A "broiler factory" on a nearby ejido provides the chickens and eggs that are a staple of the Mexican diet. Officials hope that local farms will increasingly provide a cheaper source of supply for hotel food, much of which is still transported from Mérida and Campeche.

Tropical Boomtown

The people who provide the local goods and services for Cancún's tourists are supposed to live in Cancún City—where the streets are not made of gold, but are among the few in Quintana Roo that are paved. "This is a blessing for the people," according to Guillermo Grimm. "The Cancún workers are able to live decently. They are trained to know that what is happening to them is happening because of tourism."

During the initial construction phase, daily life in Cancún City was filled with inconveniences. New residents complained that the community was far from ready; it grew faster than expected, and its services took longer to install. Constant bulldozing made the city dusty and noisy.

Moreover, many basic consumer goods—mattresses, simple chairs, appliances—were in short supply, and people of all economic classes waited desperately for housing. In mid-1975, the cheapest house available in Cancún City cost 800,000 pesos ($64,000), with interest of 15 percent on a five-year note. Such housing was not for people who earn 1,600 pesos a month.

The poor did not live in Cancún City. Rather, they lived in Puerto Juárez, a

Shops in Cancún City. (Photo courtesy Cancún Information Bureau.)

squatter settlement of tin hovels, cheap *tortilleras,* and bars along Cancún City borders. The workers were shuttled early in the morning and late at night in special buses. Unofficial estimates placed the number of squatters as high as 30,000 in 1975. They had potable water with above-ground piping, but no paved streets or sewage-treatment facilities.

Puerto Juárez was an embarrassment for FONATUR. In 1975 one of its staff members said, "It would be unconscionable of us to be building this fancy resort without doing anything for these people. We are thinking about what to do."

By 1977, the development of Cancún City began to catch up with the housing shortage. Public and private projects were under way in many of its neighborhoods. The physical plan of the city was designed to protect the residential zones from dust and traffic insofar as possible, with peripheral roads around the residential neighborhoods keeping cars away from the homes. On the master plan green zones were set aside to "refresh the air." As in most boomtowns, construction has outpaced any reliable statistics, but there is clearly steady growth.

The effects are noticeable as well in Puerto Juárez. Although many people still live there in unsanitary, makeshift conditions, many of the worst hovels appear to be abandoned. The town does not house as high a density of population as it did during the early stages of development.

On the other hand, the character of the work force in Cancún has also changed. The unskilled labor needed for early development is less in demand; carpenters, bartenders, and shop clerks, more so. As a result, many of the native Mayans seem to have left Cancún. Despite the government's effort to train the

Algae in Bojórquez lagoon; condominiums in background. (Photo by author.)

Mayans for hotel and construction work, more experienced workers from all over Mexico, many from Acapulco and other resort communities, have successfully competed for many of the better jobs.

Cancún City shows little of the regimentation characteristic of many of the world's new towns. Its housing is varied in style and size, and the shops reflect the full range of Mexican private enterprise. Yet its remoteness and small size give it a frontier character that more sophisticated Mexicans find dull. One resident, until recently a native of Acapulco, was asked what he liked most about living in Cancún. He thought for a moment and replied, "Well, it's only an hour from Miami."

From the point of view of the Mexican government, Cancún has succeeded in providing the hoped-for economic benefits. No large-scale influx of foreign workers has been needed; virtually all jobs are being filled by Mexican citizens. While it would undoubtedly have been preferable to provide more jobs for the indigenous residents of Quintana Roo, work is scarce throughout Mexico, and the project is designed to benefit the country as a whole. The workers have been provided with a new community that is spacious, attractive, and sanitary, even if not as exciting as Miami.

The Mexican government has made a real and largely successful effort to use tourism development as a key to social planning. True, some of the social planners in Mexico City were disappointed that FONATUR chose as its first development site an area that one of them described as populated largely by birds and turtles. But, from that standpoint, the birds and the turtles have also good reasons to be disappointed.

Where the Mangroves Were

The natural environment of Cancún has received much less attention than the social environment, and studies by consultants regarding the impact of development have been hard to find. Although FONATUR's sales brochures refer to a "staff ecologist," one finds only an entomologist whose primary job is to supervise spraying of mosquitoes and sandflies in the new resorts.

The natural environment has been almost totally transformed. Before man arrived, the coastal region was filled with mangrove wetlands and tropical forest. Now, it bears the scars of slash-and-burn agriculture, and scrawny cattle graze on sparse vegetation over much of the area.

The Cancún developers exhibited little concern about adding to the devastation of the nearby mainland. To build gardens and a golf course, fertile areas have been scraped for black topsoil, which FONATUR buys by the truckload. Huge quarries have been dug to obtain construction materials. An enormous quarry, two-thirds of a mile long, was a source of fill for the airport, which used a total of 9,000,000 cubic yards taken from the lagoon and sea as well as the land. In a 1975 interview, the FONATUR entomologist, who felt that the agency had been responsive to his requests to fill in the places where mosquitoes were breeding, expressed concern about this constant digging up of topsoil in the jungles, since the holes it creates become new breeding areas.

Portions of the lagoons have been filled in for condominium sites. Nichupté and Bojórquez were once bordered on all sides by extensive mangrove forests.

Those adjoining the mainland still remain. Those on the island have been destroyed. Rows of palm trees now dot the stony edges that have replaced the soft, swampy shores.

The lagoons were studied in the early planning stages of Cancún's development by limnologists from the University of Mexico, who recommended management practices to preserve their qualities. An inquiry in 1975, however, drew the response that the study had been "misplaced." Although FONATUR intended to keep untreated wastewater out of the lagoon and sea, construction of the permanent sewage-treatment facilities at that time was behind schedule. The project manager claimed nonetheless that there had been no change in the water quality of the lagoon, and that a study proved motor boats were having no impact on sea life.

Two years later, the smaller lagoon, Bojórquez, showed early signs of deterioration. Algae was blooming along its edges, though it was localized and not extensive. As to Nichupté, its vast size has provided protection for the quality of its water. A wide variety of birds—including pelicans, terns, several species of egret and heron—still fish in it. Future phases of construction, however, will test the shallow lagoon's absorption capacity.

The fate of two wildlife sanctuaries, on the other hand, has been sealed: they no longer exist. In 1972, the Mexican government designated four sites in the eastern Yucatan as refuges for marine life, flora, and fauna, including two points on Cancún island. These were quickly seized as desirable hotel sites when development began. The handsome Camino Real now sits on one. It is designed to take maximum advantage of what the owner thinks the tourists want—a view from all rooms of the clear waters, swimming in artificial lagoons as well as the sea, diving, deep-sea fishing, sunshine. On the other point, Punta Nizuc, is the Club Méditerranée. The builders here took greater care in preserving the natural features, which are lusher than in the rest of Cancún, but parts of the lagoon have been filled to provide space for villas.

With the sanctuaries gone, a small island in the lagoon immediately adjacent to the boulevard has been chosen as the site for an aviary. Covered with beautiful coconut palms and dense shrubs, the island seems ideally located. A series of large, net-enclosed cages are to be constructed and birds of the region will be displayed as a tourist attraction. Roger Margris, a French ornithologist who loves birds, jungle, and swamp, was brought in to develop the aviary. He had mixed feelings about the project. It was his duty to accustom the birds to eating totally different foods and living in small spaces, and the death rate was very high. As of the fall of 1977, moreover, the island for the aviary remained undeveloped. Other priorities seemed to have taken precedence.

Travelers to Cancún have had mixed reactions. The beach draws raves from everyone, but many feel that the resort lacks character. Thus, a New York Times writer, Ralph Blumenthal, has called Cancún "disappointingly prosaic—haphazard and sterile," citing plastic greenery in the Cancún Caribe's dining-room.[8] Several readers, however, responded to his comments by coming to the resort's defense. Denying the alleged lack of wildlife, one of them wrote, "We even saw a pet anteater a little Mexican boy had on a string."[9]

Although the impact of development on Cancún's natural environment has been significant, it could have been much worse. The sewage-treatment and spray-irrigation system avoids the ocean outfalls that, when combined with offshore winds and currents, have fouled the beaches of many other resorts. Cancún's linear layout has fostered remarkably frequent bus service—with about five-minute headways—that has proved attractive to tourist and worker alike. As a result, few private automobiles are found on the boulevard along Cancún island, reducing potential problems of air pollution and runoff.

Many of Cancún's hotels demonstrate that the designer was aware of the natural characteristics of the site. Dunes have been retained and drainage ponds created. On other sites, however, the beach has been graded and leveled in ways that may portend future problems.[10]

In light of the development at Cancún, it is difficult to imagine it as a rural reserve, where hunting is prohibited. It is perhaps less surprising that hunting is common. And during midsummer, when catching lobsters is illegal, they are widely available in the local restaurants. "There's a whole series of laws that are on the books for which implementation is not really seriously considered," according to FONATUR executive Gleeson. "Hunting turtles is forbidden, but people have to eat. . . . What can you do if that's what people eat?" Insofar as the construction of hotels on land set aside as a wildlife sanctuary is concerned, it "creates a problem of conscience for the upper and middle class who don't like to see the birds dying. But when you see a kid die, and a bird dying, you know what you have to do. There is no choice." Perhaps the next generation can find a new source of food to replace the vanishing turtles.

Preserving the Mayan Links

Laws protecting archaeological remains seem to receive more respect at Cancún than laws limiting hunting. Pablo Mayer, a determined Mexican archaeologist crusading for the protection of the national culture, and his associates from the National Institute of Anthropology and History have been working at an important archaeological site about three miles from Cancún's first-phase hotel zone.

Mexican law concerning archaeological sites is quite strict. It protects both zonas archologias (archaeological zones containing pre-Hispanic remains) and zonas típicas (historical zones containing colonial remains of the 16th, 17th, and 18th centuries). Permission must be sought directly from the National Institute of Anthropology and History before altering any protected site. If a site is uncovered in the course of a public works project, the project must stop immediately. Heavy penalties can be levied for destroying anything. Nevertheless, according to Mayer, continuous vigilance is needed.

Fortunately, there is a rising awareness of the value of the sites. Little by little, says Mayer, a new conscience is growing among authorities and the Mexican people. It has been helped by radio programs, movies, and conferences held at museums and in small towns and cities.

To protect the archaeological sites at Cancún, FONATUR has provided the institute with 1,500,000 pesos for Mayer's work. FONATUR officials were initially skeptical of the economic value of this effort, but now recognize its merit, apparently because of potential interest to tourists. "In Mexico we are just not rich enough to develop sites for one purpose alone," said Mayer. "Tourism gives us the opportunity to develop the site within the context of an economic project,

Island proposed as site for aviary. (Photo by author.)

and to get the investment of public money because of its justified basis of tourism.''

The main archaeological zone at Cancún is not immediately endangered by present development, according to Mayer, but its future is uncertain. Tourism helped preserve the zone, but tourists also present a threat. As old remains are exposed to the air during delicate exploratory work, they can easily be destroyed. FONATUR is strictly enforcing a ban on visitors, and does not inform tourists of the project's existence. Uninvited visitors are warned off a "construction" site.

Scattered remains of Mayan buildings have been found in other parts of Cancún as well. On the golf course the foundation of a small structure serves as a unique hazard for those who hook their approach to the 12th green. At the Camino Real hotel, the landscape architect managed to work similar artifacts into the hotel's site plan.

Many tour guides at Cancún offer trips to Chichén Itzá, Tulum, Uxmal, and other Mayan sites within a day's drive. The tourists are attracted by the world-renowned temples, awed and mystified by the remnants of once-powerful cities.

Déjà Vu?

No one knows for sure why the Mayan cities were abandoned. Some archaeologists have hypothesized that the sudden collapse of Mayan civilization resulted from ignorance of the surrounding natural environment. As population increased, slash-and-burn agriculture destroyed natural forest, using up an increasing amount of fertile soil. According to archaeologist Patrick Culbert, the society just "overshot" its resources:

> The curves that we could estimate for the Maya rise and decline would look very much like the Club of Rome's computer simulations of the modern world. If we

ourselves stand at the edge of a precipice—our entire world endangered by the possibility of a global overshoot—can we say any longer that the fact that the Maya overpopulated, overexploited their environment, and disappeared from the earth bears no relationship to modern problems? Instead, should we not ask whether the Maya failure can be applied to our own situation? Given an understanding of the forces that destroyed earlier civilizations, can we not look at ourselves and our society and marshal our talents and energies in a determined effort to avoid a world collapse—a collapse from which there might be no return for the human race?[11]

In ancient Mayan legends the islands off the Yucatan coast were shrines of Ixchal, the moon goddess. Ixchal was unfaithful to her husband, the sun, who pulled out one of her eyes. That is why the moon's light is dimmer than the sun's, and why, to the Mayans, the moon was the symbol of licentiousness.[12] Surely, this is a disconcerting symbol for the FONATUR official who said, "We've gone to the moon."

Remnant of ancient Mayan temple on Cancún golf course. (Photo by author.)

Faced by serious poverty and unemployment, the people of Mexico understandably might find it difficult to resist exploiting the seductive charms of the islands of the moon goddess. And in many ways the development of Cancún has proved to be a success—economically, socially, and environmentally—in comparison to most areas of the world where intensive tourism development has taken place. That it could have been better, and is in some ways a disappointing use of a magnificent site, should not detract from the remarkable achievements that have been made under difficult conditions.

If, despite the planning that went into Cancún, it turns out that the moon goddess has again been unfaithful, and that the modern Mexicans have "overshot" their resources in the manner of the ancient Mayans, the Mexicans are unlikely to be alone in facing this predicament.

Chapter 2
France Creates New Rivieras

When people around the world think of summer in France, they are likely to dream of the French Riviera, its casinos and bikinis, its beautiful people, its voluptuous indolence. In the 19th century, when pallor was fashionable, the Riviera was a winter resort. In the 1920s, it was the place where the suntan was popularized. Now, summer is the Riviera's most crowded season.

The Riviera symbolizes the glamorous side of tourism. It also represents some of tourism's worst problems. It is too expensive, too crowded, and too polluted. Along much of the coast, the steep terrain offers relatively few building sites, and these have been overexploited. Untreated sewage is dumped into the sea, fouling beaches, particularly near the larger communities.

In season, traffic jams are common, auto fumes assault the nostrils, and parking spaces are almost nonexistent. Alec Waugh described a journey from Nice to Antibes as "a trip through the wilderness of cranes, bulldozers, excavations and churned up soil that separated the airport, the race course, a vast new supermarket and an immense two-flanked block of flats." But:

> Ten minutes later . . . I was sitting on a terrace by the ramparts. On one side I looked onto the long curve of the Baie des Anges and the promontory of Cap Ferrat, on the other to the twin towers of Antibes. Beyond was the curve of the Garoupe Beach. The sea was calm and blue. A light breeze fanned us. It gave the answer to my doubts. In the old days your eyes were constantly delighted. Now they are very often not. Beauty is not spread prodigally at your feet. You have to search it out. Charming places are not obvious. But they are still there, and they are still unmatched when you do find them.[1]

Waugh's experience cannot be shared by many, for only the affluent can now afford the Riviera.

Whatever their destination, the French cherish their vacations. An estimated 80 percent of the population spends at least a week away from home, mostly during July and August. Between August 1 and 15, 1975, for example, approximately 15,000,000 French citizens were vacationing, Paris was virtually deserted, and some resorts had reached saturation point.[2]

Field research for this chapter was conducted by John S. Banta and Jacqueline B. Merikangas.

Cannes. (Photo courtesy French Government Tourist Office.)

Many French tourists travel to Spain, which has seen an explosive growth in tourism. As long ago as 1958, French officials—notably President de Gaulle—watched the summertime exodus with considerable annoyance. By spending so many francs abroad, French citizens were disrupting the balance of payments.

It was obvious to de Gaulle that the Riviera and other traditional French summer resorts could not expand to accommodate tourists at a price they could afford. But during the summer months, when the Riviera was packed, several other French coastal provinces were relatively deserted. About 1960, therefore, de Gaulle and Prime Minister Michel Debré decided that the best way to keep the franc in France was to invest substantial sums in tourism facilities along undeveloped coastal areas. The two sites that they chose were in the regions of Languedoc-Rousillon and Aquitaine.

A Riviera in the Wetlands

The government's first tourist development project was in Languedoc-Rousillon, on the sparsely populated and low-lying Mediterranean coast west of the Rhone delta. The region's future seemed bleak. Its treeless dunes were

FRANCE

N

BELGIUM

GERMANY

Paris ★

SWITZERLAND

ITALY

Bay of
Biscay

Lacanau Ocean •

• Bordeaux

AQUITAINE

LANGUEDOC-
ROUSSILLON

Capbreton
• Biarritz

La
Grande
Motte

Marseille

Riviera

Cannes

SPAIN

MEDITERRANEAN

SEA

Statute Miles   0 20   60   100
Kilometers   0 20 60 100

gradually deteriorating, the ponds becoming marshland, the marshes silting up. Nevertheless, de Gaulle and his national planners believed this could become another Riviera.

The coast offered many potential advantages. Perhaps most important was the flat offshore profile, supporting a stable, white sand beach. Behind the beach lay a varied landscape of fields, ponds, and low hills. The area could be reached easily from nearby industrial and commercial centers, and from more distant points by already-established air, rail, and highway corridors.

To develop Languedoc for tourism required extensive dredging, filling, and mosquito control. In June 1963, the *Mission Interministerielle pour l'Aménagement touristique de littoral Languedoc-Rousillon** was created and given the powers and budget to begin the massive project of transforming the area. Arthur Haulot, former head of the World Tourism Organization, described the project as *"un exemple frappant de valorisation de l'environnement par et pour le tourisme."*[3]** Ann Louise Strong, who describes the early stages of the project in her book *Planned Urban Environments,* quotes the chairman of the mission: "When . . . I surveyed for the first time all that wasteland of swamps and shores infested with shanties and tents with no sanitary facilities whatsoever, I was dumbfounded. I thought momentarily that we would never clean up all that."[4]

The mission handled all the planning and major earth moving. It also instituted controls on land prices to deter speculation.[5] "Naturally," reports Strong, "this attitude of the national government did not increase its popularity with local landowners, many of whom also resented the fact that Paris would plan the development of their land for the benefit of outsiders."[6] The mission staff were regarded as a bunch of hotshots from Paris. According to Lloyd Rodwin, in his book *Nations and Cities: A Comparison of Strategies for Urban Growth,* "The political scientists, administrators, economists, and other social scientists [in these and other such missions] could barely conceal their contempt for the architects and engineers in the . . . local communities."[7]

Highways were built, harbors and lakes dredged, infrastructure provided for a string of resort cities separated by green areas. In La Grande Motte, the first big resort community, many of the hotels and condominiums were built in the style of pyramids truncated by sundecks, resembling Mayan temples.

In 1974, a decade after the project's inception, almost a million and a half visitors stayed at the resorts of Languedoc.[8] At that time La Grande Motte had 31,000 beds.[9] It occupied 2,000 acres along two-and-a-half miles of gently sloping beach (not the natural beach, but man-made with trucked-in sand), backed by two large lagoons (also man-made). According to one observer, La Grande Motte has a "high-rise, city-like atmosphere, which attracts a high-style

---

*The mission for Languedoc-Rousillon is part of a regional planning and development hierarchy outside the straight line of government authority. A number of interministerial missions share a common office in Paris and are organized along similar lines. They work under the general supervision of a special committee of ministers (chaired by the Prime Minister) called the *Comité Interministeriel d'Aménagement du Territoire,* which considers all major planning and development decisions requiring an interministerial or Prime Minister's decree.

**The concept of "valorisation of the environment by and for tourism" is a uniquely French euphemism that does not translate well into English. There is no common English word to signify the "giving of economic value" to a place that in its natural state is assumed to be valueless. Given changing attitudes toward the land, one may hope such a word will soon become obsolete.

international yachting crowd. The boutiques boast Paris originals rather than local handicrafts."[10]

Languedoc—Parisian control, Parisian boutiques. In many ways, the pyramids of La Grande Motte are an ironic memorial to the president of France who abdicated his office when the voters rejected his demand for more regional autonomy. Nevertheless, the Languedoc project achieved the goal of stimulating investment in a neglected region.*

As for the environment, a vital wetland resource, which provided a breeding area for marine life, a bird habitat, and flood-absorption area, has been lost. Arguments have been made that the marshes were filling in anyway, but had this occurred slowly, it might have offered some opportunity for species adaptation. The Languedoc project is now so far advanced, however, and the natural environment so radically altered, that it would be hard to evaluate fully the original impact.

The Languedoc experience suggests that, even when there is planning for tourism development (in contrast, for example, to what happened in Jerusalem and Acapulco), it does not ensure a harmonious relationship between development and environment. This lack of harmony can often be attributed to pressure put on the planners to produce quick, visible results.

For their second experiment in Riviera-creation, the French were determined not to be hasty. It was with awareness of the mistakes of Languedoc that the coast of Aquitaine was approached.

---

*The development of Languedoc does not seem to have slowed the attraction of the Spanish coast to French tourists. In July and August of 1975, for example, 4,500,000 French nationals crossed the Spanish border, creating lines of cars that at times backed up for 25 miles.[11]

La Grande Motte. (Photo by David L. Callies.)

Traditional summer homes at Piqueyrot in Aquitaine. (Photo by author.)

Dunes, Pines, and Vines

Aquitaine has not traditionally been thought of as a fashionable tourist destination—not even by the French themselves. It might be somewhat comparable in reputation to the coast of southern Texas—nice, but not Nice. Charles de Gaulle's government hoped to change this image of Aquitaine, and in doing so also attract foreigners, most of whom had little awareness of the region.

The dominant city in Aquitaine is Bordeaux, quiet and aging, with traffic congestion that rivals Paris at rush hours. Its people are open and friendly, but have the reputation of being suspicious of ideas and development from outside. They have long enjoyed the sparsely developed Aquitaine coast as a site for scattered summer homes, especially around the Arcachon Basin. About 50,000 Bordelais go to the coast every weekend in the summer, and many of them are spending an increasing amount of time year-round at their summer homes.[12]

Aquitaine also has had a gradual but steady increase in tourists from outside the region, especially tent and trailer campers. It is a natural stopping point for tourists going to Spain from northern Europe. In 1970, of the 250,000 beds available to tourists on the Aquitaine coast, only 50,000 were in hotels and similar establishments. Another 75,000 were in tents and trailers, and 125,000 in second homes.

The Arcachon Basin, in the approximate center of the Aquitaine coast, hosts thousands of migratory waterfowl and a thriving oyster industry as well as vacationing Bordelais. It is also the last remaining European refuge for the sea horse. South of the basin is a large and very secluded military reservation, home of France's nuclear weapons program. This tends to insulate the area further south from the type of summer-home activity found around the basin. The coast is largely undeveloped until the boundary of Aquitaine is approached. In this southwesternmost corner of France is the Pays Basque, with the traditional resort town of Biarritz, the Adour Estuary, and the city of Bayonne.

The natural features of Aquitaine are complex and closely interrelated. A series of zones, from west to east, runs parallel to the Bay of Biscay on the Atlantic ocean, beginning with the region's most popular tourist attraction, a broad, white, sand beach that stretches the length of the coast. The tidal range of about four meters leaves the beaches wide at low tide and narrow when the tide is high. Powerful winds blow from the Atlantic much of the year. Although summer temperatures are warm, strong winds cool the beaches. Rain is not too frequent.

Immediately landward from the beach is an initial dune ridge, averaging 50 feet in height, which moderates the violent western winds. Behind the ridge, a depression known as *la lette littorale* forms a transition zone between the coastal dune and the *massif dunaire,* or interior dunes averaging 100 feet in height.

When George Perkins Marsh wrote his pioneering work on ecology, *Man and Nature,* over a century ago, he cited Aquitaine as a region of rapidly moving dunes, where wind-blown sands constantly threatened any human habitation:

> The sea is fast advancing at several points of the western coast of France, and unknown causes have given a new impulse to its ravages since the commencement of the present century. . . .

> We know, from written records, that [the dunes of Aquitaine] have buried extensive fields and forests and thriving villages, and changed the course of rivers, and . . . rendered sterile much land formerly fertile.[13]

Under an 1801 Dune Commission and its successors, maritime pine, the only plant species considered capable of surviving in the area, was planted on dunes and on the flat plain of sand that extends eastward from them. The forests brought a degree of stability to the region, and provided a major source for timber and recreation. Some of the forest is now private, but much is owned by the

Chateau Lafite surrounded by its vineyards. (Photo by author.)

National Forest Office. Access is from a narrow, paved road—paralleling the coast a few kilometers inland—from which fire roads and bike paths weave a network through the woods. The soil is almost pure sand, so there is little undergrowth.

Within the forest lies an irregular chain of freshwater lakes, some of which, like Hourtin and Lacanau, are major recreation areas. The villages surrounding these lakes, like most villages in Aquitaine, tend to consist of a few dozen shops, a handful of tiny hotels, and housing for a few hundred full-time residents; second-home subdivisions surround this core.

Eastward, the sandy forest soil gradually gives way to sparse, gravel-laden earth that appears unproductive. The look of the earth is deceiving. For in this soil, bordering the Gironde Estuary, grow perhaps the world's most famous grapes, the basis for the reputation of Bordeaux's renowned wine industry. Protected by the pine forests from the harsh sea winds, the vineyards produce such famous wines as Chateau Lafite and Chateau Latour.

The natural environment of Aquitaine, in sum, is a wall of dunes, backed by a forest of pines, backed by world-renowned grape vines. Sparsely populated, the woods and dunes are used largely by campers and, in the central section near Bordeaux, for summer homes. Preparation of a tourism-development plan for this unusual area presented a challenge.

Happiness Before Profit

By decree of October 20, 1967, the French government created an interministerial mission for planning the coast of Aquitaine, *Mission Interministeriale pour l'Aménagement de la Côte Aquitaine* (MIACA). The mission was given three objectives: (1) to preserve the natural values of the Aquitaine coast, (2) to organize development to achieve the tourism potential of the coast, and (3) to develop the faltering economy of Aquitaine. The basic objective was to create a potential demand for tourism and recreational development in the Aquitaine area without destroying it.

From the beginning, the MIACA planners opposed the *front-de-mer* of high-rise hotels that characterized the Riviera. They hoped to open the Aquitaine forests and lakes, but to leave the coast basically untouched by development. In an interview with *Le Monde*, MIACA's first president, Philippe St. Marc, explained:

> A mercantile developmental approach would consist of locating everything on the coast, denying ecological constraints, not providing for cultural investments, subdividing for the benefit of a few promoters . . . . The goal of the Aquitaine mission at the outset was to put man's happiness before profit, to imagine a new society rather than commercialized space; to greet well, rather than just greet; to promote the tourist rather than tourism; to change man himself by changing the form of leisure.[14]

The initial studies of MIACA divided Aquitaine into a series of segments, some labeled "develop" and others designated "preserve," which were later assembled into an overall plan approved by MIACA in 1969. The main thrust of the plan was the development of the interior rather than the coast. Its proclaimed aim was to integrate man into nature without destroying it, democratize access to nature, "ruralize" development, and join nature and culture.

Lake Hourtin. (Photo by author.)

The plan provided for 530,000 tourists by 1985. There were to be new, small-scale resorts on the interior lakes and a trans-Aquitaine canal linking the lakes. Resort development along the coast was to be limited, sited away from the shoreline, and separated from other development zones by wide greenbelts.

The plan was not what tourism developers had anticipated. They were not expecting to invest in low-key development sites in the interior. Traditionally, hotels had been built as near the beach as possible, and on as high a site as possible to maximize the view. In Aquitaine, this would mean building hotels on the first row of dunes. A number of developers, ignoring the plan, proposed developments of this traditional type. A stalemate ensued.

In early 1970, Premier Chaban-Delmas replaced MIACA president St. Marc with Emile Biasini, formerly a high-ranking aide to André Malraux at the Ministry of Culture. St. Marc's departure was somewhat acrimonious, and the participants disagree on the reasons behind it. It seems clear, however, that the premier, a former mayor of Bordeaux, was embarrassed that MIACA had not generated more investment in hotels and other tourism development projects in his native region.

Despite the change in leadership, the MIACA planners continued to elaborate upon the original philosophy. First, development throughout the region was to be on a small scale, consistent with the type of development that had existed in the past. (An implicit political element of the plan was the need to spread the development thinly around the region to obtain cooperation from local communities.) No large-scale high rises or concentrated rows of hotels were to be permitted on the dunes. Second, the important ecological functions of the dunes were to be recognized, and development kept off them and directed to the less ecologically sensitive areas behind. Third, the water quality of the inland lakes was to be protected by strict regulation of sewage disposal for both existing and new developments. And fourth, the plan strongly encouraged multiple use of the national forests for recreational purposes.

After some revisions in the plan proposed by the new president of MIACA, each sector to be developed was assigned a separate team of architects and planners. Within certain general guidelines established by MIACA, the teams were free to design their own plans, which were developed in cooperation with the departmental and local councils in the region. Detailed plans for each of the development areas were approved by the *Comité Interministeriel d'Aménagement du Territoire* in April 1972. At that time the government released approximately $100,000,000 for development of the Aquitaine coast over the next 10 years. Local governments were to be involved as participants in the development process in an effort to reduce the impression of Parisian control so evident in Languedoc.

Ultimately, MIACA is to dissolve and the Aquitaine development area will be totally under local control. In the meantime, much of the developable land in the region has been placed in a planned development zone, which under French law gives MIACA a right of first refusal at advantageous prices on any land sold, and hence control of development on most of the available land. After MIACA is dissolved, the regional and local plans will be the development-control mechanism.

MIACA's initial development phase provided infrastructure for immediate needs in the areas where it was directing growth. During its first four years of operation, MIACA contributed almost a million dollars to capital improvements in a new regional park. It also provided funds to acquire land for a number of large nature reserves and other protected areas.*

But developers remained reluctant to build in the interior, and a number of proposals for such development were dropped. Also, the trans-Aquitaine canal project, the first section of which was opened by Premier Chaban-Delmas in 1971, was eventually abandoned, partly on the advice of a panel of environmental experts.

Instead, the first development projects were initiated on the coast, at Lacanau and at Capbreton. Both of these major hotel-condominium projects created controversy.

Capbreton: Litigation Overcome

The Capbreton development was the target of an unsuccessful citizen suit claiming that the project represented the use of taxpayers' money to package a vast speculative venture contrary to the common good. "The foolish grandiose ambitions of a few technocrats pose expensive risks for everyone," claimed a citizens' group in a widely distributed tract. "Elsewhere similar projects are now rejected by local citizens, and in addition by the courts, because more and more often the [rulings] reject this orientation towards luxury tourism and speculative

---

*MIACA's concept of a "protected" area is hardly one of wilderness protection: "Some of the protected zones form a natural setting of quite outstanding interest and deserve both social protection and promotion, based on a policy that the largest number of people should be able to visit them."[15] In support of this policy MIACA has permitted a 5,000-bed *camp de naturistes*, or nudist camp, in a section designated as a "protected area."[16]

development. They call instead for more socially sensitive programs."

The citizens' group argued that the development would cause local taxes to rise, and force local commerce to compete with large-scale companies from outside the region. Moreover, they complained, the project would displace a local campground that provided middle-income families with easy access to local beaches.

As far as MIACA is concerned, according to a staff member, the litigation at Capbreton "was a losing case, but the lawyers for the plaintiffs were well versed in local procedure and the technical details of the law. It cost us one year delay." The plaintiffs were able to raise few serious environmental issues. The minister of tourism was sanguine: "If the work drags," he said, "it is because of sometimes difficult realities, but in the end accounting, it is worth an extra year to avoid regrets from too precipitous decisions."[17]

By the beginning of 1978, two condominiums had been built, one on the coast and one adjoining the marina on the harbor. About two-thirds of the condominium units have been sold. MIACA eventually hopes to triple the number of units, but the pace of sales leaves the construction of further stages questionable.[18]

Lacanau: An Unstable Compromise

The other MIACA tourism site that got an early start was in the town of Lacanau-Océan, a tiny community on the edge of the coastal dune about 30 miles northwest of Bordeaux. Its one-block main street contains small shops and restaurants. At the ocean's edge stand a few small hotels. Campgrounds and second homes are scattered on the inland side of the dunes. Once the terminus of a railway that brought tourists from Bordeaux, the area stagnated when the automobile made the coast closer to Bordeaux more attractive. But in recent

New tourism development at left; at right, Capbreton. (Photo courtesy MIACA.)

Downtown Lancaneau-Océan. (Photo by author.)

years, weekend visitors have been arriving in growing numbers.

MIACA calls the Lacanau-Océan project, started in June 1974, its most important development now under way. It is the first phase of a planned development of 20,000 beds, expected to take 10 years to complete. The first set of buildings, called Océanide, has been constructed squarely on top of the primary dune, in violation of MIACA's plan. Despite this, MIACA has supported the project, and in turn has received a great deal of criticism.

Océanide is being developed by one of those mixed ventures of numerous public and private participants characteristic of French development practice. The first stage of the Océanide project consists of a three-story condominium set on top of a stabilized dune more than a half-mile long, beginning at the commercial center of Lacanau-Océan and stretching south. The condominiums were built "in anticipation of" approval of the final plan.[19] Eventually, the stabilized dune is to be extended to accommodate a five-story hotel. Lower-density housing, campgrounds, and a golf course are to be built inland.

The foundation of the first building is said to be about 150 feet deep. The developer hoped this would reassure potential purchasers worried about the permanence of the dune's location. Indeed, these people might have looked down the beach and seen that German ingenuity did not prevent huge concrete blockhouses built less than 40 years earlier (as part of the Siegfried line) from literally washing into the ocean within 200 yards of the project. MIACA removed this embarrassment by destroying the remains of the blockhouses.[20]

The developer is also "stabilizing" the dune by bulldozing its clifflike front into a very gradual slope. The slope is then reinforced with concrete and covered with grass. The result is an artificial landscape that contrasts sharply with the natural dunes to the north and south of the project, where wind from the ocean sweeps up an abrupt natural dune face, swirling the sand around in a very active wind-and-water transport system. While scientists still have an imperfect understanding of these systems, many believe that the abrupt bluff generates the currents that support the regeneration cycle. Any use of artificial substitutes for dunes is a gamble, given the imperfect knowledge of the dynamics of beach systems.[21]

Stemming the Tide

MIACA, however, justifies development on the dunes by claiming they were "in a state of neglect" and needed restructuring anyway.[22] The beach 100 yards to the north of Océanide, for example, lying immediately in front of the town's tiny business district, has serious erosion problems. The town has not found a way to prevent the winter storms and spring tides from undermining the dune on which the town's business section was built. A MIACA planner concedes that erosion problems are already appearing at the base of the Océanide dune, but this can be remedied by "pumping a little sand back in place."

A German blockhouse (right), built on top of the dune as part of the Siegfried Line, now sits on the edge of the beach as a result of erosion. At left are the results of attempts to stabilize the dune by grading and fencing, and planting dune grass. (Photo by author.)

In further justifying its project in the face of these controversies, MIACA argues that the condominiums will help turn the little community of Lacanau-Océan into a "new centre of life close to the sea," which can then serve as the core of the entire development project, the remainder of which will be inland. MIACA claims that the low height of the buildings "will make them almost invisible from the beach."[23] Only a blind person, however, could miss seeing the initial structures perched on top of the dune.

MIACA planners try to put on a brave face, but they are embarrassed by Océanide. They supported the project under pressure from a combination of forces: powerful developers were interested; the site had already been abused; increasingly desperate politicians sought to lay cornerstones. In exchange for allowing the construction of the oceanfront buildings, MIACA obtained a commitment from the developers to build low-density development inland as well.

Biasini plans a championship golf course for the inland portion of Lacanau, which he hopes eventually will become a spot on the professional tour. After years of negotiation, development sites in the inland area have been sold to two French and two Swedish developers, and MIACA is optimistic that its compromise will prove successful.

But in the long run it is questionable whether Océanide and other projects like it will survive the onslaught of the sea. Moreover, any destruction of the dunes vegetation—which is a well-recognized consequence of trampling—results in blowouts and moving sands. And as sands move, they form mounds at the base of trees and girdle them. Once dead, the trees are increasingly subject to fire. If substantial deforestation should take place, it would reduce the protection the forest buffer now gives the inland vineyards from winds, sand, and salt spray. How much is "substantial" deforestation? No one can say. But grapes are notoriously sensitive to microclimatic variation. At the present time, development is not nearly at the point where it would have an impact on the vineyards, but a precedent has been set.

Today, one can sit on the beach at Lacanau and see Océanide sitting atop its artificial sand dune, which is already eroding. And one can hope to believe the predictions of MIACA that this is not the wave of the future; that Aquitaine will not consist of rows of hotels and condominiums perched atop eroding dunes; that the forest will not be blown away by the winds from the Atlantic; and that Chateau Lafite '99 will be just as good as Chateau Lafite '29. But because the world contains so many other rows of high rises hovering over beaches, it is not easy to accept the explanation that this is an exceptional case.

Plan and Reality

MIACA's plan for Aquitaine is an excellent example of sensitive environmental planning. At a time when there was little precedent to guide them, the planners produced a remarkably creative scheme for the adaptation of tourism to a unique environmental situation.

With limited funds, a lot of bright ideas, and fewer than normal bureaucratic constraints, MIACA nudges and shoves the more established governmental agencies rather than trying to dominate them. Because of its short lifespan, it seems more adventurous than most of the more traditional bureaucracies. But,

Océanide condominiums under construction. (Photo by author.)

bureaucratically, MIACA is a tool to generate consensus on a specific objective, and it is probably fair to say that its plans will never be fully realized because of shifting demand and public opinion.

For one thing, a severe recession struck between the planning and implementation stages. The planners started out in a seller's market and ended up being evaluated in a buyer's market. The planners needed high-visibility projects like Océanide and Capbreton to show that they were willing to cooperate with developers.

As a result of the recession, MIACA's objectives have been scaled down from 525,000 beds to 440,000. MIACA argues persuasively that its go-slow approach, with its sensitivity to social and natural environmental factors, is necessary to avoid completely swamping the social and economic fabric of the area. "The infrastructure is going in," says MIACA president Biasini. "If nothing more happens, it will still be a major contribution to the present inhabitants. To suggest that the plan fails if its full development levels are not met is to ignore some of its fundamental philosophical bases."

In the minds of most people, however, MIACA is a development agency, and there is an almost irresistible tendency to evaluate such agencies in terms of how much gets built. During the recession that began in 1974 little private capital was being attracted to build the hotels and other facilities necessary to attract tourists to Aquitaine. MIACA's reports were replete with enthusiastic language about development deals that were "virtually complete." But anyone familiar with the development industry knew how to read between the lines. Some of the same projects had been "almost" a reality for many years.

Biasini argues that the slow pace of development has been advantageous: "Each project, in the course of refinement, takes on only slowly a definite form—always in accord with the directives of the plan, but prudently spread out in time according to time schedules which subordinate the entire realization to the result of each stage."[24]

As of 1978, private developers were beginning to be attracted. Momentum has been growing, but slowly. If the momentum of development continues to grow, MIACA's ability to resist pressures for quick development will have been well worthwhile. But only time will tell whether Aquitaine becomes a new Riviera, remains a rural backwater, or achieves the middle ground envisioned by the MIACA planners.

A Sense of Time

Reviewing the work of regional developers, one senses that their contributions are greatly enhanced if they see themselves having a significant place in history. To develop wisely requires careful consideration of long-range values.

In its 1973 study *The Use of Land*, the Rockefeller Brothers Task Force urged governments to change their systems of incentives—whether economic, spiritual, or psychological—to convince developers that the "maintenance and enhancement of quality" is a more important goal than immediate cash flow.[25]

For regional development agencies, this change in goals requires a difficult adjustment in analytical technique. H. C. Coombs, former chancellor of the Australian National University and one of that nation's leading economists, has suggested the nature of these changes in a perceptive essay entitled "Matching Ecological and Economic Realities."

> It is not enough for men to be convinced that they are collectively wasting a heritage of resources they cannot replace and despoiling an environment to the damage of future generations. They must also be prepared to take the welfare of such generations effectively into the calculus by which they make their decisions. Men find it hard to give their own future needs and those of their immediate families an importance equal to that they attach to the gratification of present needs or desires. How much more reluctantly will they forego such gratifications in the interest of generations unborn, for the bulk of whom they can have no imaginable sense of personal concern?

This broader vision can only be realized, Dr. Coombs suggests, if the ecologists' long-range concern is internalized so that it becomes part of the unconscious motivation that molds the developer's conscious thoughts and actions.[26]

The context of regional development projects brings home the urgency with which the issue must be addressed. The technology is now available to make irreversible environmental changes over huge areas. Cancún and La Grande Motte are totally reconstructed environments built by people whose knowledge of the environmental impact of their actions is necessarily limited. Although our knowledge about the land is growing, our ability to transform the land is growing at an even faster pace.[27] As that power grows, the importance of reexamining our motivations grows as well.

Changing people's motivations is no easy task. Developers, whether private or public, are accustomed to having their status measured by "the bottom line." Countries all over the world seduce developers with tax incentives or subsidies promising immediate returns. In contrast, the rewards for producing development of long-range quality may be many years away.

Quick returns are tempting, but in the long run a developer's reputation rests on the lasting qualities of what he creates. The builders of Cancún and Aquitaine are trying hard, despite countervailing pressures, to create something that will cause the grandchildren of the Savignac and Biasini families to remember their ancestors with pride.

II MOVING

Chapter 3
Dreamtime at Ayers Rock

Shortly before his death, Charles Lindbergh visited a newly discovered tribe in a remote section of the Philippines. In an introduction to *The Gentle Tasaday,* he described his inner conflicts:

> Sitting on a dry, stony hump in the living cave, cook fires behind me and the morning sun streaming in through mists and hanging vines, I thought of what qualities were missing in the ways of civilized men. Qualities of the senses manifest themselves in tribal areas—the feel of earth and bark and leaves, the taste of rushing water, the smell of embered chips, the sound of wind. A mother nurses her babe. Naked children play along cliff ledges. Youths climb up from the stream with fish, crabs, and frogs.
>
> My tyrannical intellect grew aware of the sensate values it had been suppressing—of how greatly these values could enhance my twentieth-century life. Somehow I must strike a balance between the civilized and primitive. It was a balance that both the Tasaday and I were seeking from opposite directions. In achieving it, I did not want to renounce my civilization, and they did not want to renounce their cave-centered culture.[1]

To what extent should man try to conquer nature? Or live with nature? How do we measure our experiences against those of others who have not made great efforts to transform the earth? Do we exalt civilization? Or lament it? If we cannot go backward, can we learn something from radically different cultures that will enable us to go forward more wisely?

Lindbergh pondered these questions in the Philippines. The convergence of two different cultures at Ayers Rock, a startling landmark deep in the Australian outback, provides another perspective on them. Here, the white tourist meets—or fails to meet—the aborigine; the new wanderer meets the traditional wanderer.

Perpetual Tourists

Aborigines are believed to have arrived in Australia from Southeast Asia more than 30,000 years ago.[2] When European explorers first made contact, they were astonished by the aborigine way of life, which was more "primitive" than that of

---

Field research for this chapter was conducted by Richard J. Roddewig.

Aerial view of Ayers Rock; landing strip in foreground. (Photo courtesy Australian Information Service.)

any culture previously encountered.

The aborigines appeared to wander freely across the continent, with no places of permanent habitation. As European scholars learned more about aboriginal culture, however, they discovered that these wanderings were not random. The aborigines followed the rhythm of the seasons, climate, and topography.[3] For the most part, they would rove in small bands, often consisting of only a single family group with a few relatives and friends, or perhaps several groups totaling 30 to 40 people. At certain times of the year, many bands would converge from distant locations to feast on a local delicacy—the cones of a particular pine in the Blackall ranges, roasted bogong moths in the Australian Alps.[4]

An aborigine band would move through the country in a rhythmic but not rigid pattern, "cropping" the food resources of the environment without interfering unduly in the basic ecological balance.[5] The men, using spears and boomerangs, hunted game. Their quarry varied with the season and the region. Sometimes it was fish, sometimes kangaroos, often there was nothing.[6] The women gathered whatever was edible from the countryside. Their labor, while less adventurous than the men's, was more steadily productive.[7] Although many weeks might pass between successful hunting expeditions, the band was usually able to get along tolerably well on roots, seeds, nuts, and fruits, supplemented by a variety of lizards and small animals. The aborigines also ate insects—the "witchetty grub," a large caterpillar, was a particular favorite.[8]

Recently, some scientists have suggested that this way of life, rather than being "backward," reflected a conscious, sensible preference yielding more varied food and involving less-demanding labor than traditional agriculture.[9] The cycles of migration were adapted to Australia's rapid and dramatic climatic changes, and enabled the aborigines to make use of constantly changing natural resources. With neither herds nor crops to tend, the aborigines could move whenever they wished. They wore few clothes, slept on the ground in the open, and needed few possessions. When ready to set out, the men simply picked up their hunting tools; the women carried the remaining possessions such as digging sticks, bark containers, and grinding stones. The travel patterns reflected a deep understanding of the climatic and seasonal cycles of plants and animals.[10]

Each aborigine band apparently knew it could travel some places only with the consent of another band. For white Australians, the aboriginal rules establishing boundaries and legal rights to land are not entirely clear even today, despite extensive research. On their part, the aborigines from first contact were puzzled by the European concept of land as a commodity to be bought and sold. Mark Twain noted this on his visit to Australia in the 1890s:

> The land belonged to *them*. The whites had not bought it, and couldn't buy it; for the tribes had no chiefs, nobody in authority, nobody competent to sell and convey; and the tribes themselves had no comprehension of the idea of transferable ownership of land.[11]

The aborigine always regarded land as his to use, and to allow others to use. But he never thought of land as his to convey. Even today, he experiences a communication gap in dealing with the concept of land as property. According to a modern aborigine, speaking in opposition to proposals to formalize lease arrangements for aboriginal holdings:

> In our culture we [do] not like any leases. We know which is our country between different groups. So we can go anywhere. If you have a lease, you can't go into another boundary, another area. Someone will say go in or get back. So we can just go friendly together—they can come to our land, we can go to their land. The honour of the land is what we want. The leases make it hard. That is why we do not want any leases in the first place. We only want the grant so we can walk around. In old days our fathers' fathers' fathers just could walk anywhere.[12]

Why has the aborigine traditionally been unable to see his land as property? Because he has seen it, together with the plants and animals, the spirits, and himself, as an organic whole. He could as easily say that he "belongs" to the land as that the land "belongs" to him.[13] This attitude has its origin in the aborigine concept of creation.

The explanation of the world's origin differed somewhat from region to region, but in general it began with the "dreamtime"—a period when mythical beings, human and animal, walked the earth, engaged in epic battles, and created the landscape by turning themselves into hills, outcrops, and trees. The places where these battles took place embody the participants. A particular rock is a snake; a cave is the eye of a hawk. Beings who existed in the beginning still exist today, and will indefinitely. Some land has special significance, and boundaries are sometimes fuzzy, but all land is identified with a symbol from the dreamtime. [14]

Even today, the individual aborigine sees himself as descended from one of the symbolic dreamtime beings and thus as a member of the creature's "clan." He views the land that embodies the symbols of the creature as the land of his clan. The connection of man to land is timeless, commencing before birth and continuing after death. [15]

When an aborigine describes land in this way, he implies that he owes responsibilities to it. To encourage a particular dreamtime creature to multiply, large groups of aborigines perform rituals at certain sacred sites. These places are also the location of initiation rituals in which young men are accepted into manhood. Large numbers of aborigines from a variety of locations gather for such rituals. A traveling band may include members of many clans, and may visit in turn the land sacred to each.

For thousands of years, as aborigines made the rounds for seasonal rituals, they encountered only each other. In recent decades, however, they have seen new visitors in increasing numbers. Now, one of their most sacred sites has also become one of Australia's major tourist attractions—Ayers Rock.

A Big Rock That Turns Red

Almost as if dropped on the scrubby prairie by a giant hand, Ayers Rock sits on an otherwise flat and arid plain in Australia's sparsely populated Northern Territory. The world's largest monolith, it measures two-and-a-half miles long,

*Alice Springs, the largest town in central Australia. (Photo courtesy Australian News and
Information Bureau.)*

one-and-a-half miles wide, and 1,143 feet high—about as tall as the World Trade
Center. Its sides are steep, often almost perpendicular. They flake like the bark of
a eucalyptus tree, and are patterned with caves, clefts, and channels of various
sizes. On top, scattered potholes hold water year-round.

Besides its size and shape, Ayers Rock is impressive—indeed, world
renowned—for its color. Principally, it is composed of arkose (feldspar-rich
sandstone) that has turned reddish brown through oxidation. During the day, it
appears dull. At sunrise and sunset, however, the entire surface glows with
reflected red light. Photographs of this phenomenon can be seen on hundreds of
Australian tourist posters.

Ayers Rock and the surrounding area, now part of Uluru National Park, have
become the place that white Australians and international tourists feel they must
visit to capture the "outback experience," which shaped the national character
of Australia. Yet, as Senior Park Ranger Derek Roff says, "A lot of people don't
know anything more about the park other than that there's a big rock that turns
red."

The reputation of Ayers Rock developed not through a Madison Avenue-
style media blitz, but by word of mouth, as early visitors told others about it. The
first tourist party to reach the area by motor vehicle arrived in 1946. By 1953,
planned excursions were occurring regularly, and in 1957 buildings were constructed to accommodate them.[16] During the 1960s the average annual rate of
growth in visitors was 12 to 13 percent, reaching 30,000 in 1970-71. The next two
years saw a tremendous upsurge, and by the 1972-73 season 50,000 visitors
arrived at Ayers Rock.

To appreciate what it takes to make this journey, one must consider the
remoteness of the site—which is why, in fact, Ayers Rock serves as a symbol of
the outback. Australia is a highly urbanized nation, with about 60 percent of the

population concentrated in its five largest cities. The distance between Sydney and Ayers Rock is comparable to the distance between Charleston, South Carolina, and Cheyenne, Wyoming. Much of the highway that the tourist travels to reach the rock is a treacherous, nerve-shattering washboard covered with thick dust—providing a ride infamous throughout Australia. A small plane flies between Alice Springs, the major town in the Northern Territory, and the Ayers Rock "airport," a rocky strip of red desert dust. The trip is not for the queasy. The airport's location near the base of the rock puts it in an area of strong, shifting wind currents.

Having arrived somehow, the tourist finds no plush accommodations. The "village" at the base of the rock has about a half-dozen motels of the "ma and pa" variety, the largest with 35 rooms. Most visitors, however, stay in campgrounds sprawled randomly around the rock. The harshness of the environment explains part of its appeal to Australians, for whom the outback is as important as the Wild West is for Americans.

Tourists at Ayers Rock have four "must" items on their agenda. First, they must get up before dawn and travel to Sunrise Dune, just east of the rock, to photograph the glowing color produced by the first rays of sun. Cameras are in evidence everywhere. Elspeth Huxley called Ayers Rock "probably the most photographed boulder in the world."[17]

Second, the tourist must climb the rock—a hot, grueling, and dusty effort, often made more difficult by the wind. Old and young, fit and unfit tourists make the climb regardless of obstacles. Even people with broken legs have been seen struggling on the slopes.

Third, complementing the early morning ritual, tourists go to Sunset Dune to see the rock turn deep red at day's end.

Finally, the tourist explores the base of the rock to view the caves and rock formations. One formation, for example, represents the body of Metalungaua, the sleepy-lizard:

> The aborigines look on this boulder, which they believe is full of the kurunba (life-essence) of sleepy-lizards, as an increase centre for these reptiles. When, at the correct season, an aboriginal rubs this stone with another boulder—to the accompaniment of the correct chant—the kurunba of sleepy-lizards will leave the stone and impregnate the female sleepy-lizards who, by giving birth to their young, will increase the food supplies of the aborigines.[18]

The largest pool at the base of the rock, shown on maps as Maggie Springs, is called *Mutitjilda* by the aborigines. The pool contains not water, they believe, but the blood of Kunia, the carpet-snake man. Where the indifferent observer sees a patch of lichen on the rock's walls, the aborigine sees the "metamorphosed smoke from the burning camp of the greedy sleepy-lizard."[19]

Most tourists examine the aboriginal paintings that decorate the caves. Few people realize that some of these works were created to tell a story for the edification of pilgrims, while others were drawn merely for amusement during idle hours. For the stranger, the latter appear similar to the sacred work, while for the aborigines they have no ritual significance.[20]

Maggie Springs. (Photo courtesy Australian Information Service.)

Protecting cave paintings has become one of the most difficult tasks for those who manage Ayers Rock. Relatively little vandalism has occurred, but damage has been caused by photographers who brush chalk on the paintings to enhance the photogenic qualities. Wide ranges of temperature and humidity also take their toll.[21]

To the artists who painted the cave walls, such concerns would probably seem strange. Their art was never permanent.[22] It was considered more as a phenomenon to be experienced than a possession to be treasured.[23] Little or no binding material was added to the pigments, which were applied to a surface that received no preparation. Art objects often were discarded casually with the understanding that similar ones would be made in due course. Studies of the Mutitjilda cave in 1940 and 1960 indicated that many new paintings were added and others retouched in the interim.[24]

The aborigines probably were not concerned about permanence because they assumed that their wanderings would bring them back to Ayers Rock, giving them an opportunity to repair or even replace their creations. Now, the aboriginal way of life is changing. If no new paintings are done, it may well be because the most serious environmental consequence of tourism at Ayers Rock is its impact on the aborigines themselves.

Aborigines Search for a New Role

Bill Harney, the first ranger assigned to Ayers Rock-Mt. Olga National Park, as it was then known, found some basic conflicts between the aboriginal way of life and traditional concepts of park management.

> I soon realized that [the aborigines] were a greater lot of vandals than the unthinking tourists. Their uncontrolled dogs were in and out of the rock-holes, camel droppings littered the lead-ins to the drinking sites and the smell from the animals' bodies was more than all the advertisements could cope with . . . . Being food gatherers [the aborigines] were out gathering food wherever they could find it. The golden-nectar-laden blooms of the grevillia fell the first victim to the aboriginal children who looked upon it as a sweet. Gaping holes appeared in the red earth where women hunters had dug out a honey-ant's nest. Everywhere the acacia trees were pressed down, or hacked at, for the tasty witchetty grubs at their root and branches.[25]

The conflict between Harney's attitudes toward the natural environment and the aborigines' is part of a much greater problem—namely, defining the relationship between aborigine life-styles and values and those of Australia as a whole. This issue has preoccupied observers of the aborigines for more than a hundred years.

When the *Beagle* dropped anchor in Sydney in 1836, Charles Darwin traveled to the nearby Blue Mountains and noted that "the number of aborigines is rapidly decreasing."[26] During the following century, as concern for the plight of the aborigines grew, the government sought to provide segregated areas for them. In portions of north and central Australia considered too dry for good agricultural uses, large reserves were created within which the aborigines were encouraged to carry on a semblance of the old life.

The official policy since 1948, however, has favored assimilation. In keeping with this policy, at a national referendum in 1967 the Australian people amended the constitution, authorizing the government to undertake measures for aboriginal advancement. Though it has been successful for a few, such as tennis star Evonne Goolagong, assimilation left many more aborigines living as derelicts on the fringes of white society, victims of the poverty-whiskey syndrome. The infant mortality rate for aborigines is high—in the Northern Territory about 50 percent.[27]

Today, aborigines amount to only two-thirds of 1 percent of the population of Australia, perhaps too few to constitute an identifiable community with its own culture, and the Australian government's concern for the aborigines' future is mixed with a fear that, as Prime Minister Fraser has expressed, "We began too late."[28] Anthropologists Ronald and Catherine Berndt have described the aborigines' difficulties in finding a new role:

> At first the aborigines, dazzled perhaps by the white man's apparent wealth, want to see and know more about him—and take what he has to offer. But . . . by the limitations of their own background, they may find the results disappointing. They are not fully accepted in the new situation and they do not understand much of the new life that comes their way. Knowing they do not belong, but feeling powerless to do anything about it, they become at last frustrated and

Cave painting at Ayers Rock. (Photo by Richard J. Roddewig.)

disillusioned. They may try, then, to find help, encouragement and faith among their own people, discovering too late that in their eagerness to grasp at the white man's cultural heritage they have lost their own.[29]

Aborigine tribes never signed treaties relinquishing their land rights in exchange for some nominal consideration, as the American Indians did. The European immigrants just took over, moving the aborigines deeper and deeper into the bush. Now concern about the aborigines' status has concentrated on this issue of land rights.

Since the 1960s, Australia has undergone a mining boom. Iron, coal, copper, and nickel mines have opened, and the nation has become the world's largest producer of bauxite. The value of minerals produced rose from about $500,000,000 in 1962 to over $2,000,000,000 in 1972.[30] Australia has about one-fifth of the world's supply of high-grade uranium ore, and plans are under way to exploit these reserves at an increasing rate.[31] Much of the country's mineral wealth is located in areas of Queensland, Western Australia, and the Northern Territory that had been occupied by aborigines and never settled by whites.

Young aborigines in the cities, increasingly bitter over displacement, have begun to focus their energies on forcing the government to consider aboriginal claims to the land.* In 1973 the national government responded by creating the Aboriginal Land Rights Commission to investigate claims in the Northern Territory. Aboriginal land councils were organized to advise the commission.

One complaint of the councils was that tourists were defiling sacred sites at Ayers Rock. Council members asked that the area be placed under the control of aborigines, who would have the right to regulate and profit from tourism. They also sought to bar nonaborigines from visiting the rock for two to four weeks during annual ceremonies. While the Aboriginal Land Rights Commission recommended that aborigines be represented on a future management board for the park, it declined to give them a controlling position.

Beyond this, Australian government officials have been trying to learn enough about traditional aboriginal beliefs to protect the sacred places at Ayers Rock. They have been frustrated, however, by the difficulty of communicating with older aborigines who still adhere to ancient religious beliefs. Taboos regarding certain sites may prevent the elders from telling outsiders that a place is sacred, even when it is clear that protection will be provided only if there is such a disclosure.[33] Once again, the aborigine's concept of the relationship between man and land is so different from the white Australian's system of property rights that communication between the cultures has proved difficult.

Derek Roff, senior ranger at Ayers Rock-Mt. Olga National Park in 1975, says older aborigines tend to answer questions the way they think the questioner wants them answered. He believes that younger militants take advantage of this to exaggerate the religious significance of Ayers Rock. A committee considering which sites to protect asked Paddy Uluru—the elder recognized as having the

---

*Ironically, a leader of the aboriginal community suggested that the Australian government should follow "the great example of the North American democracies in their relations and honorable dealings with their original citizens, the Indian nations."[32]

closest totemic ties to the area—to point out sacred places. Roff recounts the scene:

> They started saying "Well then this place should be off limits to whites, shouldn't it, Paddy?" And Paddy in the typical way aboriginals will try to make the questioner happy would answer "yes." I could see that Paddy was very uncomfortable with them but I told him "all right, I won't take tours into any of those places until you figure out exactly which area you don't want whites to visit."

Subsequently, the committee asked 35 elders to visit the rock and decide which areas should be off limits. After the meeting, Paddy Uluru reported that it was necessary to close off only one ritual cave where young boys are initiated into manhood.

How the aborigines will fit into future plans for places like Ayers Rock is a question that remains unanswered. The Northern Territory Reserves Board has made an effort to appoint aborigines to the park staff. Though Paddy Uluru did not accept an offer to live and work at the park, his brother Toby Uluru is a trainee ranger. His primary job is to explain the displays at the Visitors Center. Paddy's son, Reggie, has also been hired by the Reserves Board as a trainee ranger. As the eldest son, Reggie inherits the duty to be the tribal spokesman on the rituals of the rock and has a keen interest in its traditions.

Many people would be put off by the thought that aborigines are to be valued only as "living museum pieces and objects of scientific interest."[34] On the other hand, an Australian tourism official has argued that the display of the aborigines' traditional culture, if properly utilized, "offers [them] one of the best ways to preserve the integrity of their tribal life and customs, as is desired by everyone, and at the same time, to make a living."[35]

A mixture of cultures, in fact, has already taken place, and presents, in the words of Melbourne law professor Geoffrey Sawer, an opportunity and a problem.

> The opportunity is to recreate an ecological balance between man and environment suited to something like an indigenous aboriginal life pattern, and acting to preserve the environment in something like the balance achieved before the coming of the white man. The problem is to do this in a situation where the complete isolation of the aboriginal can no longer be attained, so that aspects of the white technology and economic structure have to be adapted.[36]

Tourists from Two Cultures

Today, most aborigines visiting Ayers Rock arrive in groups, some on foot and some by car or four-wheel-drive vehicle. Phyl and Noel Wallace, whose book *Children of the Desert* is a superb photographic chronicle of the children of the Pitjantjatjara aborigines, describe a modern journey as follows:

> The coming of the white man has not stopped the desert aboriginal's seasonal walkabout, but it has changed it in many ways. Today, the preparation for walkabout includes the unaccustomed packing of such white-man things as buckets, billies, cooking pots, clothes, food, if available, and blankets. Fortunately there are also camels, donkeys, and, for a few, even old unreliable motor cars or trucks. These are used by the lucky ones who own them for carrying their possessions, but the great majority still walk, barefoot, along the time-worn tracks of their ancestors.

Women are seen carrying incredible loads on their heads, while babies and small children cling to shoulders or backs, or ride on hips. Dozens of lean camp dogs follow at the women's heels, adding to the colour, noise and excitement of walkabout. Instructions and advice will be called from group to group, a joke and a laugh will be shared, and a holiday atmosphere generally accompanies the departure. But involved in walkabout there is also deep emotion, because it is not simply a restless, meaningless movement from one place to another. There is always some serious tribal or inter-tribal reason for the journey— perhaps the meeting of relations for some vital ceremony or ritual that will benefit or affect them all.[37]

The Wallaces witnessed the preparation for a hundred-mile walk to attend initiation ceremonies:

We watched as they set out and marvelled at the faith they have in themselves and their land, that they, with young children and babies, could undertake such a journey so pitifully ill-equipped. Barefoot, they walked the route established by their ancestors; we travelled by car on the white man's road, achieving in a day what they managed in eight, and watched again as they arrived at their destination—leaner without doubt, but otherwise in excellent spirits, and quite unaffected by the rigors of their journey.[38]

At Ayers Rock, the aborigines often settle next to the white tourists' camping area. They sit all day under the shade of the mulgas and blackwoods, while tourists scramble up the rock and explore the caves. Later, while every white visitor is 10 miles away on Sunset Dune, the aborigines light their evening fires. Occasionally, one campfire group or another breaks into a chant, practicing songs they will sing later in the evening.

The aborigines make no effort to lure people into coming over to watch. As darkness falls, they simply begin singing. The white tourists usually are hesitant about approaching, not recognizing the chanting as an invitation. Many of them gather in closer to their own campfires, as the muffled and distant singing adds to the eeriness of the setting.

After a night or two of futile attempts to gather a crowd just by singing, the aborigines may approach the ranger for help. He then drives slowly around the tourist camp after dark, encouraging campers to wander over to the chanting and clapping aborigines. A hundred or so whites may gather slowly, standing in a semicircle at a respectful distance from the aborigines, who sit quietly by flickering fires.

The chanting and singing begins without explanation. A few women may rise and perform a dance, each obviously acting a part from a story. Still, there is no word of explanation. The tourists nearest the ranger whisper questions to him, but Derek Roff is hesitant to become master of ceremonies for the corroborees: "They need to explain the stories behind the dances to the tourists, but for them to do that means whites will get involved and that's no good. If I start explaining the dances and passing the hat, they will become dependent on us to do it all the time for them and that's not good." Nonetheless, when Roff is there, he reluctantly gives a brief word of explanation.

The dancers begin their performance dressed in ordinary work clothes. If the audience and atmosphere are right—that is, if there is no laughter at the singing

Corroboree of Aranda tribe. (Photo courtesy Australian News and Information Bureau.)

*Ceremonial dance of Gurundji, one of several tribes living in the Northern Territory.
(Photo courtesy Australian Information Service.)*

and dancing—some of the women dancers may "go bush." They leave the group quietly, partly disrobe, daub themselves with white ochre, and return to do a dance or two. Then, just as casually as it began, the singing stops. The audience is left wondering whether the show has ended. Soon the visitors wander back to their own campfires. Only then, in keeping with the noncommercial character of the whole evening, do the aboriginal elders pass around a hat. It reaches not more than a handful of the hundred or so whites who had been there.

Planned Outback

Studies of tourism at Ayers Rock indicate that a desire for the outback experience is a prime stimulant to white tourists. The visitors look forward to contact with aborigines and aboriginal lore as an important part of this experience; guides for the tour-bus companies emphasize aboriginal legends and rituals in their descriptions of the rock. Mysterious aboriginal campfires bring back the romance of lost explorers, camel caravans, dingo scalpers, and gold prospectors. An individual somehow becomes more Australian after having seen Ayers Rock.

Do tourists leave with what they came for? They usually get only a brief glimpse of aboriginal life in the outback. Many are disappointed that they did not have any direct contact. "A remarkable number of visitors don't even realize there are aborigines around," says Roff.

Unless a formal aboriginal song and dance presentation is staged, dissatisfaction among the audience probably will continue, as will the inefficient present method of passing the hat. Yet once staged, something will be lost in the performance. The dancers will wear paint and feathers, and the dances will be authentic, but the atmosphere will no longer be casual. Today, when a white tourist wanders over to the campfires of the visiting aborigines, he is entering their domain, their way of life as they live it now. He sees them in their tattered clothes, with mangy dogs curled up at the feet of naked, tow-headed children. The tourist hears their songs and sees their dances as they relate to aboriginal life in the 1970s—not carefully staged pseudo-events. The effect is that of tourists meeting tourists, participating in an amalgamation of the primitive and the modern.

In other ways, too, the tourist now sees a strange mosaic of the traditional outback and the modern frontier. The makeshift motels, campsites, roads, airport, and garbage dump, and the almost constant drone from the sightseeing flights, tend to destroy the feeling that Ayers Rock stands isolated in the middle of the outback. Because a desire to experience such isolation prompts many tourists to visit Ayers Rock, the distractions may leave them with a vague sense of dissatisfaction. Yet in many ways the ramshackle, unplanned collection of tents and shacks is itself a true representation of the outback.

It is questionable nevertheless whether the unplanned growth of tourism at Ayers Rock can continue at its present pace without destroying the very things that attract people. Even small numbers of tourists can cause considerable destruction in this environment of harsh climate and fragile desert ecology. Poor planning of roads and trails has aggravated the damage to native flora. In many places around the rock, trampling has destroyed wide areas of vegetation. The paths from parking lots to special points of interest are not wide enough to handle busloads of people, so many wander onto the desert grasses.

At Sunrise and Sunset Dunes, where tourists gather for 45 minutes in the morning and evening, damage is most severe; the height of Sunset Dune has been reduced by a foot since organized tourism began in the 1950s. Near Maggie Springs, another popular spot, a road passes sufficiently close to cause serious erosion. The danger of polluting the scarce water supply is a constant concern. Areas near the motels, campsites, airstrip, and garbage dump have lost almost all vegetation. The roads and airstrip have seriously interfered with drainage patterns, creating erosion around the rock.[39]

Although firewood is provided at the campsites, campers often search the bush for their own. Many a live desert scrub oak has fallen that way. Some tourists pick flowers and break branches at random. Grass fires, often started by careless visitors, are another problem.

The destruction of vegetation creates serious dust when the wind kicks up, and every car on the unsealed roads leaves a cloud in its wake. The dust has begun to have a scouring effect on the cave paintings.

If unplanned growth is a threat, however, so are planners. In fact, the first plan for the area, which proposed an ultramodern tourist village with a 400-room hotel and golf course, aroused wide protest.

Subsequent to that plan, various studies of the area were undertaken, including analyses of the impact of tourism on its delicate ecosystems. Scientists suggested relocating the village and airstrip, and redesigning the road system. For the aborigines, a residential compound and a cultural center was recommended. There, they could play their music and exhibit such skills as painting, carving, tracking, preparation of traditional tools and weapons, boomerang throwing, and dancing.

Fluted sides of Ayers Rock. (Photo courtesy Australian News and Information Bureau.)

A committee representing several departments of Australia's central government—Tourism and Recreation, Aboriginal Affairs, Northern Territory, Housing and Construction, and Environment and Conservation—has been established to review past studies and formulate an official management program for Ayers Rock, including development of a resort village. Many of the needs and values that must be considered in this study are apparent. How they should be evaluated is not.

Quantifying the Dreamtime

Once its attractiveness has been discovered, a place like Ayers Rock can act as a magnet, exerting its own special force, needing neither subsidies, advertisements, nor development agencies. Tourists get their information by word of mouth. What develops is a "collective sense that certain sights must be seen."[40] This, in fact, is how Ayers Rock became famous.

Often, however, the most attractive tourist destinations are fragile magnets. If the special qualities that attract tourists are to be maintained, the impact of increasing use must be carefully controlled. Judgments must be made about the amount of growth that can safely be permitted.

The attempt to determine the limit beyond which growth should not take place often is defined as the search for the "carrying capacity" of an area. The concept has commonly been used in relation to an area's ability to support, for example, deer or cattle. Today, planners are seeking to apply the same concept to humans. They seek quantitative measures of the capacity of each area to take human use without damage to the resource or to the recreation experience.[41]

Could the planners devise a formula to determine how many tourists should visit Ayers Rock? One proposal for determining the carrying capacity of tourist destinations has been offered by P. Stanev of the Scientific Center for Tourism in Sofia, Bulgaria. He proposed the following:

> The basic formula for determining the capacity of a specific tourist area is as follows:
>
> $$K = \frac{S \cdot k_o}{N}$$
>
> where
>
> K = the maximum capacity of the tourist area;
>
> S = the total area;
>
> k_o = the correction factor, which varies between 0.5 and 1 and is determined as a function of hypsometric characteristics, taking into account engineering, geological, hydrological, landscape and other considerations;
>
> N = the standard area per person in m² per person.
>
> The total capacity of the area in question must satisfy the following requirements:
>
> $$\leqslant K \geq \text{II}$$
>
> where
>
> $\leqslant K$ = the total capacity of individual tourist areas;
>
> II = the volume of the stream of tourists (number of visitors) to the area.

Not only is Stanev's formula subject to "hypsometric" correction, but he notes in his commentary that there is "no accepted method" of determining the "stand-ard" area required per tourist.[42]

Another formula has been proposed by Maurice Pickering, an English land-scape architect, to measure the effect of human development on the ecosystem. Called "Pickering's Principle," the formula measures ecological value by the number of species present, while the other side of the equation measures the number of "hominals" present and the nature of their activities.[43]

These formulas emphasize quantification beyond reasonable limits. Ever since astronomer Lord Kelvin propounded his famous dictum that "non-quantified knowledge is of a meager and worthless kind,"[44] formula-makers have attempted to develop quantified measures representing every value involved in a particular development decision, using some common term so that all values can be compared mathematically. The formula then should establish the point at which the harm caused by additional development exceeds the benefits, as measured by units of the common term.

"Reductionism" is the label often applied to those who would reduce all values to measurable terms. Today, many people criticize reductionism as dangerous, and accuse scientists of turning "people and nature into mere, worthless things."[45] The Vietnam war, the first conflict in which formula-makers played a well-publicized role, was a prominent target for antireduc-tionist critics. David Halberstam argued that the very process of reducing every-thing to numbers had the effect of anesthetizing moral feeling. The war, he suggests, was an "aberrant mutation" of analytical methodology in which human lives became "body counts," and persecutions, massacres, and battles were "coolly justified" by cost-benefit analyses prepared by "gifted profes-sors."[46]

Regarding peacetime decisions as well, antireductionist critics argue that analytical systems of policymaking will inevitably discriminate against such values as "ecological balance, urban aesthetics and community cohesion"[47] in favor of a "dull, destructive, political righteousness."[48] The analyst sees the world "through a slide rule darkly,"[49] in the words of Harvard law professor Laurence Tribe.

The analyst responds, however, that the fault does not lie in the analytic method but in its application; that the callousness of the analyses of the Vietnam war only reflected the analysts' brutal values. Similarly, advocates of quantified approaches to carrying-capacity planning may justifiably argue that Pickering's principle and the Bulgarian equation are not fair examples of their art. The solution, they may argue, is to incorporate more accurately measured subjective values into the analysis, not to forego analysis in favor of mysticism or simple power politics. Most analysts who study the effect of additional development on the environment recognize that unless their formulas somehow incorporate subjective values, their work will prove to be largely irrelevant.[50]*

---

*Antireductionists point out, however, that it is the formula-makers who will establish the measur-ing rods for these subjective values, and that they will be strongly tempted to weigh most heavily the values of those who are paying their bill.[51] Kenneth Boulding has satirized this aspect of cost-benefit analysis:

But can we hope to quantify all the important values affected by development decisions? In analyzing tourism at Ayers Rock, how could one quantify, for example, the nature of the outback experience sought by tourists? Or the complex mixture of tradition and aspiration expressed by aboriginal poet Kath Walker:

> See plain the promise,
> Dark freedom–lover!
> Night's nearly over,
>   And though long the climb.
> New rights will greet us,
> New mateship meet us,
> And Joy complete us
>   In our new Dream Time.[53]

Despite the seeming impossibility of the task, the search for quantified carrying capacity goes on. To a public trained to respect the objectivity of scientific judgments and distrust the narrow partisanship of politics, decisions that appear to be based on scientific reasoning attain a certain credibility because of the "media" in which they are garbed.[54]

Too often, the compromise that results is heavily *qualified* quantified analysis—a formula that elaborately dissects the easily quantifiable factors, and carefully points out that the analysis has considered only the "hard data"; that the result may be completely different if unquantifiable factors such as cultural traditions and natural beauty are taken into account. If others want to reach different conclusions on the basis of "political" or "aesthetic" factors, says the analyst, they are free to do so. However, in McLuhan's terms, if the medium is quantified analysis, the message is that unquantified knowledge is of a meager and worthless kind.[55] Thus the result indicated by the "hard data" carries a far more favorable connotation than the result suggested by the fuzzy "intangibles."*

That message—that only hard data is trustworthy—is particularly dangerous where development decisions are concerned. To know how to control development, it is necessary to understand what makes a place attractive. Ayers Rock, like other magnetic tourist destinations, has a special aura, an indefinable combination of characteristics above and beyond the ordinary attractive qualities of hundreds of competing tourist destinations. Deciphering and maintaining those particular qualities is no easy task.

Many scientists hope that someday they can provide a place in the decision-making process for values as disparate as, for instance, those sought by the different kinds of people visiting Ayers Rock. "Policy science," says one of its leading theoreticians, Yehezkel Dror, "recognizes the important roles both of

---

> There are benefits, of course, which may be countable, but which
> Have a tendency to fall into the pockets of the rich,
> While the costs are apt to fall upon the shoulders of the poor,
> So cost-benefit analysis is nearly always sure,
> To justify the building of a solid concrete fact,
> While the Ecologic Truth is left behind in the Abstract.[52]

*English economist E. J. Mishan calls such compromises "horse and rabbit stew." The analyst carefully dissects and measures the flavor of the rabbit, then casually notes that the stew is made with one rabbit and one unanalyzed horse.[56]

extrarational processes (such as creativity, intuition, charisma, and value judgment) and of irrational processes (such as depth motivation)." The "paradoxical problem" of policy science is "how to improve extrarational and even irrational processes through rational means."[57]

But that is a long-range goal, even assuming—as many would not—that it should be pursued.[58] For the moment, changes in the environment must be made through a process in which these values are given consideration, quantified or not. Decision makers need not masquerade as the maximizers of human welfare, but must recognize that "humanity is part of nature and the natural order a constituent part of humanity"; that this relationship is "something deeper and more complex" than man's analytical techniques can handle.[59]

Consider some of the decisions discussed in this book—the destruction of Languedoc's marshes, development of high-rise hotels in Jerusalem. In retrospect, few of the crucial factors affecting the wisdom of those decisions would have lent themselves to quantification. Tourists are not mere numerical abstractions, but complex individual personalities, having a variety of complex motivations. The next chapter examines the impact of an unusual type of tourist on an area that is the opposite of Ayers Rock in almost every respect—the ancient Dutch city of Amsterdam.

Chapter 4
Drifting through Amsterdam

Why do people travel? To the Australian aborigine, walkabout was neither work nor play—it was life. For most medieval Europeans, travel was a rare and dreaded disruption. The idea of traveling for pleasure is a somewhat recent phenomenon.

Travel is now so often perceived as "fun" that the origin of the word *travel* may be all but forgotten. It comes from the same root as *travail*, and throughout most of history travel was thought of as a painful chore. In the words of an ancient Arabic proverb, "There are three states of wretchedness—sickness, fasting and travel."[1]

During the 18th and 19th centuries, modes of transportation gradually improved. Larger, more comfortable ships were built. Railroads enabled the traveler to avoid rutted highways. "Instead of an athletic exercise, travel became a spectator sport," says Daniel Boorstin. "It was the decline of the traveler and the rise of the tourist."[2] It has certainly become rare to meet someone who lacks the desire to see new sights, experience new places, and escape daily routines.

Given the profits to be gained from tourism, and the desire of many countries, corporations, and individuals to share in them, it is not surprising that the tourism industry sponsors countless surveys asking why people travel. Yet attempts to simplify the motivations of tourists typically degenerate into stereotypes; subconscious motives may be more important than those reported to pollsters.

The tour bus filled with retired shopkeepers and doctors is only a part of the story. Young people are traveling in increasing numbers and following patterns much different from those of their parents. Millions travel for religious reasons. Others travel to study, to shop, to relive the pioneer life, to "take the cure," or just to get out of their apartment. There are tourists who travel to Paris to eat, or to Munich to drink.

Some analysts suggest that the motive for traveling is an urge to see another side of oneself, to discover "the unknown worlds of our potentialities."[3] Sociologist Dean MacCannell feels that members of his profession and tourists

---

Field research for this chapter was conducted by Richard D. Ducker.

are much alike; both attempt to "synthesize modern and traditional elements in a new holistic understanding of the human community and its place in the modern world."[4] A desire for deeper involvement with a different culture is often part of the motive for traveling, whether to exotic cultures in distant lands or to the bucolic contrast that the nearby countryside offers.

Those most concerned with seeking intercultural experiences often speak of a search for authenticity—culture untainted by outside contact. Wary of the fakery of "tourist traps," many of these people cherish the belief that somewhere they can find "a genuine society."[5] At the other extreme, some tourists approach travel timidly, welcoming everything that reminds them of home, and seeking the companionship of a group of compatriots.

Sociologist Erik Cohen has classified tourists according to the degree that they seek new experiences, free from traditional sanctions. The tourist who wants the most familiar experiences and official sanctions is the "organized mass tourist." The next category is the "individual mass tourist," followed by the "explorer," and, finally, the "drifter."[6]

With businesses and governments around the world trying to attract mass tourists, economies of scale have greatly reduced the cost of tourism. Charter flights and block bookings of hotel rooms have made overseas travel available for the first time to working-class families in most developed countries. At the same time, reduced fares for jet travel and other transportation opportunities have enabled young people to travel more than ever before and have contributed to the rapid growth of the least orthodox form of tourism—the new style of walkabout known as drifting.

The phenomenon of drifting, according to Erik Cohen, first appeared after World War II. The drifter was a tourist who became "both physically and emotionally involved in the lives of members of the host society" and was thus "the true rebel of the tourist establishment and the complete opposite of the mass tourist."[7]

In the late 1960s, as the number of drifters began to mushroom, the character of drifter tourism changed:

> The original drifter would typically travel without a fixed itinerary or time table, going places by whim or opportunity and staying as long as he pleased— or when necessity or opportunity spurred him on. Since he was travelling outside the established tourist circuit—both geographically and socially—he had to make use of those opportunities for lodging, eating and travelling which lent themselves and which were often those used by the local population. With the *Vermassung* of drifting, these things changed. Drifter-itineraries were gradually formed . . . [and] . . . some of these might not differ much from the itineraries frequented by the ordinary, adult tourist. The drifters and the other tourists thus frequently flow along parallel geographical lines, though through segregated institutional channels.[8]

Seemingly off the beaten path, having rejected traditional tourist behavior, drifters established patterns of their own. The emergence of drifting as a mass phenomenon led to coalescences of people with shared interests and demands that may be likened to those produced by more conventional forms of tourism.

Sightseeing boat on canal in central Amsterdam. (Photo by Bart Hofmeester.)

When tourists are attracted to a place, and begin to converge on it, they create problems, raise questions, and prompt decisions, no matter what kinds of tourists they are, or where the place is. Drifting, in fact, may be only the opposite, still largely unfamiliar face of a common coin. The people of Amsterdam, however, know it well.

The New Grand Tour

The Netherlands has been called "the gentlest, kindest place in Europe."[9] No single explanation of this reputation is entirely satisfactory. Perhaps, in part, it is a reflection of a strong religious heritage that has encouraged pacifism and discouraged violence in Dutch society. Or it may owe something to the fact that the political party structure in the Netherlands has been highly fragmented, and any effective political action could be based only on careful coalition building.[10] Some say the Dutch are determined to highlight the contrast between their own flexibility and what they see as the rigidity of their powerful neighbors to the east, the Germans. The Dutch, indeed, have always been proud of their individuality in a world dominated by larger countries.

Within the Netherlands, the city of Amsterdam represents the epitome of the independence and benevolence for which the Dutch are celebrated. James Boswell, writing to a friend in 1763, noted a distinction between the Dutch in general and "the citizens of Amsterdam, who must always wish to be free from any superior power."[11] Another traveler in that century wrote that "as for acts of charity, Amsterdam may be said to equal if not surpass all of the cities of the world. At every house almost in the city there hangs a poor's box with a chain, in which people put money as they are disposed. . . ."[12] For hundreds of years, the city has thought of itself as a tolerant place where minority groups have prospered.

For tourists today, Amsterdam is the fourth most popular city in Europe. Many visitors enjoy traveling down the narrow canals lined with gabled brick townhouses, listening to guides describe the city's history in anecdotes, perhaps in six different languages. The Rijksmuseum is the home of some of the best works of Rembrandt, Vermeer, and Hals. Another museum houses a dazzling collection of Van Goghs. Among music lovers, the Concertgebouw is world renowned.

Because of its cultural attractions, Amsterdam has long been a highlight of the grand tour. In the late 1960s, however, legions of drifters began arriving, and the city soon became a high point of European counterculture. The new tourists, less interested in traditional sights, seemed to be motivated by different forces.

To many residents of Amsterdam, the young tourists symbolized the more relaxed, peaceful society they hoped the future would bring. "It all depended on your point of view," according to historian Geoffrey Cotterell. "For some the beautiful people were standard-bearers of a new and lovelier world . . . while to others they were a squalid nuisance, badly needing to wash and probably to be deloused."[13]

Unlike most places in Europe, Amsterdam offered many special services for young people. In few other cities and countries had youth interests and activities been so legitimized, so publicized, and the points of view of young people so widely heard. The Dutch also had a reputation for tolerating those who wanted to smoke grass or hash—smiling, and ignoring the reasons for the many vacant smiles they received in return.

Some of this Dutch hospitality faded when young tourists began congregating in ever-increasing numbers on the Dam, a historic square with a national war memorial at its center. As the Dam overflowed daily with drifters, many of whom remained for the night, contributors to the War Monument Fund demanded their money back. Owners of neighboring retail stores complained of people sleeping in entryways and blocking sidewalks. Tour buses brought traditional visitors not to see the square, which has been compared with such famous urban plazas as Trafalgar Square and the Place de la Madeleine, but its notorious occupants—tourists who had become transformed into attractions.[14]

A local political group, the *Kabouters* (gnomes), provided its share of annoyance by heralding the drifters as the vanguard of a better society. One Kabouter proclamation read: "How does a new society rise from an old society?

The Dam Square. (Photo courtesy Artica Press.)

Like a toadstool on a rotting tree trunk . . . left and right the toadstools of the new society will spread. Fairy circles of elf-cities will join together in a world-encircling net: the Orange Free State."[15]

Whatever the future, the drifters on the Dam in 1970 aroused a backlash. In August, the mayor of Amsterdam gave the people sleeping on the square several days' warning to find accommodations elsewhere. Then police moved in, and a contingent of marines helped them "liberate" the Dam. The marines remained to clear dirt and rubbish from the memorial, and then marched away to the station, singing the war song "Zorg, dat je erbij komt"—"Make Sure That You're There." A large number of Amsterdammers joined in the singing.[16]

The cleaning-up effort generated mixed emotions, as might have been expected in Amsterdam. The mayor's decision was attacked from all sides. Dam sleepers felt that they had been betrayed. Even some residents who agreed with the decision complained about the ineptitude with which it was executed. In retrospect, many people thought that a wiser alternative would have been to institute the sleeping prohibition during the winter months, when the Dam was virtually deserted.

As summer ended, city officials pondered over the influx anticipated in the following year, and how to deal with it. They considered the rather unorthodox opportunities provided for their own young people. For a number of years, Amsterdam had subsidized private groups that operated youth centers, primarily for the use of residents. In the daytime, visitors to these centers could find quiet areas to practice meditation or yoga, and in the evenings there were rock groups, light and multimedia shows, and—probably most importantly—ample opportunities to smoke dope in peace. Following an outdoor concert at one of the youth centers, a Dutch observer noted: "So much hash was smoked that mosquitoes dropped dead from the sky, yet the police did not interfere."[17]

The city decided to establish alternative accommodations for young tourists, especially for those who wished to sleep outside. The result: the Vondel Park experiment.

The First Year: Free As Birds

"Heaven is our roof; we do not work; we are as free as birds," wrote the Dutch poet Joost van den Vondel. The park named after him is a beautiful, 150-acre site within walking distance of the Leidesplein, the entertainment center of Amsterdam. Vondel Park contains a teahouse, an outdoor theater, tennis courts and playing fields, ponds, creeks, wooded areas, and green lawns that benefit from the generous Dutch rain.

In 1971, the year after the Dam controversy, the city opened the entire park to people who wished to sleep out of doors, without tents. An old school on the park boundary was converted to a public facility with showers, washrooms, a baggage depot, and a first-aid station. A bomb shelter under the Vondel Park bridge was refurbished as a recreation center. A cafe was opened and managed by a special youth organization. The director of a nearby youth center, Piet Riemans, became director of the Vondel Park project.

By midsummer 1971, about 500 sleepers used the park each night. The recreation center became a focal point for youth activity. In the evening young people could enjoy films, music, and live entertainment—sometimes until 4 A.M. A sign outside the door advised that "smoking" was permitted but using or dealing hard drugs was not.

The staff supervising the experiment were enthusiastic at the outset, feeling that Amsterdam was doing something unique in the world. But the colony of drifters in the park soon aroused controversy. The Hotel and Restaurant Owners Association sent a letter to the city council demanding that quiet hours be imposed from midnight until 7:00 A.M. So much trash was produced that the sanitation department could not cope with it: waste bins constantly overflowed; plastic sacks and empty cans and bottles polluted the ponds. Lack of sufficient toilet facilities led park users to improvise in ways that many others found offensive. A newspaper in one of the southern provinces commented that Vondel Park was becoming a "modern version of a Middle Age plague house."

Project director Riemans agreed that the park was being fouled. The city allocated more money, and by early August the park had additional waste cans, toilet wagons, and sanitary personnel. In September, some of the most worn patches of lawn were replaced with new sod, and the park began to resume its normal appearance.

The Users

A 1971 survey of the young people staying in Vondel Park found that the accessibility of drugs was a major reason for their coming to Amsterdam. The city's reputation for drug tolerance was widespread. In July 1971, for example, CBS television in the United States presented a special on the subject of Amsterdam and drugs. According to correspondent John Sheehan, "Every young tourist can, within minutes of arriving in Amsterdam, buy hashish. . . . In order to know what the actual effects are of the use of drugs, we need only to study the Dutch experiment."

From the beginning of the Vondel Park project, the issue of drugs lurked in the background. Piet Riemans' attitude was, "Naturally, you may relax and smoke a 'stickie' here. I find it absolutely harmless. That is one of the great attractions of Amsterdam." Hard drugs were viewed as a different matter by the project staff.

For their part, the police were reluctant to intervene. In the last week of August 1971, however, they conducted a drug raid on the recreation center under the Vondel Park bridge. Initiated by plainclothes informants, the bust concentrated only on users and dealers of hard drugs. Smokers were left alone.

As the project completed its first year, the city was concerned that drugs were fostering larceny. Thefts from automobiles in the vicinity of Vondel Park increased. Ten youths were arrested for theft one day, 17 one week, by local police. A newspaper carried the headline "Image of Vondel Park Grows Worse Because of Thefts." In the view of one observer, "The foreigners think that here in the park anything is allowed. Smoking is okay, so why not stealing?"

A federation of social service organizations in Amsterdam declared that it would not support a continuation of the Vondel Park project in 1972 unless the city gave more attention to the growing number of destitute youth who were not leaving the city in the autumn, but staying through the winter. Youths with no

Drifters sleeping in Vondel Park. (Photo courtesy United Press International.)

money, often with mental health and drug problems, were breaking into abandoned houses, trying to find employment without work permits, and stealing to
support themselves. The Kabouter Party proposed that the city of Amsterdam ask
the U.S. government for contributions toward Amsterdam's expenses in accommodating the "so-called American youth problem."

The Second Year: Amsterdam, Here We Come

As the summer of 1972 approached, Amsterdam's new type of park received
worldwide publicity. *Newsweek* predicted 1,000,000 Americans were coming,
and project leaders spoke of 100,000 youths in Vondel Park. Airlines offered
so-called "hippie charter flights" to Amsterdam. Pan American Airways, KLM's
bitter rival for trans-Atlantic traffic to and from Holland, placed full-page ads in

The New York Times advertising such flights: "Beautiful, friendly Amsterdam, the world city where young people can best feel at home, is preparing this summer to receive you in probably greater numbers than ever before but in the orderly Dutch manner." The ad ended by exclaiming, "Open up your Vondel Park, Amsterdam, here we come!" City officials and residents were irked.

By midsummer, however, most residents of Amsterdam were breathing a sigh of relief. Although many more young drifters were sleeping in the park than had been in 1971 (85,000 compared to 51,000), there were many fewer complaints. A greatly expanded budget allowed for more facilities and workers, ranging from youth counselors to sanitation personnel. At least one observer found the situation in the park "remarkably better than last year." By the autumn of 1972, one report called damage to the park "negligible."

But the character of the visitors also had changed. A concessionaire, who felt that "hippies" were his best customers, on second thought reflected that "real hippies" were hard to find. More and more American college youths appeared with the latest and most expensive backpacks, sleeping bags, and miscellaneous equipment. There was talk of the new kind of young visitor in Amsterdam, the "hip" youth who ate at the best restaurants, stayed on the Dam by day, took the "alternative bus ride," and had a room in the Hilton but slept in the park—unless, of course, it rained. As one observer put it, "To be hip is nice but you mustn't get wet from it." During a particularly rainy week, only about 40 hardy souls remained outside for the night.

As the number of more traditional college students who were trying to be "hip" increased, Amsterdam became less a gilded cage for the persecuted than a routine stop for young people doing the countercultural tour of Europe. Every young traveler had to be able to say he had slept in Vondel Park. Drifter tourism seemed, at least at first glance, to have become institutionalized, "segregated from but parallel to" the tourism of the Rijksmuseum crowd.[18]

The Third and Fourth Years: Dealing with Dealers

On the surface, the summer of 1973 seemed uneventful. The city made a few changes in the administration of the project, such as closing the recreation center under the Vondel Park bridge. There was relatively little complaint. Few young tourists could remember what Vondel Park had been like in its heyday. Drifters came as usual; the action was absent. After a few evenings in the park, most people moved on.

Yet beneath the surface, the predictions by the youth assistance agencies two years earlier were coming true. An increasing number of those using the park had serious drug problems. Amsterdam had become a haven for runaways, for the homeless, the jobless, and those who were psychologically and emotionally disturbed. A dependent, problem-ridden group was coming to Amsterdam not as tourists but to stay. Most were unable or unwilling to find work. Some girls turned to prostitution.

Almost inevitably, these young people became hooked on hard drugs, and Vondel Park increasingly became a major meeting place. By 1973, with Asian heroin flooding the Amsterdam market, the park was a prime ground for introducing young victims to hard drug use.

By the fall of 1973, the decline of the situation in the park was obvious. Nevertheless, the mayor and aldermen renewed the project for 1974 and installed a special commission for youth tourism in Amsterdam in an attempt to bring together the Vondel Park project leaders, the leaders of the other youth accommodations, and the leaders of the youth assistance programs.

The summer of 1974 was a rather wet and cold one by Dutch standards. About 80,000 overnights were counted in Vondel Park, down from 120,000 in 1973. An American girl remarked, "This is not such a magic city as I thought. It's mainly just very expensive here." Cynicism was pervasive, even among the park staff. Everyone was bored. One project leader suggested, with considerable understatement, "Maybe they have no ambition."

The negative side effects of the Vondel Park experiment, which had been becoming more apparent each year, now largely overshadowed the positive aspects. The findings of a study commission substantiated reports of increased theft, use of heroin, and numbers of underage runaways who expected to remain in Amsterdam. Believing the city could not deal adequately with the problems, the commission recommended that the Vondel Park project be discontinued and that sleeping in the park either be banned or discouraged by closing the information center and the baggage depot and reducing the food, medical, and sanitary facilities to those required for normal park use. The commission also urged that announcements of the project's cessation be placed in foreign newspapers.

Dealt Out

The study commission's report helped tip the scales, and in January 1975 the city council banned sleeping in public places and terminated appropriations for the Vondel Park project. The council also acknowledged the severity of the drug problem in Amsterdam and initiated a "get-tough" campaign on drug and housing regulations.

Many residents gave a sigh of relief and wondered why action had not been taken long before. A tourism official commented, "Journalists and newspaper people always used to visit our offices and would ask us how we liked all these young tourists here. And we would always say, 'We are always happy to see more tourists in Amsterdam.' But in fact we really hated it!"

To help provide for young tourists who would still come to Amsterdam in the summer, the city adopted a dispersal strategy, proposing that a new camping facility be developed in the Amsterdam Woods, a city-owned regional park. An existing facility in northern Amsterdam was also to be used. This proposal ran into immediate opposition, however, from the municipality of Amstelveen, which adjoined the woods. Its councilmen worried that problems of policing the area would fall on their shoulders, rather than on the city's. Alternative plans were discussed. Finally, in late spring 1975, a new site for a camping ground was chosen, on an island in the Ij River in the northeastern corner of Amsterdam. The new location did not attract many young tourists, most of whom preferred the excitement of the city. Problem youths continued to disappear into the bowels of Amsterdam, and have remained problems for the social service organizations.

Vondel Park is still beautiful, and it still attracts many visitors. But in sharp contrast to the jam-packed days of the early 1970s, on a Sunday afternoon it may seem almost deserted. Many of the slogans scrawled by the young drifters have faded. Prominent signs in several languages make it clear that sleeping in the park is prohibited.

Contrasting Cultures

The rise and fall of Vondel Park as a tourism capital of the counterculture occurred within the brief span of five years. In microcosm, it provides an illustration of the fragile relationship between tourists and the special places to which they are attracted. The staid, middle-class residents of Amsterdam were upset at the odd behavior of the drifters. In other parts of the world, the behavior of middle-class European and American tourists may be equally upsetting.

In developing countries the tourist represents the modern, international culture that often both fascinates and repels.[19] Some commentators have argued that mass tourism aggravates relations between different cultures by encouraging both tourist and host to play stereotyped roles.[20] In the words of a citizen of Fiji:

Central Amsterdam. (Photo courtesy KLM Aerocarto.)

As our people in Fiji go about their daily tasks of serving the visitors we see an endless succession of the same little old ladies, with the same blue hair rinses, spending the same life insurance money and speaking in the same accents of the same things which have penetrated their similar perceptions. And what of little old ladies? As they climb in and out of their same cars, their same planes, their same hotel beds, as they eat the same foods, drink the same drinks, and buy the same souvenirs, is it to be wondered at that many cannot tell from one day to the next which country it is that they are presently visiting? These people travel the world like registered parcels, blindly unaware of the local populations, their aspirations, problems and tragedies. Instead of promoting mutual understanding, they promote mutual contempt.[21]

Many tourists agree with Daniel Boorstin that they are increasingly becoming make-believe actors in a papier-mâché world, that mass tourism is destroying the authenticity they seek by encouraging "picturesque" natives to perform pseudo-events whenever the tour bus appears:

Earnest, honest natives embellish their ancient rites, change, enlarge, and spectacularize their festivals, so that tourists will not be disappointed. In order to satisfy the exaggerated expectations of tour agents and tourists, people everywhere obligingly become dishonest mimics of themselves.[22]

Tour groups seek to visit genuine attractions, says Erik Cohen, but in the end they "transform and manipulate them."[23]

Even anthropologist Claude Lévi-Strauss, who tries to study a culture objectively, often feels that his presence contaminates:

A proliferating and overexcited civilization has broken the silence of the seas once and for all. The perfumes of the tropics and the pristine freshness of human beings have been corrupted by a busyness with dubious implications, which mortifies our desires and dooms us to acquire only contaminated memories.[24]

The increasing mobility of the world's populations has produced an intermingling of cultures. "Modern mobility tends to cancel out one reason for its existence," according to Garrett Eckbo, "by making alike all those places that once attracted by their differences."[25]

Cultures are, in fact, changing rapidly, incorporating influences from all parts of the world, just as Western culture has absorbed from others. A visitor to the Caribbean may complain about West Indian steel bands playing eclectic music for tourists rather than their pure native folk songs, thus creating "a distortion of the original meaning which may in fact be unidentifiable to later research workers. . . ."[26] But surely each ethnic group does not have an obligation to maintain the purity of its ways so that tourists and research workers may study them. African music has had a powerful influence on jazz and rock music; Japanese art has strongly influenced the art of Europe. These "impurities" are seldom found objectionable. Why, then, should there be an objection to West Indian steel bands playing Beatles tunes?

"Culture is not some cross to carry; it is a way of having fun," in the words of James Ritchie, an anthropologist from Waikato University in New Zealand. In the Pacific,

the level of culture continuity is tough, sinewy, but also capable of multi-form expression. Bar songs are it. Beer parties are it. Waikiki is it. Slogans stenciled on T-shirts are it. And so are electric guitars, modern dyes and paint, mimeographed newssheets, photo-montage, tape recordings, children's park and school classes, legends retold, poems created, cultural competitions. . . . What specific islanders are doing expresses their cultures as they are now. If ways can be found to enhance, excite, stimulate, encourage, promote, support any or all kinds of experimentation, sharing, enjoyment, then let such ways be explored and leave it to the culture carried by those whose culture it is to select and to determine its own fate. . . .[27]

Like the Australian aborigines, people around the world are forgetting some of the specific habits of their clans and tribes, blending them into new mixtures. The small groups into which people formerly divided themselves are being replaced by much larger categories, writes Margaret Mead. "The farther from home, the larger the category with which our minds must work. Californians become successively Americans, Westerners, and Whites as they move about the globe."[28] Tourists are both carrying and absorbing a modern, worldwide culture.

The increased mobility reflected in tourism may gradually bring about a substantial change in the relationship between people and places. The middle-class European cannot list his address as Paris and St. Tropez, but he may be able to list it as Rotterdam and Zeeland, or Birmingham and Torquay. Future demographers, instead of using little dots to represent people on population density maps, may need to use lines—or, for Swedes, Swiss, and Germans, just a blur.

It may be premature to say that the world's population is beginning a long, slow evolution toward the nomadic status once enjoyed by the Australian aborigine, and his counterpart—the modern drifter. Nonetheless, there are people, and their number may be increasing, who have adopted this kind of life-style. Some members of the "jet set"—people who, as Russell Baker put it, "live in a natural state of travel"—have literally become homeless.[29] They wander the globe to avoid spending the length of time in any country that would trigger higher tax payments. As Mick Jagger put it:

Why do you need a country? I don't think you need a country. It's not necessary any more—if it ever was. I suppose it was at one time. I think that people that play music don't need a country at all. Nor do physicists, either. Whatever skills they have, they perform that service anywhere.[30]

From the User's View

The drifters who moved through Vondel Park were adapted to rootlessness. A sense of independence accompanies an ability to move on at a moment's notice. Yet with the independence grew a disregard for the people and places they visited, and this produced a backlash.

In the beginning, most residents of Amsterdam were proud of their city's attractiveness to drifters. It was evidence of the benevolence for which the city was famous. But a pathological element emerged. Users of the park were also users of drugs that led to theft, psychosis, and violence. As this pathology increasingly became dominant, the benevolence of Amsterdam's citizens was sorely tested.

All tourism can be viewed as a drug. It can be uplifting and beneficial; it can make one feel good. But it can be abused and become destructive, to the user and to his environment. Even the botanist, who sanitizes his clothing to avoid carrying exotic seeds into the untrodden New Guinea jungle, does the jungle some harm, however negligible. Yet the tourist's impact can often be accommodated—like that of the botanist—if there is a clear understanding of what drug is being sought, what makes a place attractive, so that the destructive elements can be minimized. Ayers Rock and Vondel Park show how elusive and subtle the attractive qualities of an area can be. And when the users of the area include such exotic people as aborigines and drifters, determining what they find attractive and how their needs can be reconciled with other needs is no simple matter.

In Amsterdam, the drifters didn't participate in the process of deciding where they could stay. The users' viewpoint was represented only by stand-ins—in this case social workers, innkeepers, or merchants—people whose concern for the users' desires was mixed with, if not subordinated to, their own self-interest.

The role played by the drifters in Amsterdam differs only in degree from the role played by tourists everywhere. Were the tourists asked whether they wanted high-rise hotels in Jerusalem? No, the hotel developer spoke for the tourists' interests, and persuasively argued that he could sell the tourist that most enticing drug—the "international" high-rise, which looks the same whether in Jakarta or Dakar, and promises the tourist the security of a lodging that may not be exciting but at least won't be disappointing. To what extent will these hotels reduce Jerusalem's attractiveness to tourists? No one knows.

If tourists' perceptions of a place's attractive qualities were accurately understood, the destructive aspects of tourism could be better controlled. Amsterdam might well have been able to accommodate drifters without tolerating extreme drug abuse, just as Jerusalem could accommodate foreign tourists without tolerating the visual pollution of high-rise hotels.

For places like Jerusalem, Ayers Rock, or Amsterdam, it is, perhaps, the viewpoint of the artist that will help to provide an understanding of attractiveness. After his first six months in the South of France, Vincent Van Gogh wrote his brother: "To make a picture that will really be of the South, it's not enough to have a certain dexterity. It's looking at things for a long time that ripens you and gives you a deeper understanding."[31]

The problem of point of view will be reexamined in later chapters. First, however, it is important to consider the effects of a type of tourism that is not so much the result of a particular place's magnetism—what draws people to Jerusalem, Ayers Rock, or Amsterdam—as of a desire to "get away."

III PLANNING

Chapter 5
Sprawl Is Beautiful?

The automobile has transformed tourism into an experience that can be shared by all but the very poorest. Despite the tremendous growth of tourism, however, relatively little is known about how many people travel where, particularly within a country. To some extent, the absence of accurate data reflects a popular desire to have government keep its nose out of people's leisure time.* For statisticians, that freedom of the tourist to move about undetected is frustrating insofar as it requires expensive survey techniques to determine tourist movements.

On the European continent tourism statistics are somewhat more meaningful than in most regions because so many tourists cross national boundaries and are counted at those points. Wherever an automobile can travel in Europe, there is likely to be a tourist in the summer. In 1976, 150,000 Danes were accommodated at tourist facilities in Austria; 200,000 French, in Denmark; 420,000 Portuguese, in France; and 130,000 Austrians visited Spain.[1]**

Automobiles and a network of broad motorways have made rural Europe much more accessible than it once was, and tourism has spread to areas that even 50 years ago had been considered remote from major cities. Not only in Europe, but in developed countries throughout the world, there has been a dramatic increase in the number of people who pack up their car and drive someplace for a weekend or a week.

In response to the demand generated by widespread automobile travel, there has been increasing development of tourist accommodations designed to permit

---

*In *The Day of the Jackal*, the apprehension of the potential assassin of President de Gaulle is facilitated by a French law requiring hotel keepers to report on a daily basis the names and passport numbers of foreign guests. This peculiar French law was subsequently repealed and now in France, as elsewhere, people can travel by car without anyone knowing where they have gone or why.

**Germans, who take pride in being the world's most inveterate travelers, dominate European tourism statistics. Over 7,000,000 stayed in Austrian accommodations and 3,500,000 in Danish accommodations in 1976.

Field research for this chapter was conducted by Paul R. DeStefano, Richard D. Ducker, Christopher J. Duerksen, Richard J. Roddewig, and Eastern Tin.

115

the occupants to cook their own meals. "Self-catering" accommodations, as they are known in the trade, are not a new idea; what is new is the increasing share of the tourism market such units occupy.

Perhaps the simplest self-catering accommodation is the tent. In many countries, widespread automobile ownership has greatly increased the popularity of camping. Sometimes, trailers or recreational vehicles are used, but tent camping is especially popular with people who cannot easily afford such luxuries. In France, some campgrounds are owned by factories, and workers obtain use of the site as a fringe benefit.

Houses and apartments designed for recreational use are also increasingly popular. Many are rental units, but more and more people are buying their own second homes, often a condominium. Once a privilege of the rich, the second home has now become a goal for a large part of the population.

Demand for second homes has been felt throughout Europe. The number in the Alps is expected to triple by 1985.* In Norway, there is already one second home for every five year-round homes, and by 1990 the ratio is expected to be one to three.[2] In Sweden, a 1967 study found one household in every seven owning a second home. The ratio has undoubtedly increased substantially since then; by 1980, it is predicted that Sweden will have 5 to 10 times as many recreational dwellings as farm dwellings.[3]

Other urbanized countries are experiencing the same phenomenon. In Australia it is common for urban families to buy lots in recreational subdivisions and do their own building. On weekends, middle-class Mexicans pour out of Mexico City toward cottages in Cuernavaca and other resort areas. Japan, too, is seeing a boom in the construction of second homes, reflecting a recent trend to family vacations.

The new mobility that tourism reflects seems to represent a basic change in life-style. In Germany, only 13.5 percent of disposable income is being saved.[4] In all of the wealthier European countries, demand for televisions, stereos, dishwashers, and other such goods has flattened out. People are, however, seeking more leisure time, which they want to spend in places more "home-like" than traditional hotels. The increasing use of cottages, condominiums, campgrounds, and trailers has dramatically affected traditional patterns of geographic dispersion and caused social and economic changes on the Continent as well as in many other parts of the world.

The Impact of Self-Catering

The growing demand for self-catering accommodations has had at least three major impacts: (1) on the location of tourism facilities, (2) on the labor requirements of the tourism business, and (3) on the retail and service suppliers of tourists.

Geographically, the location of a self-catering accommodation is much more flexible than that of traditional hotels. Since tourists arrive by automobile, access to the facility is not dependent on public transportation. The automobile is available to take the tourist to shops, cultural events, sports, or other recreational

---

*In Garmisch, Germany, a sheik from Oman recently purchased a 150-room hotel for his second home.

activities, so the accommodation need not provide such services nor be within walking distance of them. And, since few people are needed to manage self-catering accommodations, they need not be located near sources of abundant labor.

As a result, self-catering accommodations tend to spread throughout the countryside. Because there is less dependence on specific sites, land costs often are much lower than for more traditional types of tourist development. Cheaper land, in turn, has helped to make self-catering tourism available to more people.

The social implications of this growth may be significant. In many communities, jobs available in the hotel trades have declined sharply. Beyond this, the availability of cooking facilities in the new accommodations means that tourists are less dependent on local restaurants. Grocers may obtain some benefits; yet many tourists arrive with their cars already full of food.

Changes in social and geographic patterns have also led to a sharp decline in land prices in some tourist centers, and a gradual rise in land prices over a larger region. Nonetheless, the various cost reductions have created more opportunities for tourism for more people.

This chapter examines areas affected by an increasing number of small-scale tourist accommodations, the spread of which is hard to control. A few cottages here, a few there, individually seem innocuous. Gradually, however, the increments can transform the environment.

Most of the world's more advanced countries try to regulate this type of development through systems of physical planning. Government agencies prepare some type of overall plan for a community or region and grant permits for new development consistent with the plan. The Dutch planning system, for example, has had to deal with scattered tourism development in the province of Zeeland.

Kleine Schaal

If there is any place where one might expect an appropriate use of scattered recreational housing, it is in the Dutch countryside, where *kleine schaal* (small scale) is a way of life. In the 1930s, Karel Čapek noted:

> The Dutch seem to have founded something like a small-scale style of building. Their houses are smaller than anywhere else; the livingrooms are about as tiny and airy as birdcages. . . . There is a certain cosiness and frugality with regard to size which, where this nation is concerned, constitute nothing short of an ingrained formal law. . . . Everything that the nation builds and establishes on its small territory is somehow in harmony with the size of the country. Here people do not bite off more than they can chew, by overdoing things either in architecture or their way of living.[5]

Reliable statistics on dispersed tourism, or sprawl, may be difficult to obtain, but on the coast of the Netherlands at the end of June no statistics are needed. Long lines of cars full of tourists can be seen heading out of cities—some pulling trailers, others carrying tents, many just carrying food to stock their summer home.

Many of the tourists are going to the Netherlands' most isolated province, Zeeland, in the southwestern corner of the country. Here, three major rivers empty into the North Sea through a system of inlets, bays, and estuaries. The land

Kleine schaal—small scale, as represented by town of Den Hoorn. (Photo by author.)

is uniformly flat, except for a row of sand dunes that protects it from the North Sea. The horizon often seems endless. Most buildings are small: church steeples and windmills provide orientation for miles around. Old dike walls, farm houses, and neat rows of trees blend into a harmonious whole.

For centuries, Zeeland was distant in every sense from Amsterdam and the other sophisticated cities of Holland. A 19th-century traveler commented, "Zeeland is somewhat mysterious even to the Dutch themselves; very few of them have seen it."[6] Zeeland's people were traditionally quiet, deeply religious farmers; few newsworthy events happened in the remote province.

Then, in January 1953, Zeeland attracted worldwide attention. Huge waves, caused by strong westerly winds and abnormally high tides, damaged or destroyed approximately 300 miles of dikes, leaving almost 55,000 square miles of land inundated. More than 1,800 people drowned, and 72,000 were left homeless. Saltwater ruined much of the farmland for years.[7]

Subsequently, a commission established by the Dutch government to study the future of the delta area recommended a large public works project to dam off all the major arms of the sea except the shipping routes to Rotterdam and Antwerp. By 1961, the first inlet was dammed, creating a freshwater lake, the Veerse Meer. Two other inland lakes were also created out of former bays.

The keystone of the delta project was to be a single huge dam—the

Oosterschelde—connecting the islands of Schouwen-Duiveland and Walcheren, which would block the strong winds and tides. But concern spread throughout Holland about the environmental impact of the dam. It was thought that it would surely spell the end of oyster, mussel, and shrimp fisheries; saltwater marshes, which provided breeding and feeding grounds for marine animals and birds, would be destroyed. Many cities feared that the new freshwater body would become increasingly polluted by canals connecting it with Holland's industrial rivers.

Environmental groups objecting to the proposal carried their message to their elected representatives. In November 1974, the Dutch parliament adopted a compromise plan. Studies were to be carried out to determine whether a partial dam with massive floodgates would be feasible.

The Oosterschelde controversy created among the residents of Zeeland a substantial awareness of environmental-impact problems. That awareness did not, however, bring into focus another major environmental problem, namely, the steady stream of tourism development. In contrast to a single, massive project like the Oosterschelde, tourism development in Zeeland involves the construction of many different campgrounds, second homes, and other accommodations. Growth results from countless small decisions, each having only a minor effect. Nevertheless, the aggregate has had a major impact on the region.

Down the Delta Route

The tourism boom in Zeeland, as in many other places, began with new construction to facilitate transportation, providing easier access to the area. A series of roads and bridges, known as the Delta Route, has put most of Zeeland within two hours of Rotterdam. The number of visitor-nights spent in the province grew from less than two million in 1959 to over six million in 1970 and approximately seven million five years later. Most of the tourists are interested in camping. Camper trailers account for over 5 percent of the vehicles registered in the Netherlands.[8]

In 1975, the Ministry of Economic Affairs encouraged an increase in the number of campers by offering to pay 50 percent of all infrastructure costs for new campgrounds (as well as other tourist destinations) as a way of boosting employment. It also played a strong role in promoting tourism by advertising in other countries and by financing new hotels. The ministry establishes "zones of tourist development," one of which is the North Sea coast, where large stretches of land are still only sparsely used even at the height of the season. Tourism officials have suggested the shore should be made more easily accessible along its entire length.

The Dutch need no officially promulgated statement to tell them that Zeeland's wild North Sea coast is attractive. Most of Zeeland's tourists come from urban centers in the Netherlands, where population density is among the world's highest and recreation space is scarce. (A recent study found that metropolitan Rotterdam, for example, has about 4 square yards of recreation space per person, approximately the size of a billiard table.)[9] Other tourists come from the industrial centers of Belgium and Germany.

Zeeland's major attractions are its beaches, backed by a solid line of dunes

that keep the sea from inundating the land, much of which is below sea level. The Dutch, acutely aware of the perils of erosion, have consistently prohibited construction on the dunes; people going to the beach cross the dunes on wooden walkways to avoid trampling the stabilizing grasses. Concern over evacuation in case of flood has led to a road pattern that provides access to the beach only by routes running perpendicular to it, with no beachfront highway. The strip behind the sand dunes along the North Sea coast of Schouwen-Duiveland and Walcheren, however, has become crowded with campgrounds and second-home developments.

The developments vary greatly in size and quality. At the end of the spectrum are the few tents or trailers that a farmer is licensed to permit on his property during the summer months. In contrast, some campgrounds cater to several hundred trailers, providing a broad range of facilities such as laundries, stores, and swimming pools. There are also large, highly developed "mobile home" parks, some of which contain cabins and accommodate movable trailers.

Walkway constructed to protect dunes. (Photo by author.)

Finally, there are large second-home developments with residences that may be suitable for year-round occupancy.

Planning in Zeeland

Conscious of their limited land area, the Dutch for many years have relied on physical planning to control development. Under their system, basic planning policies are established at the national level and implemented in greater detail by the provinces and local governments.

The provinces are responsible for preparing regional plans, which outline basic policies for future provincial development, and for overseeing municipal planning procedures. It is at the municipal, or local, level that public control of land development has its greatest impact.

Each municipality is *encouraged* to draw up a structural plan that functions as a general land-use guide for future development, and is *obliged* to draw up a development plan *(bestemmingsplan)* as a prerequisite for any major development. The development plan indicates the ultimate use of the sites covered, along with a set of applicable land-use controls for the same areas. Because all construction permits must be consistent with the development plan, planners regularly find themselves in negotiation with developers seeking to change it or to obtain an exemption or conditional permit.[10]

The public has several opportunities to participate in the planning process. A local development plan undergoes a one-month review and comment period—often including public hearings—before adoption by the municipal council. If the plan is approved by the municipal council, it goes to the provincial council, which must also approve it. Then, the first draft plan is again displayed for review and comments; objections may again be filed. Beyond the provincial council, objectors may appeal to the Crown. The appeal is heard by the Council of State, an agency appointed by the monarch (on the government's nomination) that hears administrative appeals on many subjects. It may either approve or reject a local plan.

The Council of State usually relies heavily on the recommendation of the Ministry of Housing and Physical Planning, which may appeal a plan to the council even if local objectors do not. Only about 10 percent of all plans are appealed to the council, but these include virtually all of the largest and most controversial plans, and those thought to have the greatest environmental impact.

The Ministry of Housing and Physical Planning has adopted clear national policies toward tourism development. Second-home complexes with low-development densities are discouraged because they occupy scarce open space and because they typically cannot afford high-quality facilities for disposal and treatment of sewage. Instead, the ministry favors high-density clusters of recreational accommodations, preferably connected to and serviced by commercial centers in existing villages.[11]

A Conflict in Scale

On paper, at least, the planning system provides a logical framework for ensuring that major development decisions reflect these overall national policies. In

Many older second-home developments in Zeeland are visually unobtrusive. (Photo by author.)

practice, the local planning process in Zeeland does not appear to be guiding growth as much as rationalizing it after it takes place. The pattern of development that has emerged is quite different from that called for by national policy. High-density clusters arouse the most opposition. Scattered, low-density development slips through with little protest. The negative attitude toward large tourism developments reflects a common feeling that *kleine schaal* must be retained to avoid destruction of the rural landscape.

One organization that has protested against large campgrounds and second-home complexes is the Zeeland Foundation for the Coordination of Nature, Landscape, and Environmental Protection. It received support from a 1974 study sponsored by Delft University, which said that the number of campgrounds was outrunning the province's ability to provide fresh water, sewage treatment, and roads, and was adversely affecting the visual environment.[12]

The Zeeland Environmental Federation also has objected to large recreational development—specifically, to a proposal for the shores of the freshwater lakes created by extensive diking of the delta after the 1953 flood. These lakes have provided excellent opportunities for boating and sites for many small-scale tourist projects with easy access to boat harbors. The federation has argued that large, space-consuming developments not only mar the landscape, but contribute to a never-ending push for more outdoor recreation facilities in the Netherlands—particularly from foreign countries.

In response to such criticism, most local governments have demanded that developers limit the scale and density of projects to avoid creating an impression of intrusiveness. Except in a few of the larger towns, little development has been permitted involving high-rise buildings that would be visible over the skyline of the dunes. One developer, whose proposal to build a four-story condominium in the small village of Zoutelande was denied, appealed the decision all the way to the Council of State. The council upheld the denial, saying that such high buildings would be inconsistent with the scale of the landscape and would adversely affect the skyline.

Height limitations have done much to eliminate visual intrusiveness in Zeeland tourism development. So, too, have screening requirements. Many developers have been required to plant solid walls of trees around the perimeter of their projects. Some of the older second-home developments, where the trees are fully grown, are almost invisible to the passerby. But the present development pattern (scattering small-scale facilities over the landscape) has made it considerably more difficult to provide efficient sewage-treatment facilities at reasonable cost. Moreover, the small-scale approach has undoubtedly used more land than would have been used for concentrated, large-scale developments adjacent to existing village cores.

In Anticipation of the Plan

Why has the national policy of high-density clusters been honored primarily in the breach? One reason may be that approval of a development plan under the Dutch system can take two to five years. This is a frustrating and expensive process for developers who spend substantial sums to buy land and prepare plans. Because of pressure from such builders, a shortcut procedure has evolved for smaller developments. A person who wants to build a few second homes may obtain the permits he needs from the municipality "in anticipation of the plan."

Campground near Westerschouwen; the North Sea lies beyond the dunes. (Photo by author.)

Three types of dwellings: in background, Vlissingen apartment buildings; in center, summer homes among trees; in foreground, trailers and tents crowd field.

Although the provincial executive council must approve all such permits, the approval need not entail formal planning criteria. Rather, decisions are based on unwritten land-use control concepts of local and provincial administrators.

If camping facilities are at issue, an even shorter cut is available—namely, local campground licensing ordinances, which set minimum standards for sanitary and washing facilities, availability of drinking water, and so on. The licensing system also allows a municipality to impose conditions regarding the layout of the campground, the permitted number of overnight campers, and the amount of open space. Once obtained, licenses for small camping areas are renewed almost automatically, without any review at the provincial level. This procedure may, therefore, have more influence on local land-use patterns than does the planning system. One consultant calls it a separate "sub-surface planning system."

In addition to these means of circumvention, a certain amount of illicit development appears to take place with the tacit consent of local government. Small, primitive camping areas will sometimes expand into full-scale campgrounds by incremental violations. Municipalities are constantly trying to change local land-use policy to rationalize not only nonconforming uses but illegal land use as well.

Although plans are able to control development, they do so only if they can be enforced against violations. The Delft University study has pointed out that still another obstruction to implementation of the planning system is that enforcement is hampered by judicial roadblocks. Individual camping trailers are

(continued on page 129)

BAVARIA: MAD LUDWIG'S BACKYARD

Travel is such an important status symbol in Germany—two or three vacations a year are not unusual for a middle-class family—that children may be embarrassed to admit to their peers that they stayed home during a school vacation. In 1973, Germans passed Americans as the world's biggest spenders on tourism, and there is no ceiling in sight.[1]

A favorite destination for German tourists is the German countryside itself, particularly Bavaria, which leads all states in Germany as a destination for both winter and summer tourism.[2] Bavaria's attractions include not only magnificent natural features like the Alps, but an atmosphere rich with diverse products and ghosts of history.

One of the most notable figures in Bavaria's past is Ludwig II, the famous mad king who reigned a century ago, creating convoluted castles—like Neuschwanstein, Linderhof, and Herrenchiemsee—and promoting the operas of Richard Wagner. Ludwig had peculiar notions about whom he entertained. He was said to be so fond of his favorite gray mare, Cosa Rara, that he once invited her to dine with him. According to a biographer, "Soup, fish, a roast and wine were served; Cosa Rara ate with hearty appetite and then, to mark her appreciation of the unusual honor shown to her, proceeded to smash the costly dinner-service to smithereens."[3] Today, many Bavarians are wondering whether hordes of tourists, who have accepted Bavarian hospitality with a hearty appetite, will end the meal by smashing the china.

A major controversy in Bavaria involves the question of whether mountains should be preserved for hiking, hunting, and active recreation, or should be subdivided for second homes. Active recreation is very important to the Germans. Swimming, riding, skiing, and hiking are among the most popular vacation-time pursuits. Bavaria's wooded areas are crisscrossed by footpaths maintained by regional hiking clubs.

These recreational opportunities have led many Germans to choose Bavaria as a site for a second home. In the early 1970s, the construction of second homes in the state boomed, with an annual increase of 6 percent projected for alpine areas.[4] Prior to the 1950s, few people could afford a retirement home in the country, and only the very rich could buy a second home. But in Germany, as in many other places, widespread automobile ownership has been accompanied by general affluence, less costly development, and a shift to self-catering tourism. Because Austria has legislated against ownership of land by foreigners, the second-home construction on the Bavarian side of the border has multiplied.

The sprawl has put increased pressure on the natural resources of the alpine areas. Conservation authorities have been disturbed by the picking or trampling of various plant species; the presence of humans in traditional animal breeding and feeding areas has tended to force many animals higher into the mountains, where food is relatively scarce. In mountain towns such as Garmisch, pollution from automobiles spoils the clear air. Roads to serve

Bavarian Alps, near Berchtesgaden. (Photo courtesy German Information Center.)

isolated second homes in the countryside have created substantial environmental damage in the form of erosion, siltation, and landslides.

The most common complaint about second homes is that they destroy the peace and quiet of a stroll through the woods. The average German feels that owners of woodlands have an obligation to permit hiking through them and doesn't like hiking through a subdivision. In addition, many Bavarians express concern that second-home residents contribute relatively little to the local economy, while requiring the construction and maintenance of expensive roads and sewers.

The state government of Bavaria, which has been wrestling with the second-home controversy, is responsible for reviewing and approving all substantial development proposals. Since 1972, it has declared a number of mountain areas off limits for second-home construction. In 1974, the state planners touched off a controversy by publishing a draft plan that would have prohibited second homes in the entire alpine region along Bavaria's southern frontier. The plan recommended that tourism be concentrated in higher-density clusters in or adjacent to towns.

Local hiking clubs, representing mainly residents of Munich and other Bavarian cities, supported the ban, which they felt would preserve the peace and quiet of the mountains. Their view was buttressed by a widely read book, *The Landscape Glutton,* published in 1975, whose author argued that if second-home construction were allowed to run its course, it would "consume" the landscape between Munich and Milan in 10 years, turning the entire alpine region into a suburb.[5] Some of the plan's supporters were also motivated by resentment of the north Germans' haughty attitude toward the citizens of "cuckoo-clock-land."

But the plan aroused strong opposition. Construction workers resented efforts that would deprive them of a source of badly needed work, and many farmers had family members employed by gas stations and restaurants that depended on tourism. A recession in 1974 made these jobs especially important. The recession also lessened the apparent urgency of the problem by reducing the volume of second-home construction. With fewer mountain homes being built, complaints died down.

When the State Development Program was finally adopted by the Bavarian parliament in March 1976, it omitted the controversial ban on second homes. Instead, a map delineating an alpine area where second homes "should not be constructed" was included only as an advisory document for local governments and regional planning associations. State planners hoped to secure both performance standards that would reduce the extent of environmental damage and zoning for uses compatible with the capacity of the land.

scattered throughout some of the most beautiful and fragile dunes in Zeeland because the municipalities have been unable to prove to the courts' satisfaction that each trailer doesn't have "grandfather rights," though it is obvious the number of trailers has increased many times since the regulations were adopted.[13]

The attitude of provincial authorities toward recreational development, in contrast to that of local officials, has been more favorable toward the large, self-contained projects encouraged by national policies. A huge project with accommodations for up to 14,000 on one freshwater lake received support from the provincial council, despite the fact that the provincial planning division, the local water board, environmental and citizen groups, and many members of the provincial legislative body felt that if the development were to be allowed at all, it should be postponed for a number of years.

The provincial council has rejected certain plans because the proposed recreation developments would not be connected to municipal sewer systems. Since the refusals were based only on the lack of adequate sewage collection and treatment, however, the province may not be in a position to reconsider other environmental issues once the sewage collection and treatment problem has been solved. Developers who were rejected earlier will again be knocking on the province's door. Old promises are long remembered in a region like Zeeland, and several observers who would like to control growth see some real problems ahead.

In retrospect, one of the key factors affecting growth on the island of Schouwen-Duiveland—one of the fastest-growing parts of Zeeland—was a 1972 regional plan which discussed the great importance of the recreation industry for economic development. Although regional plans have no binding legal effect on land use, they are expected to give local municipalities a good idea of what kinds of development plans will be approved by the province. The policies contained in the 1972 plan were very general. Two aspects, however, have been cited frequently by proponents of recreational growth. First, an appendix to the research section projected that the number of overnight accommodations along the seashore would rise from an estimated 48,200 in 1970 to around 95,000 in 1990. The latter figure is now cited as "the plan" by prospective developers. Second, on the plan's map, broad areas were colored as potential sites for permanent recreational accommodations and boat harbors. Therefore, the developers argue, this map commits the province to granting approval of development plans for those areas.

Little attention was focused on either of these aspects when the plan was given its public display prior to adoption. At that time, public concern over the problems of development was not nearly so great as it has since become. With the change in attitudes, many national and provincial officials realize that the 1972 regional plan was wholly inadequate in its consideration of environmental impact. The plan survives, however, through inertia.

Unlucky Experts

In urban areas, the Dutch system may be effective in controlling development. In such areas, demand is heavy in relation to the land that is available, and the planners are rationing a scarce commodity.[14] Extensive use is made of public ownership of land and systems of land price control.[15]

When applied to scattered, small-scale development in a rural area like Zeeland, however, the Dutch system is much more problematic. Many Dutch observers would agree that the planning system does not seem to have been an effective vehicle for controlling the environmental impact of new development in rural areas.

Certainly, though they may disagree on planning policies, the three levels of government in the Netherlands at least have developed a consciousness of environmental problems before the problems got out of hand. Gradually, there seems to be a response to new concerns. But inertia persists: permits are issued "in anticipation of the plan"; informal commitments have been made to old friends; trailers have made creeping encroachments that the courts will not stem; powerful associations and corporations have purchased land for recreational development. National planners thus would be well advised to pay more attention to local attitudes and pressures that contradict national policy. All too often the planners seem to assume their policies will be implemented, and then have no way to cope with what really transpires.

S. J. Simon, who wrote a series of colorful books on strategy in playing bridge, had one character called the "unlucky expert." This was a man who had mastered the technical rules and always played his cards perfectly. He generally lost, however, because he always assumed his partner and opponents were also following the rules perfectly. "Just bad luck," he used to say.[16] The planning system in the Netherlands seems to have its share of unlucky experts.

In that respect, however, Dutch planners are not alone. Britain, long regarded as the fountainhead of planning wisdom, is undergoing serious self-reevaluation of its planning system. Because of the prestige of British planning, and the fact that variants of it have been exported to countries all over the globe, it is worth evaluating in somewhat more detail than other planning systems.

Cultivated Nature

An appreciation of the English planning system requires an understanding of the English attitude toward nature. A "natural" scene drawn by an Englishman would probably include a thatched cottage with roses and neatly kept lawn, nestled in a pastoral valley where sheep graze, with clumps of carefully placed trees enhancing the composition.

The English are unfamiliar with an environment untouched by civilization such as one finds in the American tradition. In England, that kind of environment disappeared many centuries ago. Instead, "cultivated nature" has long been idealized. Natural areas the English find beautiful do not "abound in grand and sublime prospects," Washington Irving observed, "but rather in little home-scenes of rural repose and sheltered quiet."[17]

The concept of "cultivated nature" may seem a paradox to Americans, who tend to equate nature with wilderness. Yet in a world growing increasingly crowded, attitudes toward nature in densely populated countries like England merit a close look.

The British conception of nature is an attempt to pull together two distinct and conflicting attitudes that compete for dominance in the national character.

On one side is a penchant for neatness and orderliness that John Betjeman likes to satirize:

> Now houses are 'units' and people are digits,
> And Bath has been planned into quarters for
>   midgets.
> Official designs are aggressively neuter,
> The Puritan work of an eyeless computer.[18]

Contrasted with this is enchantment with the mysterious forces of nature, best summarized in Wordsworth's famous lines:

> One impulse from a vernal wood
> May teach you more of man,
> Of moral evil and of good,
> Than all the sages can.

> Sweet is the lore which nature brings;
> Our meddling intellect
> Mis-shapes the beauteous forms of things:—
> We murder to dissect.[19]

In the absence of a wilderness tradition, popular culture in England traces the worshipful attitude toward nature to an almost mythical people who occupied the British Isles some 2,000 years ago—the Druids.

Although very little is known about the Druids, they are popularly associated with pantheism, a belief that the natural world is the physical embodiment of the creator and is, therefore, sacred. They are said to have conducted their worship services in the forests, in places "naturally adorned, . . . brought to perfection by Dame Nature herself."[20] Early Roman explorers reported that the Druids held nothing more sacred than mistletoe, a plant that appeared on trees as if by magic and that was not susceptible to any form of cultivation. When it was found on an oak, the tree became sacred.[21]

Today, the Druids still symbolize the mystical qualities that residents of the British Isles attribute to the land in which they live. With the lines "Ah faeries, dancing under the moon, a Druid land, a Druid tune,"[22] William Butler Yeats conveys an image familiar to English, Irish, Welsh, and Scotch alike.

These two characteristics, a penchant for neatness, and the attribution of mystical qualities to nature—or, more simply, rationalism and romanticism—pull the British in opposed directions. The British planning system tries to bring them together.

"Sheer Joy to All Who Saw It"

Planning is an act of faith, according to Lewis Keeble, a noted English planner: "My own inward picture of the planned region . . . [makes me certain that it] . . . would give such sheer joy to all who saw it that no civilised country would thereafter remain content until it had secured similar conditions for itself."[23]

For a half century, British planning has been dominated by the philosophy of the "garden city." The garden city is to the city as the British idea of cultivated nature is to nature. The planners of the garden city school, who flourished around the turn of the century, were visionary evangelists revolting against the "smoke-beshrouded towns" of industrial England.[24] They and their present-day successors have dreamed of a time when the countryside would be "free from all

Coach travels a Devon lane in 1920. (Copyright National Geographic Society.)

unnecessary objects." Towns would be without "peripheral clutter," would have "a clear structure," and would contain all types of open space, from the formal flower garden to the "wild landscaped park."[25]

The garden city movement was a reaction against what was viewed as an inexorable drift of population from the countryside to the metropolis. What was to be avoided at all costs was suburbanization, the separation of man from his job and loss of contact with the countryside.[26]

Both the substance and the tone of the movement can be discerned from the words of its founder, Ebenezer Howard, who wrote in 1898:

> It is wellnigh universally agreed by men of all parties, not only in England, but all over Europe and America and our colonies, that it is deeply to be deplored that the people should continue to stream into the already over-crowded cities, and should thus further deplete the country districts.
>
> The key to the problem how to restore the people to the land—that beautiful land of ours, with its canopy of sky, the air that blows upon it, the sun that warms it, the rain and dew that moisten it—the very embodiment of Divine love for man—is indeed a *Master Key*, for it is the key to a portal through which, even when scarce ajar, will be seen to pour a flood of light on the problems of intemperance, of excessive toil, of restless anxiety, of grinding poverty.[27]

The first garden city experiments were company towns or publicly financed new communities. As the underlying philosophy became popular, planners sought to control private development in order to bring the benefits of the garden city philosophy to as many people as possible. England began in the 1920s to impose controls on proposed development through the Town and Country Planning Act. For years the British have praised this system, which has been copied freely throughout the world as a model for solving land-use conflicts.

As presently constituted, the British system involves three levels of planning below the national level. At the regional level, an economic planning council prepares a "strategy plan," to be approved by the national Department of the Environment, which projects economic growth trends for the region and suggests various corridors where growth might occur. At the county level, each council is responsible for preparing and submitting to the Department of Environment a "structure plan," which is to deal with broad land-use policies, identify problems that require action, and determine priorities for dealing with these issues. At the municipal level, the authorities prepare detailed plans consistent with policies set forth in the county structure plan. It is these "local plans" that actually guide development decisions.

The British system of planning has undergone many changes since its

(continued on page 137)

The rocky coast of Devon. (Photo by Alan Taylor.)

AUSTRALIA: REDISCOVERING THE BUSH

The desire to escape crowded urban areas for a countryside vacation is not confined to small, densely populated countries. It occurs as well in places where land hardly seems scarce, such as the Australian state of New South Wales.

Despite its vast size, Australia is a remarkably urbanized nation. Some 80 to 90 percent of its 13 million people live in urban areas. The country has approximately the same amount of land as the lower 48 United States, but only a small amount of it is within easy driving distance of cities.

Within a few hours' drive of Sydney, Australia's largest city, tracts of agricultural and dairy land are being developed into second-home subdivisions or divided into larger tracts for weekend farmers who desire to own 40 acres in the country. Australians, concluded a recent study, have made "a nostalgic rediscovery of 'the bush.' "[1]

Many purchasers have bought lots with a small down payment. Rapidly increasing prices of land throughout Australia in the early 1970s made such speculation attractive. On some lots small homes are erected on weekends by the owners themselves, often members of the building trades from Canberra or Sydney.

The impact of this development is beginning to cause concern. Land on and immediately adjoining dunes is being subdivided with little concern for damage. Farmers are unhappy at the increased property taxes that follow rising land values. Although the increased value benefits older farmers who are about to retire, it hurts younger ones who need additional acreage. In addition, heavy holiday traffic during the summer—particularly at Christmastime and on some weekends—is a source of local annoyance.

The subdivision and development of land in New South Wales is extensively regulated by planning laws. Planning in Australia has traditionally been one of the powers of the state governments, with much of the administration delegated to local government.[2] Local governments prepare planning schemes, and submit them in draft form to the state planning agency, which has the power to coordinate the planning activities of the various local governments.[3] If the agency gives tentative approval, the scheme is then exhibited for at least three months, and persons affected by it may object to its proposals. Local councils deal with the objections and report on them to the state Minister of Planning and Environment, who then decides whether to approve the scheme. If he asks for major alterations, a second exhibition leading to possible new objections may be necessary.

Much of the real decision making takes place when developers propose amendments to the planning schemes. Amendments are subject to procedures similar to those for the original scheme. The result is that any substantial development proposal must be approved at the state level. In 1974, the state planning agency reviewed nearly 10,000 separate items, compared to only 2,000 five years earlier.

The state planners became concerned about the long-range effects of sprawling rural subdivisions. They questioned whether demand would ever catch up with the supply of lots, and they worried about the economic and environmental effects of providing roads and services for such a large area.

Planners would have preferred to see more concentrated development projects. But local sentiment opposed high-rise buildings or other vestiges of urbanization. Few such projects received local approval, while subdivisions were more favorably treated. State planners were hard pressed to find fault with any individual subdivision, and they lacked any satisfactory overall policy, so they relied on the familiar tactic of delay.

Developers, in turn, criticized the complex permitting process. They felt that far too many minor matters were being referred to the state planning authority.[4] Critics said the state planners spent too much of their time supervising local handling of individual cases and too little time in statewide comprehensive planning.[5] Other observers felt that planning in Australia failed to give adequate consideration to environmental impact. Drafting a system that would satisfy both these concerns was not an easy task.[6]

In 1974, the Minister told the state planners to come up with proposals that would speed up the process and restore greater local authority. In March 1976, after numerous studies, hearings, and reports, the Minister introduced his

Murray River, separating New South Wales and Victoria. (Photo courtesy Australian News and Information Bureau.)

Sydney. (Photo courtesy Australian News and Information Bureau.)

proposed legislation. Each local government was to adopt a "local environmental plan," consistent with regional plans of the "structure" variety. For development-control purposes a four-category system was proposed: (1) permitted uses; (2) uses permitted only upon a finding of the local council that they comply with regional and local environmental plans; (3) major development requiring the Minister's consent; (4) prohibited uses.

In May 1976, before this legislation was considered, the Labour Party took over the state government. The new government withdrew the legislation and began new studies.

The problems of New South Wales reflect the same paradox found in the English planning process: (1) the planning system has been too slow, costly, and complex, but (2) complex as it is, the system has failed to give adequate consideration to issues involving environmental impact, and (3) attempts to reform the system have been so slow that the reforms seem obsolete by the time they become effective.

inception. Today's planners, however, have not found a new unifying concept to replace that of the garden city, despite the fact that that concept predated widespread automobile use and seems obsolete to many. Moreover, to planners of 75 years ago, tourism was not a relevant factor in the development of the countryside. Tourists traveled by rail or boat, and then dispersed by foot or carriage to centrally located hotels in recognized centers such as Brighton or Bath. They had little impact on the countryside.

In today's England, automobile ownership is commonplace, and sprawling tourism has had a substantial impact. The percentage of tourists who stay in informal, self-catering accommodations is steadily increasing. Many people vacation in "caravans," the British term for trailers and mobile homes, which now account for some 18 percent of principal vacations, compared to 6 percent two decades ago.[28]

The area of England that has experienced the most rapid growth in tourism, and is now the leading destination for English tourists, is the South West. It is usually defined as consisting of the counties of Devon and Cornwall.

Devon and Cornwall

The South West's share of all British tourism increased from 16 percent in 1960 to 22 percent in 1970.[29] A 1973 survey found that the South West attracted 20 to 25 percent of British vacationers. More than 8,000,000 tourists visit the South West each year.[30]

Primarily an agricultural region, the South West has few major centers of industry or trade. The climate is the mildest in Britain, and visitors are often surprised to see palms growing in sheltered gardens along the coast. Tourists are more attracted by the rural simplicity and pleasant climate than by any specific centers of activity.

Devon and Cornwall lie on a broad plateau breaking sharply at the coast, with cliffs descending to the sea, while inland are the rolling hills of Dartmoor. The plateau is broken by numerous steep-sided valleys and rocky outcrops known as tors and heads that were left by the last glaciers.[31] To the west the land becomes even more rugged as it narrows toward England's westernmost point, Land's End.

Growing numbers of people seek to own vacation homes in the South West. An official 1975 survey showed nearly 11,000 second homes in the region, with the number expected to rise to as many as 45,000 by the end of the century.[32] Some observers, however, think these official forecasts are much too low, one planner suggesting that the area might have to absorb nearly 10 times that many. A citizens' organization, Shelter: The National Campaign for the Homeless, calls second homes a "social affront" that penalizes "low-paid rural workers who can not afford to buy or build at present prices and are therefore being squeezed out of their own communities."[33] Although the number of second-home owners in England in proportion to the entire population is still quite low when compared to many other European countries, it is rising rapidly.

The type of second home varies widely. Some, following the thatched-cottage ideal, are tucked unobtrusively into the hedgerows. More and more frequently, however, the second homes are "static caravans," that is, house trailers kept permanently in large parks and used by their owners for vacations and occasional weekends.

Long-time residents of the South West view the influx dourly, complaining that the tourists are causing development to spread from established towns and villages into the surrounding countryside. During a period when Devon's population increased by only 15 percent, the extent of urbanized land area doubled.[34] Some Devonians even blamed tourists for the inconveniences associated with a 1976 drought, saying "there would always be plenty of water for the residents of Devon were it not for the fact that the county is . . . a vast summer playground for the whole of Great Britain."[35]

Predictably, attitudes about future development for the South West follow competing lines. One viewpoint is represented by tourists and retirees who seek places in the countryside, joined by the builders and developers who earn a living providing them. Having left Birmingham or Manchester to escape from urban ills, the newcomers simply want a thatched-roof cottage, or perhaps the best available substitute, a small mobile home.

Opposed to these interests are farmers and villagers who try to retain long-standing life-styles. In the face of the social change brought by rapid development, they worry about increases in housing prices and losses of valuable agricultural land. These people often find allies in the conservationists, who speak of the need to preserve the amenities that attract—but could be destroyed by—large numbers of people. If development is necessary, argue conservationists, it should be concentrated in high-density clusters, in and near existing towns and villages. That way, farmland and open space can be retained, while existing urban services and facilities can be used.

Counting Up Jobs

Conflicts over development in the South West are being fought out through the planning-system hierarchy, with the level of detail increasing at successively lower levels of government. The initial battlefield involved the strategy plan prepared by the South West Economic Planning Council.

The regional planning councils were created during the mid-1960s by the Labour Party government. Although ostensibly charged with providing overall policy guidance for the entire planning process, they were primarily designed to serve as economic development agencies.[36] The British economy was expanding rapidly. Many people were concerned, however, that much of the growth was being attracted to metropolitan London, while other parts of the country were losing population. For the South West Economic Planning Council and others, therefore, the goal was to promote overall economic growth in the region, which meant fighting the drift of industry and population to London.[37]

This orientation toward regional growth and abstract economic data is still characteristic of the regional councils, which tend to be primarily concerned with overall numbers of jobs. They have little interest in the way physical facilities are located; their goals are more often expressed by tables than by maps.[38]

To economists who sought true national planning, regional councils have been a step forward, but have involved many compromises. David Eversley, who

was instrumental in creating the first of the councils, says that a civil servant assigned to a regional staff saw himself one step from Siberia.[39] To Whitehall, the councils seemed nothing more than petty regional boosters, to be kept as passive as possible.[40] But the members of each regional planning council—typically representatives of industry and labor unions—put substantial pressure on their staffs to project increasingly greater shares of the national economic growth for their particular region.[41]

The context of regional planning looks much different today than it did when the councils were established. In the mid-1960s, it was generally assumed that national economic growth would continue indefinitely at a high rate, and needed only to be channeled to the appropriate location. In the less-prosperous 1970s, however, the regional planning councils find themselves fighting with each other for a share of an increasingly small pie. The Labour Government's Community Land Act and Development Gains Tax, designed to remove all possible profit on the appreciation of land values that accompanies development, hastened the withdrawal of private capital from the development process.

Moreover, local attitudes have changed dramatically since the 1960s, when most regions could be expected to welcome substantial economic growth. In the intervening decade, increasing suspicion has become attached to growth, and more and more rural areas are striving hard to protect their quality of life.

Most importantly, the tide of immigration to London, once thought inevitable, has reversed. To the planners' surprise, the total number of jobs in greater London dropped from almost 4,500,000 in 1961 to less than 4,000,000 in 1974.[42] Whereas at one time the rest of the country was trying to lure growth from steadily expanding London, the city is now depopulating and the rest of the country is ambivalent about accepting the emigrants.

Despite these changes, the planning process plods onward. In 1974 the South West Economic Planning Council published its proposed regional strategy plan. The plan projected a 32-percent growth in the region's population by the year 2000, and claimed there was no practical way to prevent it. Pointing out that the median income of the region stood below the national average, the plan argued that economic development was needed to provide the income necessary to furnish services to the growing population. New tourism facilities were encouraged as a source of economic development.

Peter Wilsher, in the business section of the *Sunday Times*, called such regional plans "repositories for dead and out-of-date figures, which then go on feeding inexorably into the planning system." The 600,000 immigrants to the South West might never materialize, he said, "But the Plan, judging by experience, will grind on, just as if they were arriving with the next bus. By and large, if there is one thing worse than statistical incompetence, it is blind faith in statistical infallibility."[43]

The emphasis on the use of overall economic statistics as the basis for planning is part of a general trend within the English planning movement. Economic planners in London have sought greater centralization of authority and deemphasized local control.[44] This has led to frequent clashes between planners and local citizens who seek to conserve existing amenities.

The Conservationists Reply

Numerous local and national conservation groups concerned about the environmental impact of population growth have attacked the South West regional plan. The Council for the Protection of Rural England, for example, published a critique charging that the regional council had viewed stimulation of economic activity as the sole purpose of planning. Critics felt that using the below-average income levels of the region as an excuse for greater stimulation of economic activity ignored an important point: most of those coming to the South West were, in fact, leaving industrialized regions with higher average incomes; they represented people seeking to exchange a higher income level for a higher quality of life.

The regional plan was also criticized for assuming that planning could never change population trends. Why, asked the critics, did the planners not question the wisdom of the national government in proposing to build the M-5 motorway squarely through the heart of Devon?[45] To conservationists, the idea of attracting more tourists to provide more jobs for more new immigrants was a bootstrap argument.

Procedurally, conservationists were concerned lest the regional plan's pro-growth bias effectively prevent their opportunity to participate in the county and

Devon countryside. (Photo by Alan Taylor.)

local planning process. The law provides for extensive citizen participation in the preparation of structure plans, but requires all structure plans to "have regard to" regional planning policies. Regional plans, however, are prepared with only minimal citizen participation. As regional plans are adopted, therefore, the policy choices available to structure planners are circumscribed before citizen participation gets under way.[46] Why permit extensive citizen participation in the preparation of structure plans, the Council for the Protection of Rural England asked, if "the most controversial policy decision of structure planning—how much (if any) growth a county should take and where it should go—is likely to be taken at regional planning level," through a process in which the public plays little part?

Nevertheless, in August 1975 the Secretary of the Department of the Environment endorsed the regional plan. In doing so, the government approved a philosophy of growth quite at variance with that apparently held by many of the region's citizens. This conflict between national policy and local interests has slowed the work of preparing the county and local plans.

Seeking a Structure

As of early 1978, the counties of Devon and Cornwall were still preparing structure plans. In each, increased tourism development is recognized as posing problems that require action. Planners have been formulating broad policies, which they hope will serve as a guide for future tourism development. The process, however, has been slow. Neither Devon nor Cornwall met the target date for submitting its structure plan for departmental approval.

After it has received a structure plan, the Department of the Environment is required to consider objections. Usually a hearing officer will come to the area and hold an inquiry at which the county planning authority and other persons may be heard. The department may approve the plan, modify it, or refer it back to the planning authority. This process of departmental review typically takes 18 months.[47] Given the lengthy nature of the planning process, the structure planners have tried to think in long-range terms.

Devon county planners identify four major policy areas—settlement patterns, minerals, holiday development, and conservation. Zones are to be designated for development of tourism facilities in some areas, whereas in others such development is to be prohibited. The Devon county planners anticipate that Exeter and Plymouth will be the major growth areas. Adoption of the plan (and approval by the Secretary of the Environment) is expected sometime after 1978.

Once a county like Devon adopts its structure plan, the local district councils proceed to adopt their own plans. In theory, at least, the policies in the structure plan will be binding upon local plans throughout the county. For a community such as Plymouth, the local plan will consist of a map and a written statement intended to provide a detailed elaboration of proposals sketched out as matters of broad policy in the structure plan. Aside from the requirement that it follow structure-plan policies, Plymouth has great latitude regarding the specifics of the local plan, which does not have to be approved by the Department of the Environment.

Many counties, accustomed to the detailed specificity of earlier develop-

Mobile-home ("caravan") park. (Photo by Alan Taylor.)

ment plans, have had difficulty with the concept of the more generalized structure plans. The Department of the Environment has cautioned planners to "concentrate on those issues which are of key structural importance," and not to prepare overly detailed plans.[48] But critics have challenged the emphasis on location of major structural facilities and growth centers, at the expense of policy guidelines needed to control growth in areas away from major urban concentrations. The chairman of the Countryside Commission has complained that most structure plans were giving short shrift to issues of rural conservation and recreation.[49]

The slow pace at which structure plans throughout England have been completed and reviewed has motivated the Town and Country Planning Association to call for a parliamentary inquiry. Noting that London's structure-type plan had been pending for 12 years, and that similar delays had occurred elsewhere, the association pointed out that no local plans can be completed until the structure plan for the area has been approved. The first few local plans were approved in mid-1976, and a complete system of structure and local plans will not be available until sometime between 1980 and 1982.[50]

Filling the Vacuum

In the meantime, the process of deciding individual applications for "planning permission" (i.e., requests for permits to build structures or undertake other types of development) has been where the real action is. Without structure plans

Yachts on the Salcombe River. (Copyright National Geographic Society.)

for guidance, development-control planners (that is, planners involved in the process of granting or denying applications for planning permission)* have advised local councils for almost 10 years on the basis of a document known as a "handover statement." In Exeter, the handover statement was made up of the old pre-1968 development plan supplemented by various policy declarations issued by the local district councils, and a motley collection of circulars and "bottom drawer plans." Planners involved in development control have had little contact with the structure-plan process, and increasingly doubt the usefulness of the

---

*Although "development control"—the process of granting or denying applications for planning permission—is considered a part of planning in England, in practice development control is quite separate from the process of preparing plans. Moreover, not only are the processes separate, but the people who administer them, though all called "planners," form two distinct groups. More academically oriented members of the planning profession tend to treat development control as a poor relative, calling it "mundane parcel-by-parcel review, the servicing of the development clientele."[51] Development control tends to attract planners with less academic training and different professional qualifications from those who are preparing structure plans.[52] But from the perspectives of developers and local officials, development control is more important than structure planning. The planners dealing with day-to-day development decisions consider themselves the "real" planners, while viewing the structure planners as "likely to escape on the one hand political accountability and forfeit practical relevance on the other."[53]

During the last 10 years, the British planning system has provided few general policies that are useful in resolving conflicts over the environmental impact of development, including the second-home development that is of particular concern to the South West. At the same time, "peripheral clutter" increasingly dominates the English countryside. A national land-use survey from aerial photographs shows a sharp increase in the percentage of land occupied by scattered development in rural areas. For example, in Cornwall between 1963 and 1972, five times as much open land was lost to scattered development as was lost to the expansion of urban areas.[55]

The desire to impose more centralization and rationality on English planning has left the planners pursuing an outmoded goal through ponderous procedures incapable of adjusting to changing conditions. The countryside threatens to become an amorphous mixture of urban and rural uses, satisfying neither the rationalist's desire for orderly development nor the romanticist's desire for community with nature. And those who have appropriated a bit of the countryside for themselves find it looking less and less like what they were hoping to find.

Has the English planning process been a failure? As Gordon Cherry, a planning historian, notes, in the 1960s "planning lost its positive, prescriptive, long-term, image and relapsed into adaptive, short-term incrementalism."[56] Many observers believe that structure plans will end up being placed quietly on the shelf.[57] "We have been at [planning] for forty-five years," says planning lawyer George Dobry, "and we have run out of steam."[58]

Coping with Sprawl

Is it merely fatigue, or are problems like those created by the scattered development associated with self-catering tourism just not suited to solution by the type of planning systems used in England and the Netherlands, in New South Wales and Germany? The countryside in these nations is increasingly being filled with scattered recreational development. The national planners favor high-density recreational clusters, but these clusters typically arouse great public opposition. They are highly visible targets—for those who make sophisticated environmental arguments and for those who do not want an area to become citified.

Sprawl, on the other hand, increases almost imperceptibly through permit procedures at the local level. Each project is too small to attract much attention. The developers are local people, friends and neighbors, and it is hard to say no to them. The result is that the sophisticated developer, the designer of large, well-planned projects, gets stalled in controversy. The little developer, who crudely chops up land into lots, gets through.

As for tourists, ideally they might like to appropriate for themselves one of those humble dwellings where Wordsworth felt they would be received into the bosom of the living principle of things. As a practical matter, they may end up with a small house trailer in a caravan park. Often, however, this is considered preferable to an apartment in an urbanized project.

The tourists continuing to flock to Zeeland and the South West of England have been staying longer, and many eventually turn their weekend home into a place for retirement. In a period of tight economic conditions, the lower cost of living in rural areas is a prime attraction. The trend to rural areas seems likely to continue—with the planning systems unable to impose any grand pattern on it.

Whatever the trend, no garden cities have recently appeared. Does the failure to achieve the garden city goal—shared in principle by planners in most countries—merely reflect deficiencies in the planning system? If so, a number of approaches to curbing recreational sprawl may be considered.

First, planners could work harder to convince the public of the need to stop recreational sprawl.

Second, planners could try to override local sentiment against high-density clusters, hoping the clusters would absorb the market and deter sprawl. (Some dangers of overriding local sentiment are discussed in the following chapters.)

Third, a detailed environmental analysis of each development proposal, large or small, might be undertaken. The analysis would presumably demonstrate the superiority of large projects. Many planning systems seem capable, on paper, of doing this. The analyses are rarely performed in any meaningful way for small projects, however, because: (1) the impact of the individual decision is so small; (2) the perceived public concern is low; (3) the cost of assembling the facts, making the analysis, and presenting the arguments about the impact is high.

Fourth, some economists have proposed to overcome the high transaction costs of the third alternative through a system of incentives and penalties designed to reward efficient development and penalize inefficient development, and to do so automatically.[59] As yet, however, this kind of system is largely theoretical.*

The list of procedural solutions might be extended. Perhaps, however, the availability of so many untried solutions suggests a need to reexamine the basic premise. Is it better to try to concentrate tourists in garden cities, rather than let them sprawl all over the countryside? Are planners correct in assuming that large, cohesively planned, high-density development is better than sprawl? Or is there something wrong with the garden city?

Thinking Small

For many years, planners have suggested that the environmental impact of development—not only recreational development but development in general—could be reduced if developments were concentrated in large projects. With good logic and rational argument, people have been urged to "create a balanced environment for living . . . [with] the proper proportion of various land uses [through] development on a large scale."[61] They have been assured that: ". . . large scale urban development . . . should be encouraged . . ."[62] because "an

---

*The idea of making the polluter pay has found a warm reception in Japan and Western Europe, but attempts to implement the theory have met with indifferent success. Moreover, the technique seems better adapted to pollution-control problems with a limited number of variables—rather than to more complex planning decisions—though it might be incorporated as an element in a more comprehensive planning system.[60]

Woody Bay, Lynton, Devon. (Photo courtesy British Tourist Authority.)

increase in scale [will] significantly increase the developer's opportunity to achieve quality."[63]

But people in rural areas, where sprawl occurs, usually reject this advice. Scattered subdivisions, if sufficiently small in scale as to seem relatively innocuous, tend to win local approval rather easily. Officials who must come face-to-face with potential developers (often neighbors and local voters) are reluctant to disapprove a small project when they are unable to prove some immediate and serious environmental impact caused by that specific project. The fact that many such developments will have a serious cumulative impact is not often viewed as a politically legitimate basis for denying an individual project.

In recent years, the rather incoherent expressions of public opinion in favor of the little project have been garnering some intellectual support. E. F. Schumacher, whose book *Small Is Beautiful* attracted worldwide attention, claimed that "Small-scale operations, no matter how numerous, are always less likely to be harmful to the natural environment than large-scale ones, simply because their individual force is small in relation to the recuperative forces of nature."[64]

But planners warn that each septic tank contributes its bit to the eutrophication of the waters, that each camper adds to a potentially hazardous increase in traffic, and that each new cottage subtracts something from the rustic image that made a site attractive in the first place. The sprawl of small-scale development sneaks up in the same way as middle-aged spread—one more helping of potatoes here, a couple of beers there, with no immediately visible impact. From this perspective, Schumacher is like the well-meaning but potentially lethal friend who urges, "Just one more helping."

Clearly, the countryside can handle *some* development without being destroyed. But the local official, who must confront the question of who gets the opportunity to build, may well have trouble looking a neighbor in the eye and saying, "Your proposed development is the one too many." Thus, the difficulties faced by planners when they try to cope with recreational development in rural areas raises a basic question: can it be that small-scale tourist development is inherently incapable of being planned?

Cultivating the Mistletoe

English planning tries to combine rationalism and romanticism, neatness and the Druid tradition. Perhaps recreational development is less compatible with the former than with the latter. The urge to escape from an urban area may be an urge to escape rigid planning.

In many parts of Europe, in particular, the reaction against high-density, neatly planned cities is apparent. In countries like the Netherlands, the attitude toward scale of development has been shaped by 30 years during which government policymakers felt obliged to give the consumers higher densities than they wanted. In her book *Planned Urban Environments*, Ann Louise Strong quotes a Dutch official:

> I think nearly everyone would like to have a one-family house with a garden. . . .
> On the other hand, . . . apartment houses can be built in large numbers and at
> cheaper costs. . . . I am afraid that, when we have overcome the housing

shortage, people will dislike to live in what we are building now. They will want to build a house outside of town. [At that time the Dutch were building 87 percent of their apartments in buildings of four or more stories.][65]

The great increase in European recreational development may represent a counterpart to the American rush to the suburbs. In a residential neighborhood in Rotterdam on a summer day, the tall buildings and minimal open space create a hygienic but oppressive atmosphere. It is small wonder that come summer the occupants run to the country.

Mistletoe, the plant sacred to the Druids, grows wild in European forests. Hiding among the leaves, mistletoe has a characteristic rare among plants: it is absolutely incapable of cultivation, living off the tree that is its host.[66] Even in ancient times it was noted that "the mistletoe cannot be planted in soil, nor will it be forced to attach itself to another tree."[67] It goes where it wishes.

Perhaps modern man retains some of the primitive admiration for the plant that refuses to be cultivated. Maybe there is something about the motivation for selecting a campground or vacation home in a rural area that is incompatible with the rigorous analysis and stern self-control required for comprehensive planning. Perhaps it is necessary to shift the attack, to learn to mitigate the effects of sprawl rather than to try to cultivate the mistletoe.

Chapter 6
The Coast in Sickness and in Health

Are tourists going to someplace or trying to get away from someplace? Most tourism shares some of each motive, but the tourists flocking to the scattered countryside destinations discussed in the last chapter are primarily seeking a temporary escape from the urban environment. This kind of tourism might be characterized as predominantly centrifugal—a force moving away from a center. In other places, however, the force is primarily centripetal—toward a center. Jerusalem and Ayers Rock are obvious examples, as was one of the earliest types of tourists centers, the seaside spa.

Taking the Cure

Theories dating back at least to the Middle Ages have attributed curative properties to the special features of certain places. Inland spas like Vichy and Bath were fashionable long before travel for pleasure became popular.[1] In the 18th century, the notion that bathing in the sea had medicinal value took hold in Europe, and subsequently coastal towns began to compete for the trade of the leisure classes.[2]

> Then all, with ails in heart or lungs,
>   In liver or in spine,
> Rush'd coastward to be cured like tongues,
>   By dipping into *brine*.[3]

The first seaside resorts attracted members of the nobility and other socially prominent people, who in turn attracted social climbers. Patrons traveled by carriage and stayed for weeks, or for an entire season.

With the coming of railroads in the 19th century, the clientele of the seaside resort was greatly expanded, both in Europe and America. The new patrons belonged to the middle classes. Often, they stayed at the resort for only a week, or even a weekend. Towns that built up a steady following among the growing middle classes found that tourism could be a sound economic base, resulting in a relatively long period of stability.

Field research for this chapter was conducted by Paul R. DeStefano, Christopher J. Duerksen, Phyllis Myers, Lewis J. Smith, and Eastern Tin.

SYLT

SCHLESWIG-
HOLSTEIN
Hamburg

NORTH

SEA

N

WEST GERMANY

* Bonn

.Frankfurt

BAVARIA

FRANCE

.Munich

Garmisch-
Partenkirchen
.

SWITZERLAND

AUSTRIA

Statute Miles   0   25   50   75
Kilometers   0   50   100

The resort communities tended to share common features. Their overall development pattern was typically a T-shape. Tourists from inland traveled by rail, arriving at a railway station that stood at the intersection of the "T." Nearby, a pier, a pavilion, large hotels, restaurants, and shops provided attractions for day or night strollers. Resort hotels stretched along the beach on either side of this juncture, while housing for workers extended landward along the rail line.[4]

Tourists have flocked to the seashore for over a century. Their motives for doing so have changed, however. Belief in the curative properties of sea bathing, still held by many older Europeans, has largely been replaced by the desire for a "healthy tan."* More importantly for seaside resorts, the numbers of tourists, the way many of them get to the shore, and the kinds of accommodations provided for them also have changed. Three resorts that have experienced these changes are the German city of Westerland, the English borough of Torquay, and the Mexican town of Zihuatanejo.

Sun and Calisthenics

In Germany, belief in the salutary benefits of bathing in the sea remains widespread. Moreover, German physicians often prescribe a vacation as a remedy for general or specific maladies, particularly among older people. The tax-deductible vacation, to be spent at one of 490 places granted official "cure" status by the government, is known as "taking the cure."[5]

Westerland, one of the most popular cure centers along the German North Sea coast, is located on the island of Sylt, at the northwestern terminus of the German rail and highway network, not far from the Danish border. The island, part of the state of Schleswig-Holstein, is connected with the mainland by a long causeway, crossed by a railroad over which auto-carrying trains bring hundreds of thousands of tourists every year. Some tourists take the cure; many simply take a vacation.

Westerland is the only sizable city on Sylt. Military bases guarding Germany's northwestern frontier occupy much of the island, and nature reserves protect broad expanses of rolling dunes and wide marshes that host large flocks of migrating waterfowl. Low tide exposes extensive flats between Sylt and the mainland; these flats provide vast feeding grounds for birds.

Early Roman explorers reported that Germans were sun worshipers. Today, sunrise finds Westerland tourists lined up on the beach for group calisthenics. Afterward, they occupy numbered spots in the sand, complete with a high-backed settee that faces away from the strong wind blowing off the North Sea. (These winds, on a warm day, make 70 degrees feel like 50.) Swimming in the surf is popular with all ages, despite the cold water and chilly wind. Alternatively, one can escape the urban atmosphere of Westerland by traveling either north or south to less-crowded beaches or wild dune areas. In the evening, visitors may shop in branches of fashionable European stores or dine in a variety of restaurants offering *haute cuisine* or pizza.

---

*The association of a suntan with health, and pale skin with illness, is a 20th-century phenomenon. It arose in the 1920s and persists today despite physicians' warnings of the risks of skin cancer from overexposure to the sun. In earlier times, a pale skin signified freedom from the rigors of outdoor labor.

Calisthenics after dawn, in Westerland. (Photo by author.)

Tourism in Westerland has grown gradually but steadily. Initially, accommodations consisted of small hotels, supplemented in the peak season with rooms rented by homeowners. An estimated 70 percent of the households in Westerland offer tourist lodgings.[6] At the peak of the summer season every room is taken, while the occupancy rate between October and May is only about 5 percent. Increasingly, however, responding to a proliferation of tourists in the urban area, medium-sized hotels and modern buildings, offering apartments for rent or sale, have replaced smaller hotels. During the 1950s and 1960s, as these changes occurred, the total number of visitors tripled.

At first, the citizens of Westerland viewed the intense building activity as a welcome sign of economic progress. Lured by the prospect of more visitors and expanding profits, they apparently considered the construction noise and turmoil a temporary inconvenience. Their attitudes changed, however.

The Condominium Boom

Since 1968, new high-rise condominiums and apartments have accounted for virtually all of Westerland's residential development. Meanwhile, the number of hotels and rooming houses has declined. Reflecting the worldwide growth of self-catering tourism, tourists now arrive in Westerland in automobiles, bringing along their favorite brands of beer and sausage, and stay in kitchen-equipped apartments rather than hotel rooms. Between 1969 and 1973, the number of beds available to "overnight" tourists—those who wanted traditional bed-and-board facilities—declined almost 20 percent.[7]

Dune on island of Sylt. (Photo by David L. Callies.)

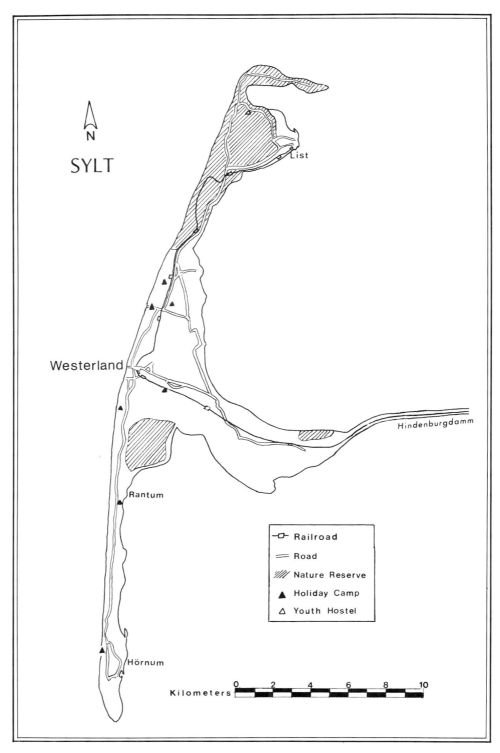

SYLT

List

Westerland

Hindenburgdamm

Rantum

Hörnum

	Railroad
	Road
	Nature Reserve
▲	Holiday Camp
△	Youth Hostel

Kilometers 0   2   4   6   8   10

Downtown Westerland. (Photo by author.)

The shift in tourism patterns in Westerland affected a wide range of local businesses. Although a few supermarkets flourished, many small restaurants closed, and hotel employment declined.

It is not surprising, then, that in the late 1960s residents began to complain about out-of-town speculators trying to cash in on the booming tourist industry. Residents felt that developers were channeling sales profits back to the mainland, while local citizens were bearing increased tax burdens to finance additional public facilities—sewage treatment, water supply, solid-waste disposal—needed to service new development. Local taxes were high, well above the average for comparable cities in Schleswig-Holstein, and kept rising. Although Germany has a revenue-sharing system, it has been of little benefit to Westerland because each locality's share is based on permanent population. Westerland is crowded in summer, but its permanent population is small—and declining. Since 1950, the permanent population on the island of Sylt has dropped almost 10 percent.[8]

Westerland residents also noted that condominium owners were offering their units for rent when not using them. The new units, containing more modern conveniences than rooms in private homes, took business away from older entrepreneurs. As a result, the permanent population questioned whether the city's policy of encouraging new condominiums and apartments properly reflected their best interests.*

Tourists also were concerned. They felt that the quality of the city's life-style had declined. The beaches got so crowded that many people were unable to obtain a reserved space at the main beach, and had to drive to less-crowded beaches north and south of the city. This caused traffic jams on the narrow island roads.

Increased traffic brought severe air pollution. A university group found pollution levels equal to record highs in the heavily industrialized Ruhr valley five years earlier.[9] An article in *Der Spiegel* labeled Westerland "*Das Ruhrgebiet der Weissen Industrie*"—the Ruhr of the beach-recreation industry.[10] Because of

---

*Similar opposition to new condominiums has occurred in Japan, where the boom has also had an adverse effect on traditional inns, and on the economy of tourist communities. Instead of buying meals in local restaurants, tourists bring food from Tokyo. The condominiums stay vacant except on weekends, and even then are used only a small portion of the year, so patronage in local shops has declined. Many of the condominiums replaced hotels and inns that required permanent staff, which has meant a decline in employment. (This kind of change is occurring in the area around Mt. Fuji, discussed in chapter 9.)

Strong opposition has arisen in communities where shopkeepers and innkeepers feel they are being deprived of their livelihood. In 1973, the city of Atami, a popular resort community near Tokyo, declared a moratorium on the construction of condominiums and second homes. The city also sought and received approval from the Ministry of Home Affairs to levy a special tax on the ownership of existing condominiums and second homes. This tax cost the average condominium owner about $80 a year and the second-home owner about $200, and was expected to bring the city $500,000 each year. Other cities have followed suit.

New high-rise condominiums visually dominate older structures in Westerland. (Photo by author.)

A large salt marsh on Sylt. (Photo by author.)

the wind off the North Sea, the pollution was noticeable only on occasional calm days. It was a particularly serious problem, however, given Westerland's status as an official cure center, based on the reputed therapeutic values of the iodine-laden North Sea breezes. Too much lead, sulphur dioxide, and carbon monoxide in the air might cause the government to revoke that status, ending the flow of visitors taking medically prescribed, tax-deductible vacations.

In the eyes of Westerlanders, all of these problems had one cause: overcrowding. This, in turn, they felt, was the result of an official development policy that dated back to 1967, when the State of Schleswig-Holstein prepared a regional plan for the North Sea islands.

The First Regional Plan

Schleswig-Holstein state planners in the late 1960s were concerned that the steady growth of tourism would threaten Sylt's nature protection areas. Although tourism was seen as the island's most important economic base, the planners maintained that preparation of local plans to promote tourism "... must take into account that the natural carrying capacity of the island is limited and cannot be increased without threatening its recreational value."[11] Their plan did not specify a method for determining carrying capacity, but directed that Sylt's population—21,553 in 1966—should not exceed 26,200 by 1975, an increase of only 20 percent in nine years.

To protect nature, increase tourism, and curtail growth, the plan recommended that new construction be concentrated in existing urban areas, particularly Westerland. The rest of the island was to retain its low-density character. Only in Westerland, said the planners, should buildings over three stories be permitted. Major traffic and parking improvements were proposed to ease congestion. The plan also recommended that the tourist season be lengthened by providing upgraded, *indoor* "cure center" facilities.

In 1967, this policy of concentrating new development appeared sound enough. By 1971, however, many citizens had second thoughts about the merits of high-rise development. Their resistance came to the fore in a battle surrounding a proposed apartment complex called Project Atlantis.

A Focus for Protest

Promoted by the well-known Stuttgart developer Hans Bense, Project Atlantis anticipated construction of a group of condominium buildings ranging up to 30 stories—much higher than any existing structure—and containing 750 dwelling units as well as shops and offices. The development was to be located on the beachfront in central Westerland. Particularly appealing to local officials was Bense's offer to build a new cure center, with an indoor pool and health club facilities. A center of this kind had been recommended in the 1967 plan, but the city fathers had been worried about financing its substantial cost.

Proposed site for Project Atlantis in foreground; condominiums in background. (Photo by author.)

Older homes on Sylt. (Photo by author.)

In the spring of 1971, amidst growing citizen unrest, city officials held a public hearing on the *Bebauungsplan* (analogous to an American "planned unit development") for Project Atlantis. Under German law, the local town council has to recommend that the state approve such a plan for a project that involves major changes in existing plans or patterns of development. Then, the project must be approved by the state as consistent with the regional plan. Despite substantial opposition, the town council voted to recommend approval of Project Atlantis and forwarded it to Kiel, the capital of Schleswig-Holstein, for the required approval—usually automatic—of the state Minister of the Interior.

Many Westerland residents were outraged by the decision. They formed a loosely knit organization known as the Citizens' Initiative to Halt Apartment Construction, which circulated petitions, collecting over 14,000 signatures— some estimates go as high as 20,000—of island residents, second-home owners, and tourists. Popular support of the petition reflected the ability of organizers to use Project Atlantis as a symbol of development excesses on the island.

The petition placed much of the blame on "outside speculators":

Rental to cure guests constitutes the basis of existence for most families on Sylt. Outside financial groups are beginning to take more and more of the primary financial resources out of the hands of Sylters. They build and build. This is possible for them because with enormous competitive advantage, inexhaustible investment capital and manyfold tax advantages, they compete with local residents of uneven resources. The rental business in recreational areas is quite lucrative to outside speculators. That corresponds with the laws of the free market economy. But it is our legitimate democratic right to represent the rights of Sylters and their guests with priority.

The citizens pointed out that the state of Schleswig-Holstein was obligated to hear their objections in making its decision. A full-scale study of the project's impacts was demanded, together with a moratorium on apartment construction pending a "comprehensive inventory" and a new development plan. "We just cannot afford to continue to leave our future planning to speculators," the Citizens' Initiative concluded.[12]

The petition drive was initially motivated by the economic concerns of the 70 percent of Westerland's households who rented rooms to tourists. Support for the drive, however, went far beyond this group. Island residents outside Westerland feared greater pressure on their already-crowded beaches and roads, and resented the way the height of the proposed structures would intrude on their rural landscape. Visiting tourists suffering from traffic congestion gladly added their signatures.

In complaining to the state, the Citizens' Initiative emphasized the threat of hordes of visitors to the state-designated nature protection areas on the island, recalling the concerns of state planners in the 1967 regional plan. The petition drive attracted support from across the state, including significant elements of the press and well-connected owners of second homes on the island. Although hopeful, the Citizens' Initiative was not optimistic. The state government had

Beach in outlying part of Sylt nature reserve.(Photo by author.)

Rental chairs on Westerland beach. (Photo by author.)

broad powers, but rarely used them in opposition to the wishes of local government.

During the state review, the debate between the citizens' group and Westerland officials inflamed tempers. Even the local newspaper, previously tame and noncommittal, published articles urging the halt of further construction on Sylt and supporting citizen demands to allow more public participation in the local planning process.

Under pressure from the Citizens' Initiative, Westerland's "cure director"—the town's foremost tourism official and advocate for Project Atlantis—was almost forced to resign. City officials, surprised by the extent of the opposition, seemed unsure how to react to citizen unrest. They pointed out that the 1967 state plan said Westerland needed high-density development, new and better tourist accommodations, and additional cure-center facilities. Project Atlantis would provide these facilities without placing a burden on the local tax rate. What could be more consistent with the state's plan?

The Minister of the Interior pondered for over a year. Finally, in mid-1972, he reversed local approval of the project. He said that Project Atlantis would increase noise and air pollution because of the additional traffic it would generate. He questioned whether adequate fresh water was available, and particularly noted the impact of additional crowds on the nature protection areas:

Currently some guests living in the city of Westerland are forced to go to
beaches in neighboring communities during the tourist season. This necessity
would be increased considerably by Project Atlantis. . . . Through this increased use of these beach areas, the projected dune areas will be particularly
endangered. Also, the increased automobile traffic with its indiscriminate
parking patterns cannot be effectively prevented, therefore leading to further
impact on protected scenic areas.

The Atlantis decision made it clear that a new overall development policy was
needed.

A More Precise Plan

Since both supporters and opponents of Project Atlantis had based their arguments on the same ambiguous provisions of the 1967 regional plan, state officials
recognized that that plan provided no useful guidelines for making a difficult
decision. As a first step toward drafting a new plan, a consulting firm was hired
to study environmental limitations to development on Sylt.

The consultants took a survey among tourists and found considerable
dissatisfaction—complaints about noise, crowds, automobile traffic, the cost of
hotels and restaurants, the construction of high rises, and the loss of open space
on the island.[13] Beach users in Westerland had only 8 square meters (about 86
square feet) of space per person. The consultants estimated that the "general
tolerance level" was about 12.5 square meters. The only way to reach an acceptable level, they said, was to ban new permits to expand the bed capacity.

In 1975, the state adopted a new regional plan, based in part on the consultants' recommendations. In response to the Atlantis controversy, the plan directed that "high rises and other development projects of extreme height, width,
or mass . . . are to be permitted only under limited circumstances." It recommended giving priority attention to the task of improving existing facilities and
extending the tourist season, but said, flatly, "Construction of additional
weekend housing on the island is forbidden."[14] Moreover, recognizing that
Sylt's dunes and unspoiled natural areas were essential to the island's special
appeal, it called for protection of these "natural values." Sylt's various communities would have to agree among themselves before major projects with
potential impact on the dunes could be undertaken.

Probably the most basic change imposed by the new plan was the specific
limit placed on future growth: "For the entire island, the amount of land covered
by new development may not exceed 10 percent of the total covered in 1973."[15]
Thus, while the state did not follow the most drastic recommendations of the
consultants, the strict standards of the plan effectively prohibited substantial
new development.

The legality of many sections of the Schleswig-Holstein plan for Sylt was
untested. For example, it was the first state plan to specify exactly how high
buildings can be. There is substantial controversy in Germany about the legality
of such detailed planning by the state in light of constitutional and legislative
guarantees of "self-determination" to local governments in the field of land-use
planning.[16] But an increasing number of German states have prepared specific
plans, moving further into the traditional domain of local governments.

The state was instrumental in the formation of a local planning organization to implement state policies through the consolidation and refinement of local plans. Citizens who protested against Project Atlantis turned to the more difficult task of formulating these plans. First drafts of the revised local plans were reviewed by the state, and their adoption was expected in 1978. Thereafter, the state anticipates that special financial assistance programs will be established for needed beach and roadway improvements.

Most Westerlanders apparently endorse the new policies restricting further development. In a 1978 interview, a member of the City Construction Office said that Westerland expects no major new construction in the future. It sees itself as having "reached its limits of growth."

The new planning efforts at the state and local levels reflect a dramatic change in citizen and governmental attitudes. Following the stormy debates that characterized the Project Atlantis controversy, plans are no longer viewed as bureaucratic ends in themselves, but rather as a means to reflect a deeper respect for the interaction of environmental, urban, and economic systems on the island of Sylt.

Although it will take many years before the effects of current planning efforts can be measured, there is something different about the new plans that suggests a probability of success. The generalities of the 1967 state policies have been tested against the tough decisions emanating from the Project Atlantis controversy and found too vague. The new policies are much more specific. Perhaps of greater importance, citizens who initially protested against Atlantis

Walkways protect dune vegetation on Sylt. (Photo by author.)

Torquay, with Pavilion in foreground. (Photo courtesy British Tourist Authority.)

realize the significance of planning policies and are actively participating in the creation of new plans.

That Westerland should provide a classic example of citizen involvement is noteworthy, given the German tradition of citizen deference to government decisions. The same phenomenon, however, is repeated in many parts of the world. In England, too, there is growing dissatisfaction with development policies, as indicated in chapter 5. The unrest is apparent even in communities with a long conservative tradition, such as the sedate seaside resort of Torquay, on the southern coast.

Rushing with One Impulse

Torquay first gained fame in 1820 when the Duke and Duchess of Kent chose the town as the place where their ailing infant daughter might regain her health. She did. Unfortunately, the duke caught cold while admiring the view of nearby Tor Bay and died.

Overcoming this setback to its reputation, Torquay developed into a fashionable health spa. The Russian royal family built villas overlooking the bay, bringing to the area a prestige that attracted many social climbers. By mid-century, Torquay was a summer refuge for the elite of Britain and continental Europe.

The town's setting is among Britain's most picturesque. An early travel writer described Torquay as a resort that "spreads its beaches, promenades and pleasure grounds in a great semicircle below the cliffs, and makes of the cliffs themselves a delightful terraced garden."[17] By the mid-1800s, Palladian villas, gleaming white through the trees and shrubs, covered the surrounding hills.

In 1859 the railroad reached Torquay, and tourism began to grow among the middle classes.[18] "Our seaport towns have been turned inside out," noted the London Times the following year. "Down comes the Excursion Train with its thousands . . . all rushing with one impulse to the water's edge." Many new hotels were built in Torquay to accommodate weekend visitors from Birmingham and other inland cities.

The tourists arrived at what has been called the most glamorous, grandly sited, and well-planned of England's resorts. It is one of three towns overlooking Tor Bay. Another, Brixham, was home port in 1850 to Britain's largest fishing fleet. Although never catering to tourists in numbers approaching those of Torquay, Brixham has been sought out by many visitors—particularly artists—who enjoy its quaint, old-world charm.[19] The third town, Paignton, situated between Torquay and Brixham, has always served a catching-up function, accommodating the overflow and secondary growth induced by Torquay.

In 1974, as part of a nationwide reorganization of local government in Britain, Torquay, Brixham, and Paignton were joined together and collectively designated Torbay. Governmental power over the towns and surrounding area fell to the newly created Torbay District Council, which follows policies established by the Devon County Council.[20]

The Torbay area has been growing swiftly since World War II, and today is one of England's most popular tourist destinations, attracting 1,500,000 persons each year.[21] A major expressway from the north is expected to induce still more growth.

Four out of five tourists who come to the Torbay area—most of them by car—stay in self-catering accommodations, where they do their own cooking.[22] Much of Torbay's new development has occurred on the fringes of the three communities, transforming their characteristically "neat, contained shape," according to one observer, into "formless chaos."[23] Cheaper land in and around Paignton, for example, has been found especially attractive by developers of caravan (trailer/mobile home) parks—sometimes featuring maximum density and minimum landscaping—which now occupy several hilltops overlooking the bay.

The cliffs and valleys of central Torquay, with a charm missing on the fringes of Paignton, also continue to draw people. While Torquay's traditional hotels have suffered because of the increased demand for self-catering accommodations, builders find that high-rise apartments appeal to both retirees and tourists. Because vacant land is scarce, developers have concentrated on sites that already contained structures, many dating from the mid-19th century. In a country where 15th-century structures are not unusual, these Victorian-era

Ashcroft, a Victorian home in Torquay. (Photo by Christopher J. Duerksen.)

buildings were until recently considered too modern to be of historic interest. Today, however, their beauty is increasingly appreciated.

Originally, developers who sought to erect high-rise apartments on these sites met virtually no opposition. It was generally acknowledged that the apartments were major contributors to Torquay's economic base. But because of a new activism among Torquay residents, developers are finding a cooler reception.

Part of the opposition to new development results from concern about the general environmental effects of rapid growth, primarily congestion and pollution. Residents complain constantly about crowded conditions and traffic problems during the summer season. Air pollution from auto emissions is conspicuously unpleasant, especially in the town centers and along the shore drives. Water pollution has become an issue, because a growing amount of raw sewage is dumped into Tor Bay through two outfalls. There is no ongoing water-quality monitoring system where the sewage is dumped.* Torbay may lose its reputation as a healthy community, residents fear.

Another impetus to citizen activism has come from the threat to Torquay's visual appeal. Residents feel that at some point the replacement of old Victorian buildings could prove irreversible, resulting in a complete change in the town's character and a loss of the qualities for which it is renowned. This issue was brought into focus by a proposal to demolish the Torquay Pavilion.

"As Uniform and Tasty as its Cooking"

John Betjeman has neatly satirized the English taste in urban design by comparing it with the English taste in food:

> In a few years this country will be looking
> As uniform and tasty as its cooking.
> Hamlets which fail to pass the planners' test
> Will be demolished. We'll rebuild the rest
> To look like Welwyn mixed with Middle West.[24]

In 1971, the Torquay Pavilion failed "to pass the planners' test" and was slated for demolition. Built on the edge of Torquay harbor, the Pavilion is, to say the least, eclectic. But somehow its white exterior, art-nouveau ironwork, copper domes, and octagonal summerhouses combine to lend a holiday atmosphere to downtown Torquay. The manicured lawn, tropical plants, and waving palms that line walkways about the Pavilion amplify a feeling of gentility and graciousness.

After its opening in 1912, the lavish, 2,000-seat theater was used for concerts, lectures, and films, and served as the town's central meeting place. Its music festivals during the 1930s were world famous. By the 1950s, however, the theater began to show wear about the edges and remained open only during the summer months. Maintenance costs rose, and deterioration set in. In 1971, the planners recommended that the Pavilion be torn down.

Hearing of the demolition plans, Sheila Hardaway, a lifelong resident of

---

*Torbay's lack of sewage-treatment facilities is not unusual in Britain. Even major cities such as Newcastle and Edinburgh dump raw sewage in the ocean. The British place great confidence in offshore currents and have actively resisted the recommendations of other Common Market nations regarding water-quality standards.

Torquay, decided enough was enough. She had suffered quietly while dozens of Victorian homes were razed. This was the time and place to stand up against the bulldozers that were destroying Torquay's character.

Mrs. Hardaway and a small band of cohorts, calling themselves Friends of the Pavilion, set about rousing the public to save the old theater. When the local council refused to respond to friendly overtures, the group organized noisy public meetings and protest marches. They obtained over 10,000 signatures on a petition to get the Pavilion designated as a national landmark.

The local council still refused to budge. The central government, however, was more responsive. The Department of the Environment listed the structure as having great architectural and historic value, in effect prohibiting its demolition. This forced the local council to seek an alternative use for the existing structures.*

"As Though Embosomed"

Mrs. Hardaway had bigger things in mind than the Pavilion. Having saved one landmark, she saw an opportunity to reverse local policy toward development in general, and organized a watchdog environmental group to overlook activities in her neighborhood. Similar groups soon sprang up in other neighborhoods. They shared a common goal: to prevent the replacement of Victorian structures by high-rise apartments catering to the tourist market. A brochure authored by Mrs.

---

*The local council subsequently agreed to lease the Pavilion to the Rank Organisation for conversion to a dancing and entertainment center. As of 1977, the deal was stalled because Torbay licensing justices refused to issue a liquor license, citing police complaints of summer rowdiness in the harbor area. Mrs. Hardaway testified in favor of the license. "You can't bring out a pot of tea in a place like this," she told the local newspaper.[25]

The Pavilion. (Photo by Alan Taylor.)

Contrasting structures in Torquay. (Photo by Alan Taylor.)

Hardaway explained the goal in a style heavy with Victorian symbolism:

> There was a time when man's hand complemented and did not vie with the
> natural environment. The homes nestled amid hills, as though embosomed; and
> no home, no building, violated the contour of the land but instead blended with
> it. The natural environment accepted and assimilated the human scene, so that
> both joined and became one in the manner of a good and lasting marriage.[26]

Builders had erected a number of especially unattractive high-rise apartments in neighborhoods of Victorian buildings, or on sites that interfered with
traditional views. As the new structures became more prevalent, public opposition mounted. Increasingly, the council responded to citizen pressure and denied developers' applications.

With other Torbay citizens, Mrs. Hardaway continued the fight. Neighborhood groups have become quite expert at working within England's
development-control process, primarily through established procedures, while
using petitions, demonstrations, and other confrontation tactics only as a last
resort.

The Dynamics of Local Planning

In Torbay, as elsewhere in England, to develop land a person must obtain
"planning permission" from the local planning authority. On receipt of an
application, the authority's planning staff examines the proposal in light of
applicable land-use plans, studies, and special conditions. The staff then provides recommendations and comments to elected members of the local authority's planning committee.

As indicated in chapter 5, England has experienced serious delays in the
promulgation of comprehensive land-use plans and policies. The county structure plan covering Torbay—as of early 1978—has not been completed, and local
plans cannot be considered until the county plan has been approved. Meanwhile, planners in Torbay—and elsewhere—continue to approve or deny specific development proposals. Relying on a variety of studies and hunches, they try
to adapt these proposals to varied goals. If England has any working planning
policies at all, notes planning law expert Neal Roberts, they must be found
within the process of development control.[27]

For Mrs. Hardaway and other concerned citizens, a major point of access to
this process results from the fact that the local Torbay planning authority—like
others throughout England—must maintain a public register listing all development applications received. No other public notice is required in ordinary
cases, but some local authorities voluntarily give special notice to neighbors and
neighborhood associations. While citizens' groups may comment in writing to
members of the local planning committee on any proposal, there are no statutory
requirements that the committee take these comments into account. Members of
the public may attend meetings of the planning committee, but are not allowed
to speak.

Torbay's local planning committee may grant development approvals with
or without special conditions (such as height limitations or landscaping requirements), or it may refuse permission for specified reasons based on established planning principles. Within six months after denial of permission, a
developer may appeal to the Secretary of the Department of the Environment,

Older building in Torquay undergoing renovation. (Photo by Christopher J. Duerksen.)

who assigns an inspector and ultimately—as much as 18 months later—makes a decision on the basis, at least in theory, of the inspector's report.[28] If permission is granted, third parties, such as citizen groups that oppose the development, have no right of appeal.

In a few cases, the Secretary of the Department of the Environment bypasses the local authorities and "calls in" a development application. Since citizens' groups cannot appeal local approvals, they sometimes lobby for a call-in if they think they have little chance of defeating an application at the local level. Local authorities themselves sometimes ask for a call-in to avoid making controversial decisions. No one has a right to demand a call-in, however, and the department need not give reasons for its decision to assume or decline jurisdiction.

When a list of planning applications is published, Torbay's organized groups divide applications among area leaders, who visit the proposed sites and prepare written comments. While the process of writing comments is time-consuming, planners and amenity groups in the Torbay area think it has worked quite well.

Developers in Torbay have not been pleased. In 1976, they persuaded a new planning committee chairman to abolish the practice of sending automatic notice to neighborhood associations.[29] The developers complained that the planning committee often rejected applications solely on political grounds, that is, to appease local amenity groups. They also felt that the committee's receptivity to citizens' views had eliminated any kind of certainty from the system. The chairman of the Torbay Hoteliers' Association accused the Torbay District Council of being "antitourism" and threatened revenge at the polls.

Finding a Balance

Notwithstanding the attitudes of developers, planners working in the Torbay development-control process feel they have tried to strike a balance. On one hand, they understand the need for expansion, which many believe essential to Torbay's economic well-being; on the other, they see the need for preservation of the area's unique character, which many perceive as an important contributor to economic success.

Controls have been tightened in many older areas, and the Torbay District Council has made a particular effort to limit the size of new buildings to achieve harmony with surrounding structures. The Torbay planning authority designated four "conservation areas" where the council can prevent destruction of any building and can exercise especially strict control over development.

In addition, the council appointed a full-time conservation officer, Alan Taylor. (He established his credibility by buying and remodeling as his own

Rehabilitated 15th-century farmhouse. (Photo by Alan Taylor.)

home a five-century-old farmhouse with thatched roof.) The council also tightened up controls over the undeveloped areas on the fringes of the community. Jack Henwood, the chief planning officer, remarked, "We've just about had our whack" with trailer parks, which also are now being discouraged.

Controversies over development issues in Torbay have not ended. A number of large development companies abandoned the area reportedly because of such problems. But the community is taking a balanced and thoughtful approach. Like many other places, Torbay needed to see a few atrocious examples of what uncontrolled development could produce before deciding something had to be done. The planners and most council members appear to realize that growth is inevitable. They are concerned that an overly restrictive policy will make it difficult for young people of modest means to locate in the community. Yet they hope that by designating more conservation areas they can protect the most attractive parts of the community and that, for other areas where redevelopment is proposed, they can rely on strong design controls to minimize local opposition. In this way, they will try to retain most of the amenities that originally attracted people to Torquay, while providing opportunities for a new and less elite generation of visitors and residents.

An Aristocratic Vision?

Development-control controversies like those in Westerland and Torquay often elicit charges and countercharges of elitism. Thus, it may be argued that Mrs. Hardaway and her band of preservationists are a new elite, lacking the titles and wealth of the Duke of Kent and the Russian royal family, but determined to protect their own prerogatives from the onrush of more common people. In a similar vein, an American journalist has characterized the entire environmental movement as an attempt by the "leisure class" to thwart development that would benefit the working classes. "The environmental vision is an aristocratic one" that "can only be sustained by people who have never had to worry about their security."[30]

Such generalizations suggest that the author relied on ideology more than on observation. If true, his theory would lead one to expect welcoming festivities when expressways or urban-renewal projects invade lower-class neighborhoods, and little opposition to the Concorde or additional residential development in middle-class suburbs.

Many of the newcomers who rent high-rise apartments in Torquay are far wealthier than the owners of the dowdy Victorian terraces. The strongest opposition to Project Atlantis in Westerland probably came from small shopkeepers and rooming-house owners—citizens who would hardly qualify as people who never had to worry about their security. They saw large, modern facilities as a serious competitive threat, and that made them oppose Atlantis.

For each example of a particular class favoring development, another can be cited of the same class opposed to development. To demonstrate that such opposition is not the property of the idle rich, or even the middle class, the experience of FONATUR, the Mexican tourism development authority, in the seaside town of Zihuatanejo may be considered.

Multifamily homes in Zihuatanejo. (Photo by Phyllis Myers.)

The Real Mexico

The economy of the village of Zihuatanejo has long been supported by the rich coastal waters of the Pacific, a prolific resource for both commercial and sport fishing. For many years, a few venturesome tourists arrived in Zihuatanejo in small planes to seek big game fish and savor "the real Mexico." They liked the village's rustic simplicity—barefoot children and Brahman bulls ambling along dirt paths, women peddling shell necklaces, small cafes with fresh clams and wine in two-foot pitchers to fend off the midday heat. The Bay of Zihuatanejo may have reminded some people of Acapulco long ago.

Lying in pleasant disarray among the hills that curve around the bay, Zihuatanejo's 15 small hotels in the early 1970s attracted some 12,000 tourists annually, a majority from other parts of Mexico. Even the most expensive of these establishments offered no air conditioning or elevators. Listening to waves beat against nearby cliffs, guests dined in the open air. To reach the beach, they descended hundreds of stone steps.

Many residents of Zihuatanejo lived in hovels on the hills and mountains, without running water or toilets. Few roads or streets were paved. During the rainy season stagnant pools formed everywhere on the impermeable soil. Zihuatanejo, like many small Mexican towns, had wells and minimal running water in rusty old pipes, but no sewage system. In parts of the town, sewage flowed through the streets, descending slowly down a gentle grade toward a mud flat, a cesspool in which children swam, adults washed, and women collected their daily household water.

Zihuatanejo is located in the state of Guerrero, which is isolated from centers of commerce, industry, and education. Guerrillas roam the hills. Police regularly search cars and buses for contraband and drugs. Income is only half the national average. Unemployment is widespread. The incidence of malaria has been high.

In 1971, the Mexican government's tourism development agency, FONATUR, negotiated a loan from the World Bank to develop the coast around Zihuatanejo. A new resort community called Ixtapa was to be built a few miles up the coast, while Zihuatanejo was to become a secondary, lower-key resort and service center for Ixtapa.

The loan was conditioned on adoption of a suitable urban plan for Zihuatanejo. According to a bank official, it is "a *sine qua non* of all our tourism projects that there be subsidiary investment in a tourist area to help the people." The plan called for potable water and sewage treatment for a population of 20,000 in the first stage, with room for expansion to 50,000. A "neater" town was envisioned, with straight streets replacing the dirt bypaths. The hillsides would be cleared of shacks, and squatters moved into new housing in the town. Lighting, telephones, and sewage treatment were to be provided.

The plan aroused little opposition as long as it was only on paper. When the government began to acquire land in 1972, however, the citizens became suspicious—as a result of past experience with government expropriation—that compensation would be inadequate. Much of the land FONATUR had to acquire for redevelopment was *ejido* land, held in common by the peasants (*ejidatarios*) who lived and worked on it. The government convened a number of meetings with ejidatarios, assured them they would be treated fairly, and persuaded them to sign an agreement. The details of negotiation were not worked out specifically.

The Federal Law of Agrarian Reform entitles each ejidatario to compensation for the value of buildings constructed or improvements made on his land. He is also to be given "two urbanized lots equivalent to the commercial agricultural value of the land." Moreover, the ejidatarios as a whole receive a 20-percent equity interest in the development project.

This kind of compensation seems generous. No profits, however, are expected on the Ixtapa-Zihuatanejo tourism development project for a long time—perhaps not until 1995—so an equity interest had little immediate value. The ejidatarios did not want to wait 20 years or longer. To secure the land, therefore, FONATUR agreed to advance money based on estimates of eventual profits. After extensive negotiations, each ejidatario in Zihuatanejo received about $9,000.

The size and location of the urbanized lots to be given to ejidatarios was another source of dispute. Eventually, they were promised two urbanized lots each, serviced with water, sewers, electricity, and access roads. FONATUR initially proposed that the size of the lots be 400 square meters (approximately 4,300 square feet); the ejidatarios demanded 2,000 square meters; they agreed to 1,260 square meters.

The ejidatarios also objected to the original plan for Zihuatanejo, which foresaw a town with straight streets and new houses. In 1975, a revised master plan was promulgated. In it, new roads followed the original winding pathways. Many existing houses were to be renovated, rather than replaced. Residents in shacks high on hillsides could remain, but officials insisted no more would be permitted to settle. It was hoped that low-cost housing, as well as access to materials for building new houses, eventually would eliminate the hovels. A new school was proposed to train 180 people every three months. They would serve as low-level, semiskilled assistants in hotel services and construction work, and in installing and repairing air conditioners and other electrical equipment. Several small ejido factories, producing clay bricks and other building materials, opened in an industrial zone, and a consumers' co-op was also started. New laws required that wandering pigs, chickens, and burros be kept penned to allow a more sophisticated atmosphere.*

In Zihuatanejo, as in Torquay and Westerland, citizen opposition provoked changes in the plan for tourism development. The ejidatarios consented to the government program when promised a minimum of interference and an opportunity to participate in anticipated profits from future land appreciation. Nevertheless, they remained suspicious and determined not to be pushed around. As development proceeded, the women gathered daily to wash and gossip at the old community laundry area, ignoring a more modern washstand intended to replace it. The old life-style would not be swept quickly away.

The Glare of Others' Views

Those who sought to bring new development—and more tourists—to Westerland, Torquay, and Zihuatanejo might reasonably have believed that they were creating benefits for the entire community. Seaside resorts, after all, depend on tourism. But people do not always see change as advantageous.

Torquay's citizens decided that replacing historic buildings with modern apartments was not healthy. The planners saw modernization as a tonic for the tax base, but failed to anticipate the side effects stemming from the loss of community character.

Similarly, in Westerland municipal officials thought new condominiums would cure many of the community's fiscal problems. But the citizens saw the new development as benefiting outsiders and the municipality at their expense.

In Zihuatanejo, planners from Mexico City at first prescribed an orderly life, with tenants in new housing on straightened streets. Citizens preferred the old patterns.

That is not to say that the citizen groups were right. If they emerge as heroes, it may only be because their point of view has often been ignored. That point of view, however, is no more universally correct than the developer's. The rooming-house owner in Westerland would like to avoid competition; Mrs. Hardaway seeks to preserve the quiet gentility to which she has become accustomed; the ejidatarios of Zihuatanejo would like to earn some money in land speculation. Others could characterize these motives as selfish. But in assessing the environmental impacts of development, selfish values of existing residents can no more be dismissed than can the aspirations of potential tourists because a developer will make money satisfying them.

Planning expert Neal Roberts has said that the current problems of the British planning system demonstrate a need to take the planner "out of the shadow of his professionalization and make him more aware of the glare of

---

*Not everyone liked this kind of change, including at least one tourist. *The Washington Post* on April 27, 1975, quoted a New York tourist who had been going to Zihuatanejo for 13 seasons: "There was an ecological soundness about the roaming animals and a countrified charm that is now gone forever."

Community house, Zihuatanejo. (Photo by Phyllis Myers.)

others' views."[31] The planners in Westerland, Torquay, and Zihuatanejo made decisions that, to their surprise, created adverse public reaction. Residents of these communities reached what George Young has called a "psychological saturation level" with tourism, causing a growing loss of good-will toward tourists and toward development in general.[32]

The decisions made in Westerland, Torquay, and Zihuatanejo would have been better if the planners had been exposed earlier to the glare of others' views. As a first step, this would require improved communications. Experts must communicate to the public in language that people can understand. Economists must be found who will translate their academic jargon into statements that begin, "Look, you folks would make more money if you do it this way." Scientists must recognize that "the great issues derive from the stormy clash of incommensurable values, backed by the hunger for justice or selfish advantage."[33]

Increasingly, in the United States and elsewhere, new ways are being found to encourage public involvement in major decisions affecting community development. Ivory-tower diagnoses based on abstract statistics too often have been mistaken. In parts of the United States, "sunshine laws" have been adopted that require public decisions to be made in open meetings where the public has a right to be heard.

These kinds of initiatives move beyond the formal setting in which only the sophisticated can successfully participate. They suggest that planners must become "street smart." If the commitment is made to take planning out of "the backrooms and drafting rooms and bring it into the streets and meeting places," says University of Wisconsin planning professor Anthony Catanese, "planning would lose much of its elitist imagery and become more identified as something that people do. The professional planners would lose their ivory tower, intellectual auras and become more like champions and friends of the people."[34] Environmental planning needs to be viewed not as the application of objective planning principles, but as a problem of people living with each other and with the land around them.[35]

As technology provides more sophisticated means of collecting and analyzing data, the risk increases that the planning process will become politically obsolescent. In too many academic circles the prestige and credibility of planning depend on the use of high-technology systems of quantified analysis, dazzling in the laboratory but not credible to people in places like Westerland, Torquay, or Zihuatanejo.

Planners often seek to overcome their increasing distance from the public by intensive questioning. What are your goals? What should we be planning to achieve? Surveys, questionnaires, and committees abound, and planners are sometimes deluded into thinking that they can predict public reaction. But the level of abstraction inhibits public response. Often the public placidly agrees with policies in the abstract, but violently disagrees with their implementation.

The extent of planners' success in predicting public reaction to development projects will vary with the extent to which they realize that they themselves are part of the mixture of human beings known as the public, and that they can't afford to disregard the mixture's complexity. As René Dubos puts it, "each human being is unique, unprecedented, unrepeatable."[36]

IV MEDIATING

Chapter 7
The Ancient Lights of London

This chapter and the next examine how disputes over new development proposals are resolved in England and Japan. Tourism development provides the context for the disputes, but other types of development could have served equally well.

People throughout the world are banding together to fight for the qualities that make their neighborhoods attractive to them.[1] In this militant atmosphere, planning often seems an abstract irrelevancy; forestalling disputes becomes less important than resolving them.

Anything that brings new people to an area usually has some impact on the people already living there. Disputes between existing occupants and newcomers are not new. Throughout history, societies have striven to resolve conflicts between the need for new development and the desire to protect existing interests. What is new is the increasing complexity of development disputes and the escalating amounts of time and money needed to resolve them.

Concern over these costs has led some American commentators to call for simpler dispute-resolution systems by which neighbors would resolve their own arguments, without need for a complex public policymaking process.[2]

Prior to this century most development disputes in England and America were treated as private matters. In recent decades, however, both countries have moved away from the idea that neighborhood squabbles are private disputes. Government regulations replaced arguments about "nuisances"; courts invalidated attempts to delegate decision-making power to neighborhood groups. Every argument about the proper height of a fence became an occasion for publicly endorsed rules, and at least potentially the cause of administrative hearings and litigation.

Perhaps we should reevalute this trend. The idea of neighbors solving their own disputes certainly offers a welcome touch of nostalgia in an increasingly bureaucratic world. Private solution of this type of neighborhood dispute would help clear the calendars of overburdened courts and public agencies. This goal is strongly sought by the Chief Justice of the United States, who has called for

Field research for this chapter was conducted by Christopher J. Duerksen.

"swift resolution" of environmental disputes to "avoid the waste involved in suspending execution of large projects to which vast public or private resources are committed."[3]

The possibility of adopting simpler systems may be considered by examining a rule that once served as the basis for resolving numerous development disputes: the doctrine of ancient lights.

Time out of Mind

Under English common law, the doctrine of "ancient lights" guaranteed access to sunlight for firstcomers. As London grew, with buildings abutting each other on small lots, the English courts established a rule that "the owner of a house will be restrained by injunction . . . if he makes any erections or improvements so as to obstruct the ancient lights of an adjoining house."[4]

The law was not the guardian of the *nouveau riche*. According to Blackstone, "it is necessary that the windows be *ancient*, that is, have subsisted there time out of mind; otherwise there is no injury done." The homes of the well-established citizens—those who had been there "time out of mind"—were to be protected. Only if a window had let in sunlight for 20 years was it said to have established a right of "ancient lights." Once such a right had been established, however, the owner could obtain legal remedies against any neighbor who threatened to interfere with his sunlight.[5]

When English common law was transported to America, the "ancient lights" rule atrophied. American commentators noted that "the doctrine is not much relished in this country," because of the rapid growth of cities and villages.[6] The Maryland Court of Appeals, for example, said that such a rule would "greatly interfere with, and impede, the rapid changes and improvements which are here constantly going on."[7]

The change reflected a basic shift in U.S. attitudes toward property in the 19th century. America began with a "static agrarian conception" of property as a right to undisturbed enjoyment. Rules based on "first in time first in right" originally encouraged development by promising security against future disruption. But as the fever of economic development spread, the nation turned to a "dynamic, instrumental and more abstract view of property that emphasized the newly paramount virtues of productive use and development."[8] In the words of Dan Tarlock, professor of law at Indiana University, "the law was creating a presumption, loosely defined, that in the long run and the short run, the benefits of an activity outweighed any adverse consequences."[9] Like many other rules that favored the first appropriator over the potential developer, the right of ancient lights grew dim.

In a recent book, Morton Horwitz, professor of law at Harvard and a specialist in legal history, shows how various American courts, all espousing a common philosophy favoring development, changed a wide variety of common-law rules that had benefited firstcomers. Was there a plot among the judges, Horwitz asks, to promote development?

> Viewed retrospectively, one is tempted to see a Machiavellian hand in this process. How better to develop an economy than initially to provide the first developers with guarantees against future competitive injury? And once development has reached a certain level, can the claims of still greater efficiency

through competition be denied? By changing the rules and disguising the changes in the complexities of technical legal doctrine, the facade of economic security can be maintained even as new property is allowed to sweep away the old.[10]

This kind of historian's perspective, as Professor Horwitz acknowledges, was not available to the judiciary of the day. They were merely following to a logical conclusion the subconscious confidence in "progress" that pervaded the 19th century, particularly in the new world.

The doctrine of ancient lights, and the American rejection of it, represent contrasting examples of policies toward growth and development. In 18th-century England, the first builder had a right to sunlight that his prospective neighbor could not disturb; in 19th-century America, the new builder had an absolute right to build, regardless of the impact on his neighbor.

To the modern Englishman the idea of a "right" to build, or to prevent a neighbor from building, seems anachronistic. The substantive rights exemplified by "ancient lights" have largely disappeared. Except in extreme cases, the Englishman has only procedural rights to receive notice and express opinions on neighborhood controversies. Land-use decisions are made by the national Department of the Environment with only minimal guidance from adopted rules or policies. (See chapters 5 and 6.)

Policy may be lacking, but the process of decision making is clearly established. Thus, if a hotel operator in London opposes the construction of a new hotel, he has no doubt which forum will hear his dispute. The local city council will decide the case in passing on application for "planning permission"—that is, for permission under the planning laws to construct a building or undertake any other form of development. The council listens to those who are trying to protect existing values and those seeking to create new ones.

In one sense, therefore, the old battle of ancient lights is being replayed before these local councils. Today, however, the ancient lights that London residents want to preserve are not literally lights, but "amenities" based on the "existence of shared values on aesthetic matters or pleasantness of surroundings."[11] While incapable of measurement in footcandles, these values are as important in London as sunshine.

The process by which the council resolves the disputes is called development control. The British system of development control has been operating for almost a decade without much overall policy direction, however. Because planning policies have been poorly defined, and appeal to the courts has been effectively unavailable, the development-control process has increasingly come to be viewed as a battle between neighbors to be decided more on the basis of relative noise levels of the contending parties than on the basis of overall development policies.

As an example, tourism development in London in the late 1960s and early 1970s may be considered. The problems that often arise in the wake of the tourist were compounded by an intensive subsidy program for hotel development. The result is reminiscent of the problems found in Jerusalem, discussed in the prologue.

Tourists per Pound

As England's currency has faltered, her attraction to tourists—some 11 million in 1977—has increased.[12] The millions of tourists who annually flock to London not only pay homage to the city's great monuments—St. Paul's, the Tower, Parliament, and so on—but also congregate in the pubs of Soho, applaud in the theaters of Covent Garden, and fill the shops of Oxford Street, the most popular destination of all. The devalued pound makes the price of these attractions seem like bargains to most visitors.

For many Americans, London provides a gateway to the Continent, and a comfortable, English-speaking refuge from it as well. Of the total number of visitors in London each year, Americans account for about 20 percent. Another 20 percent arrive from other parts of the British Isles. About 40 percent are from continental Europe—including shoppers on a one-day spree—and 20 percent from other parts of the world, a significant number being free-spending Arabs.[13]

In return for its hospitality, London obtains economic benefits—foreign currency, tax revenues, retail sales profits, restaurant and hotel earnings, and so on. Tourists spent over a billion dollars in London in 1973, and the volume of tourists has been rising steadily since.[14] Such figures, however, represent a relatively recent phenomenon.

Only 30 years ago, tourism in London was negligible. Hotels were deteriorating, and postwar priorities put housing and industrial development first. Then, around 1960, the jet airliner transformed the tourism business. Large numbers of Americans began to arrive. At the same time, however, restrictions on building and increases in taxes put a damper on all new construction. Not surprisingly, by the end of the 1960s the supply of London hotel rooms was strained to the limit. Tour groups were turned away, and visitors complained loudly about the quality of the hotels. Nonetheless, the sinking value of the pound contributed to a rise in London's appeal to tourists.

For policymakers, in the face of the weakening British economy, tourism began to look like one of the few profitable sources of foreign currency. In 1969 the government hurriedly adopted a Tourism Development Act, intended to secure economic benefits from the boom and improve the balance of trade. The act included a Hotel Development Incentive Scheme, authorizing government grants and loans. The tourist board would pay up to 20 percent of the total cost for new construction or for the alteration of existing hotels to provide at least five additional bedrooms. Given the favorable climate for hotel investment that economic conditions, tourist demand, and government subsidies provided, over 50,000 hotel rooms were added as a result of the subsidy program.[15]

Local planning authorities, especially in London, catered to hotel growth by quickly approving most applications for planning permission. In cases of refused permission, the central government often reversed the decision on appeal. In the beginning, almost every hotel proposal eventually went through.

The controversy over whether subsidized tourism development of this sort will produce the economic benefits anticipated has been considered in the prologue. Even allowing for such benefits in London, however, they were not sufficient, in the eyes of some British observers, to outweigh other problems caused by the hotel development boom that followed the 1969 subsidy law.

Bayswater hotels. (Photos by author.)

Thus, in the early 1970s, architectural critics almost unanimously denounced the new hotels. The highly respected *Architectural Review* commented:

> What distinguishes hotels from any other [buildings] of this size is that . . . not one qualifies for publication, as a building, in the *Architectural Review*. . . . It seems likely that, as the years go by, the hotels of 1968-1973 will be widely recognized as a very undesirable accretion to our architectural heritage. . . . The new hotels, which will last two generations and took perhaps two years to build, all look as if they had taken about two hours to design.[16]

One newspaper critic censured the plethora of new hotels as "scars of London's hotel gold rush." Other architects used terms like "visual illiteracy" and "chaotic pile."

Some of the most destructive hotel development involved not simply creating flashy new eyesores, but razing or remodeling homes in residential districts. Here, the strongest opposition to accelerated hotel development came from displaced residents. Housing in central London was—and still is—scarce and expensive. Many older buildings that were converted or demolished to make way for hotels had contained accommodations for persons of moderate income. By one estimate, hotel construction displaced 1,000 residential dwelling units each year.[17]

To evicted residents the generalized economic benefits of tourism were no consolation. They had the immediate problem of finding housing in a market where the cost was rapidly rising. Even for residents who remained, the change in the character of an area brought about by new development and conversions was in itself unsettling. One London neighborhood that fought the process was Bayswater.

The Wrong Side of the Park

Bayswater, a neighborhood in the London borough of Westminster, lies northwest of Hyde Park. It's the wrong side of the park, residents of more elegant Mayfair would say. An area of modest dwellings—traditionally genteel but not fashionable—Bayswater since the mid-19th century has attracted middle-class families who wanted to live near central London. Its early solidity as a residential neighborhood was attested to by John Galsworthy, who set his series of novels *The Forsyte Saga* in the area.

In 1900, Bayswater felt the impact of Paddington Station, which became a major point of embarkation for young people from the Midlands seeking their fortune in London. The blocks near the station spawned rooming houses and small hotels, usually by conversion of existing residential structures. The area still has a remarkable variety of accommodations, ranging from individually owned row houses and apartments, to hotels, rooming houses, and public-housing projects. It also retains essentially the same architectural character that it had in the 18th century. Many of its structures, listed officially as historic buildings, are protected by the government from major changes to their facades.

The tiny hotels that dot Bayswater often contain fewer than 10 rooms. Family-operated, they typically provide a night's lodging plus breakfast for less than $10. Even though they could easily afford more, tourists often choose these "bed-and-breakfast places" because of the loving care the buildings receive—

Bayswater underground station. (Photo by author.)

each room is a room rather than an abstract "dwelling unit." It is of Bayswater's buildings that William Blake wrote:

> The stones are pity, and the bricks, well wrought affections
> Enamel'd with love & kindness, & the tiles engraven gold,
> Labour of merciful hands: the beams & rafters are forgiveness:
> The mortar & cement of the work, tears of honesty: the nails
> And the screws & iron braces are well wrought blandishments
> And well contrived words, firm fixing, never forgotten,
> Always comforting the remembrance: the floors, humility:
> The ceilings, devotion: the hearths, thanksgiving.[18]

The 40,000 people living in Bayswater tend to be younger, have fewer children, and be better paid than the average resident of Westminster Borough. Although voting records show a high population turnover, estimated at one-third each year, a substantial portion of the residents consider Bayswater more than a temporary home and hope to preserve its desirable characteristics. It is this group that has often come into conflict with those seeking to profit from tourists and short-term residents.

In the mid-1960s, plans were made to bulldoze a number of deteriorating but architecturally significant homes in Bayswater as part of an urban renewal plan.

Trash accumulates in front of Bayswater hotels. (Photo by author.)

Citizens opposed to the plan succeeded in having large sections of Bayswater designated as Conservation Areas, protecting them from demolition. Having defeated massive urban renewal, residents thought they had won the most critical battle they would face. Their elation proved premature.

In 1969, when the government introduced its hotel subsidy program, Westminster's borough planners looked at various neighborhoods to see which seemed most suited to tourism development. Bayswater already contained many hotels and boarding houses. Wealthy residents south of Hyde Park had more political strength with which to oppose hotel construction. So Bayswater was designated a "hotel area."

This had a dramatic effect on the community. Conversions of apartment buildings to small hotels increased. Land prices rose sharply, forcing out the poor. Many residents of small apartments or rooming houses, especially single people, were evicted to make room for tourists.

Older residents of Bayswater now associate tourism with noise, litter, aesthetic degradation, and the displacement of neighbors. In just five years, one street, Queensborough Terrace, lost 60 percent of its residential accommodations to hotels. In some areas only very old residents have remained, many not knowing what to expect next.

Parsons of once-full churches that now stand half empty on Sunday mornings blame tourism for the dispersal of their congregations. Small shopkeepers, greengrocers, butchers, and fishmongers, who depend on permanent residents, say tourists are putting them out of business because larger new hotels tend to buy food from wholesalers outside the neighborhood. The decline in traditional commerce, however, has been accompanied by an increase in the number of restaurants, pubs, and dance places.

Though many kinds of people patronize the hotels—salesmen, young people from the country seeking jobs, thrifty vacationing couples—two groups are perceived as creating the greatest problems: youths on vacations and low-price tour groups. Many students choose Bayswater during their visits to London because accommodation there is cheaper than elsewhere. Complaints about them often reflect a gap in generations and life-styles. In the words of one resident, the young people tend to be "energetic and high-spirited," and thus naturally noisy, particularly when they stumble back from bars or discos at 2:00 or 3:00 A.M.

As for tour groups, their buses regularly block traffic in Bayswater's narrow streets. Parked with the motor running during the lengthy loading and unloading process, a tour bus also assaults the sight, hearing, and smell of all in the area. With buses and taxis occupying scarce parking spaces, irate residents often have difficulty reaching their homes, much less finding a parking place.

Another source of irritation has been substantial accumulation of litter, especially around hotels. Visitors discard candy wrappers and cigarette cartons. Stacks of milk bottles are left on the curb for pickup; many are smashed before the milkman arrives. Large and obtrusive dumpsters full of rubbish line the streets, because the alleys behind hotels are too narrow for many trucks.

The face of Bayswater has also been marked by alterations to buildings. Replacing small windows with huge picture windows will change a building's facade and its relation to surrounding structures. Many hotel conversions in-

Buses at Leinster Square. (Photo by author.)

volve substantial remodeling—to the detriment of an entire block.

Faced with changes like these, the residents took action. In 1972 a group of them organized the Bayswater Residents' Association. Its secretary, Carol Baker, has said that the members would not have minded an expensive Dorchester-type hotel in Bayswater, but that was not what they were getting.* The association reviews planning applications, received regularly from the Westminster planning department, and submits detailed reports on them. Members spend much of their time persuading local politicians and planners to rectify problems such as bus parking and discouraging new conversions to hotels. They are quick to complain if a neighbor attempts an unobtrusive conversion.

The Sussex Gardens Dispute

Although the Bayswater Residents' Association is frequently at odds with hotel proprietors, sometimes an alliance is formed between residents and existing proprietors to oppose new hotel development. When the London Hilton was built, one observer noted, "the snooty neighborhood hotels, like the Dorchester and Grosvenor House, reacted like a dowager who finds herself forcibly attending a Tupperware party."[19] Bed-and-breakfast places at the opposite end of the scale, moreover, may not only resent the impersonality of the newer commercial hotels, but see them as a direct threat.

---

*"Dorchester guests get drunk in their room, not in the street," observed John Whatmore, a Bayswater member of the Westminster Borough Council. (This comment was made before a group of Arab investors purchased the Dorchester.)

An instance of various forces combining to oppose new hotels occurred in 1974 when the Grand Junction Corporation announced its plan to develop a three-block area in Sussex Gardens, a section of Bayswater near Paddington Station. Although owned by Grand Junction, the blocks contained many bed-and-breakfast places operated by tenants who had been in business for 20 years or more. The corporation sought to evict them, gut the interiors of the buildings, and open a series of block-square, modern hotels, complete with private baths, room service, restaurant facilities, and higher prices.

The Sussex Gardens (North Side) Tenants' Association, representing a group of families operating bed-and-breakfast places in Sussex Gardens and Norfolk Square, protested. They were joined in their opposition by many other residents, who feared that if the Grand Junction plan were carried out, the displaced proprietors might seek other apartment buildings to convert into small hotels.

Given strong and bitter opposition, and sensing potential defeat, Grand Junction withdrew its initial proposal and hired another architect, who submitted a plan to convert the structures into a series of hotels that would be larger than the existing bed-and-breakfast operations, but smaller than the block-long establishments originally envisioned. The developers filed a new application for

Flats for sale. (Photo by author.)

planning permission with the Westminster Planning Committee in June 1974. It did not assuage the opposition, but triggered another debate, with statements and letters submitted to the planning committee and the press.

In the view of the developer's architect, Alan Anderson, the Sussex Gardens area was in danger of becoming a slum. Hotel operators, he said, were not spending enough money on maintenance, and the buildings would soon become useless unless they underwent substantial upgrading. General deterioration, poor sanitary facilities, and obsolete plumbing and wiring posed a serious threat of fire. A renovated Sussex Gardens hotel complex, according to Anderson and the developer, would be an asset to Bayswater, already designated as a "hotel area." It would not reduce residential accommodations, since the site was already occupied by hotels. Facades would not be changed; there would be no significant increase in the intensity of use or in traffic.

The secretary of the Sussex Gardens Tenants' Association, David Andrews, counterattacked. He said that many of the proprietors had been in Sussex Gardens for 20 or 30 years and stood to lose not only their businesses, but their homes. He also argued that London had a serious shortage of inexpensive hotels. The tenants' position was supported by local merchants, who feared that larger hotels wouldn't buy supplies from the neighborhood stores, and by neighborhood residents, who—other threats aside—felt that the new hotels would attract more tour buses and produce traffic congestion.

In Want of a Plan

The local planners looked around for policies that would help them make an intelligent decision. When the government instituted its tourism subsidy program in 1969, however, no planning policies accompanied it. Administration was put in the hands of the Secretary of Trade and Industry. There was to be no participation by the Department of the Environment, apparently because it was assumed that the development-control process could accommodate new hotels without advance studies or particular requirements.

In 1964, under a special law, the preparation of a structure plan for Greater London was made the responsibility of the Greater London Council, which devoted countless man-hours to the effort.[20] In 1974, the plan was still two years away from adoption.

True, in the absence of a plan, the Greater London Council's planners did publish (in 1971) a discussion paper on tourism and hotels in London. "The Greater London Council is glad to play its own part in furthering tourism," said the paper, but it offered no real guidance for deciding where hotel development should occur. A hotels and tourism policy adopted in November 1971 also provided little guidance. It contained such policies as:

1. That, while the importance of tourism in London and the country as a whole is acknowledged, it must not be allowed to prejudice the conservation of the housing stock.

2. That planning by the London borough councils should seek to encourage hotel development outside central London.

3. That proposals for large new hotel projects in central London should be carefully examined to ensure that they will not be prejudicial to good environ-

Sussex Gardens. (Photo by author.)

mental conditions and will not be likely to exacerbate housing and employment conditions.

The lack of direction from the Greater London Council perhaps was to be expected since its role was only advisory. Real power in the development-control system resided with the Westminster City Council,* which had expressed serious concerns about hotel conversions. It adopted the following hotel guidelines:

a. The hotel proposal should not involve a significant reduction in the amount of residential accommodation in the area unless the area has been considered to be unsuitable as a future predominantly residential environment.

b. Within conservation areas, the intensity of use and massing of the proposed hotel should be such as not to disrupt the essential character of the area and should be in keeping with any other requirements of the area.

c. In regard to traffic generated by a hotel the proposal should not have an adverse environmental effect upon the surrounding area and this traffic, when stationary, should be capable of being contained within the curtilage of the site [i.e., on-site parking is required].

d. In the absence of other factors to the contrary, hotels should be encouraged on sites which are in close proximity to public transportation, major terminals, tourist attractions or local complementary facilities, e.g., shopping, restaurants, etc.

e. In the absence of other factors to the contrary, hotel developments should be encouraged when replacing obsolete land uses and when they could help to bring about a substantial renewal of any such area.

It was to these guidelines that the town planning committee of the City of Westminster turned in June 1974, when the proposal for the redevelopment of Sussex Gardens came before them. Mr. Anderson argued that his proposal fit neatly within the guidelines: (1) there would be no reduction of residential accommodations since the area was already occupied by hotels; (2) the facades of the structure would not be changed; (3) there would be no significant increase in the intensity of use or generation of traffic; (4) the site was in close proximity to Paddington Station and major tourist attractions such as Hyde Park; (5) the existing buildings were in a deteriorating condition.

The city's planning staff reviewed the applications and issued a report. It noted that the proposed rehabilitation of the area would be welcome and would be consistent with its architectural character. It also noted, however, that strenuous objections had been filed on behalf of the tenants, shopkeepers, guesthouse owners, and the community at large, and in the end recommended against granting planning permission for the redevelopment, saying, "These local objections merit the most serious consideration."

The grounds for refusal were that the formation of the new hotels would result in the loss of existing small hotels on the site. Although the guidelines said nothing about protecting small hotels from big hotels, only about protecting residences from new hotels, the planners came up with a rationalization that meshed with the concerns of residents: if the existing small hotels were con-

---

*The city one thinks of as London is much larger than the "City of London," which encompasses only a small area around the financial district. The area commonly thought of as London includes many other "cities" and "boroughs." The City of Westminster takes in the area known as the West End, which now is roughly in the center of London.[21]

verted to big hotels, then perhaps other residences would be converted to small hotels. The planning staff thus recommended refusal of planning permission.

Sensing defeat again, the Grand Junction Corporation withdrew its application before the town planning committee could act upon the staff's recommendation. Alan Anderson felt that by this time so many tasteless new hotels had been built under the government's development scheme and had created so much public antagonism that it was impossible to deal with the planners in rational terms. In his view, attacking the planning system was "like fighting a huge feather pillow."

On their part, the planners felt the Sussex Gardens case demonstrated that, despite their ingenious effort to find consistency, the existing guidelines were not really responsive to public sentiment. In October 1976, the policy on which the Sussex Gardens decision was really based—protection of small, economical hotels—became officially embodied in an Advisory Plan for Central London.[22] Local residents lauded this action, but many felt it came too late.

Planning without Plans

In the absence of meaningful policies, English planners seem little more than mediators. In a neighborhood of small hotels, a developer wants to build a bigger hotel. Existing residents complain that the amenities of the neighborhood will be destroyed. A simple, common neighborhood controversy, but one that can serve as an allegory for a wide range of similar controversies having common antagonists: people who have moved into an area and are enjoying certain values vs. people who want to move in and obtain similar values.

Could this dispute have been resolved if the government had adopted some simple rule—analogous to the doctrine of ancient lights—and let the neighbors bargain among themselves? Successful bargaining of this sort would seem to require a limited number of parties having interests affected by the dispute, and clearly established government policies. In Sussex Gardens neither of these conditions was present.

Those who opposed the new hotels included not only the hotel operators being displaced and their residential neighbors, but a variety of merchants, and even the tourists who were regular customers of the existing hotels.*

The developer appeared, by contrast, to be alone. But his subsidy represented the backing of the influential trade ministry, and he might have solicited support from those business establishments that would have profited from the more affluent tourists he hoped to attract. These tourists themselves were, as usual, represented only by proxy. (See chapter 4.)

All of the groups who appeared at the Sussex Gardens hearings or signed petitions felt their interests were affected. It is hard to suggest that any groups should have been excluded from the process. And it is hard to see how such numerous and diverse interest groups could resolve their problems among themselves.

---

*The report of the planning staff noted somewhat disparagingly: "A petition has also been received containing a very large number of signatures, but these are almost entirely from pupils and staff of schools in various parts of northern England together with those of other one-time visitors from abroad."

Moreover, the days of simple policies such as ancient lights—or its opposite—seem hard to recapture. Today the English face difficult choices between growth and conservation in a rapidly changing society where policies need reevaluation almost constantly.

For example, it was always an article of faith in Britain that everyone wanted to move to London. A key planning policy has been to divert people away from London.[23] But the ink on the plan to discourage growth was hardly dry before the government learned people were deserting London at an alarming rate. British planners finally conceded that London could be a sink as well as a magnet, and were "overwhelmed—by a feeling of our own blindness in not seeing before some of the things that were happening under our noses."[24]

The shock triggered, in some instances, a complete reversal of government policy. For example, the local plan for the Waterloo area of London was adopted in September 1977, after five years of public debate. Within a month after its adoption, planners for the Greater London Council were studying the possibility of using land near the new National Theatre, which the Waterloo plan had earmarked for family housing and public open space, as the site for "a comprehensive scheme involving up to one million square feet of offices, conference facilities, a housing association project, luxury flats, and the headquarters of a major oil company. . . ."[25]

In the absence of overall planning policies, loud shouting has often replaced clear thinking. A former planning minister, Richard Crossman, summed it up in his diaries: "There isn't any planning law, it's all planning lore, planning mythology."[26] The tourism development case is a typical example. The developers shouted loudly about the need for hotels, and the system responded. Then the residents shouted about the tourists' nasty habits, and the system responded by lurching into reverse gear.

The absence of planning policies forced the development-control planners to make ad hoc decisions. The result was that no one feels that "right" decisions have been made. By responding to superficial demonstrations of short-run concerns, the planners overreacted both ways, which need not have happened if thoughtful planning policies had been in effect from the outset. But as it was, everybody lost.

In the English context, attempts to simplify the process of resolving disputes must overcome the presence of a multiplicity of affected interest groups and rapidly changing government policies. Predictability and efficiency have been sacrificed in favor of flexibility to deal with changing conditions. Neither the forces of growth nor the forces of conservation feel satisfied with the present system—which may suggest it is doing something right.

In London, as in Jerusalem, the worst examples of thoughtless hotel building have detracted from the special qualities that make the city so attractive. To the tourist, however, the overall impact on London is far less damaging than on Jerusalem, because London's special qualities are far less fragile. A city with a diverse and dynamic image can absorb mistakes that seem tragic in a city with an image of timelessness and solidity. Henry James spoke for most tourists when he said: "The truth is I am so fond of London that I can afford to abuse it—and London is on the whole such a fine thing that it can afford to be abused."[27]

Chapter 8
The Ancient Lights of Japan

In the preceding chapter the doctrine of ancient lights symbolized the enduring conflict between development and conservation. The same kind of conflict occurs in Japan, where there are currently numerous disputes about the right to sunshine. These "sunshine cases" offer a context for examining the Japanese system of resolving conflicts—a system sometimes cited as a model of simplicity that over-litigious Americans might emulate.[1]

Winter Sun

To understand why sunshine has become a matter of contention in Japan requires some knowledge of the Japanese climate and Japanese housing.

Japan's largest cities, and much of the country's industrial development, are located on the Pacific coast of central Japan, south of the Japanese Alps. The seasons in this region are distinct and change with precision, a phenomenon that can be attributed to the location of the Japanese archipelago between the world's largest continent and the world's largest ocean.[2]

The Sea of Japan separates the islands from the Asian mainland by some 500 miles at its broadest point. Beyond the sea to the north and west are the steppes of Siberia and North China over which, in winter, a powerful air mass develops. It emits blasts of cold air that cross the sea, accumulating great quantities of moisture, which is deposited in the form of heavy blankets of snow on the sparsely populated northern slopes of the Japanese Alps.

Because of the loss of moisture as the air crosses the mountains, Japan's major cities, located to the south, experience dry weather throughout the winter. Temperatures range from the 20s to the 50s, but are almost invariably accompanied by sunshine and frequently by a brisk northwest wind comparable to the chinook of America's Great Plains.

During the pleasant spring, Siberian air masses and the tropical Pacific maintain a shaky truce, after which Pacific air masses take over. Around the middle of June, a brief rainy season known as baiu begins, bringing heavy clouds, high humidity, and abundant rain, particularly to southern Japan. As

---

Field research for this chapter was conducted by John G. Gissberg.

summer advances, the rain lessens, but the weather remains hot and humid. The summer extends well into September, with increasing chance of typhoons. Then, as the Siberian air mass strengthens, temperatures drop and the humidity declines.

Because of the mild winter climate, traditional Japanese homes are not centrally heated. Instead, most have southern walls containing movable panels that are thrown open during the middle of sunny winter days.[3] The sunshine warms the house enough to allow housewives and children to discard their heavy sweaters and jackets for a brief time in the afternoon. At night the house is closed as tightly as permitted by the thin siding, in the hope of keeping out the wind and retaining the warmth generated by portable kerosene stoves.

During summer months as well, sunshine plays an important role. Blankets, mattresses, and clothing are hung outside to combat the high humidity that dampens everything hidden from the sun's rays.

The importance of the sun notwithstanding, until very recently Japanese law provided no guarantee to homeowners that access to sunshine would not be blocked by construction of taller buildings. This created little concern as long as the Construction Standards Act prohibited high rises. Gradually, however, confidence in new technology overcame traditional fear of earthquakes. And, as high rises appeared, a chorus of complaints grew.

A Sea of Roofs

Aerial photographs of Japanese cities show a sea of roofs. Unoccupied space is scarce. Public streets, for example, account for less than 6 percent of Tokyo's land, compared to 23 percent of London's and 43 percent of Washington's.[4] Small wooden houses are crowded cheek by jowl. Yards are minimal. The rich and the poor live in the same neighborhoods, the houses of the former distinguished not by the expanse of surrounding lawn, only by the size and quality of the house itself.[5] Even the homes of the wealthy, however, are modest in size compared to homes found in most other industrialized countries.[6]

As a result of these dense housing conditions, the shadow created by a new high rise may fall across a number of dwellings. In response, homeowners have formed small neighborhood groups to battle high-rise developers.

In 1967 several groups organized the Building Construction Pollution Countermeasures Association. The association, now a national organization, claims involvement in about 80 percent of the sunshine cases in the Tokyo area, as well as in other disputes involving road construction and land development. It has helped persuade many local governments to draft guidelines for developers, specifying the hours of unblocked sunlight that must be available to neighboring property owners.

The governments were under pressure to devise some means of controlling the impact of new high-rise buildings. (Most Japanese cities had zoning and building codes, but these codes generally provided only minimal restrictions.) Guidelines for this purpose were adopted without specific statutory authority, with local land-planning boards relying on the willingness of builders to observe them. A typical city's guidelines might specify that new buildings should permit all other property owners at least two hours of sunlight in commercial districts, and four hours in residential districts, on December 22, the shortest day of the

N

JAPAN

SOVIET
UNION

SOUTH

KOREA

Tokyo
Yokohama
Nagoya   Mt. Fuji
Yokkaichi   Atami
Hiroshima
Osaka

P A C I F I C

O C E A N

Statute Miles 0   50   100 150
Kilometers
               0   100   200

year. Many cities have guidelines that protect other amenities as well as sun-shine.

The View from the Bath

The resort city of Atami, an hour from Tokyo by high-speed train, is one of Japan's most popular vacation spots. The city is particularly concerned about its amenities. Its guidelines warn builders to protect neighbors "from unusual winds generated from the construction; from interference with scenic views; from direct interference with television or radio reception; [and] from noise and pollution from traffic around the site."

Builders are not expected to achieve perfect compliance, but the guidelines require them to obtain written consent from neighbors who would be affected. This formalizes a Japanese practice of visiting all neighbors prior to construction of a building to offer gifts and apologies.

From April 1972, when it was created, through 1975, Atami's land-use board heard 145 sunshine cases. The one that attracted most attention involved two hotel owners.

Atami's central attraction is its picturesque harbor, through which ferries make regular runs to offshore islands. The harbor is surrounded by steep hills, where hotels, inns, and apartments offer occupants a marvelous view and access to sunshine.

Construction along Atami Harbor. (Photo by John G. Gissberg.)

In 1961, Mr. Shigeru Baba purchased the four-story Minoya Inn, which had been constructed about 25 years earlier on the side of a steep cliff overlooking the southern end of the harbor. The wooden structure, nearly flattened against the cliff, had only eight main rooms. Mr. Baba added five stories, enabling his establishment to accommodate approximately 60 guests. All rooms faced the harbor. In the lingering twilight, the inn's communal baths offered a sweeping panorama of fishing vessels slowly approaching port. At daybreak, guests would wake to the rays of the rising sun and relax at the open windows of their rooms.

In the late 1960s, construction began on a hotel next door to the Minoya Inn. As work neared completion, it became apparent that one side of the new building would block a small portion of the inn's view of the harbor and city. After the hotel was completed, Baba approached his new neighbor with consternation. This led to a series of meetings, with Baba eventually receiving a small payment.

Soon after this, the property between the Minoya Inn and the harbor was purchased by Ryuuichi Fujima, a man Baba considered an old friend. Fujima had sold another inn he owned and operated for many years, and was eager to move forward quickly with construction of a new hotel. He invested nearly all profit from the sale of his old inn, borrowed money from the local bank, and received a generous loan from the national small-business agency.

In an earlier era, Fujima undoubtedly would have had no difficulty seeking and obtaining a construction permit from the local authorities. The project was consistent with local zoning. But Fujima's proposed 11-story structure would have totally blocked the sunlight and view from most of Baba's rooms.

Because of the city's guidelines, Fujima had to obtain his neighbors' consent. Everyone cooperated except Baba. The spectacular harbor view, the sunrises, the moon coming up over the rolling Pacific—these would be lost, Baba argued, and with them would go his inn's appeal to tourists.

Fujima reduced the height of his hotel and made other alterations, but could not get Baba's approval. Therefore, when he presented the architect's drawings and neighbors' seals of consent to Atami's land-use planning board, one seal was missing.

Faced with the first lack of unanimous consent to a project subject to the development guidelines, the Atami planning board directed Fujima to hold two formal discussions with Baba, even though the two had already discussed their differences more than 20 times. The meetings produced no compromise. Baba demanded compensation sufficient to guarantee a livelihood for his children and their children. Fujima, on the other hand, felt he had already conceded more than enough by eliminating the four top floors from his original plan. He was convinced he could not make a living, let alone repay his loans, with a structure less than seven stories tall.

Although Fujima's application met all the requirements of the Buildings Standards Act, the city implored him to reduce the hotel's height by yet another story, so that it would block only the view from Baba's first floor. It was on this floor, however, that the baths were located, and the view from the baths was highly prized.

Fujima agreed to the one-story reduction, though concerned whether he could still break even. He had been without real work for over a year and was under pressure because of mounting construction cost estimates. If he further

Baba's inn on hillside at left, with new addition in center. At right, hotel built in 1960s. In foreground, foundation of Fujima's hotel. (Photo by John G. Gissberg.)

delayed construction, he risked losing a significant capital gains tax advantage from the sale of his old business. Finally, the planning board approved his application in July 1974.

Baba subsequently filed suit for an injunction to halt construction of Fujima's hotel. The judge made a special inspection of the site and asked the parties to meet for further negotiations in the courtroom. No settlement could be reached.

A Case of Self-Help

As the dispute between Baba and Fujima continued, a somewhat similar case arose in the city of Musashino, a suburb of Tokyo. Musashino had adopted

Fujima's hotel at a later stage of construction. (Photo by John G. Gissberg.)

guidelines similar to Atami's. A local builder, Yamamoto Kensetsu, built a five-story apartment house in violation of the guidelines. He could not get his neighbors' consent. When the building was complete, the neighbors distributed leaflets to prospective tenants, berating the landlord's antisocial conduct. The city, angry at Kensetsu's breach of the guidelines, refused to extend water to the building. Kensetsu responded by hooking up a garden hose between the water pipes of the apartment house and the pipes of the building next door, which he also owned.

View from Baba's balcony showing intrusive construction. (Photo by John G. Gissberg.)

When the city refused to provide sewer connections, Kensetsu tapped in his own connection to the public sewer. Then the mayor, Kihachiro Goto, backed up a ready-mix truck to the manhole in front of Kensetsu's building and filled the sewer with cement. Kensetsu parried by diverting the sewer to a pit in the backyard.

With battle raging in the streets and sewers, Kensetsu's attorneys argued in court that he had complied with all applicable laws and deserved an occupancy permit. The city maintained that Kensetsu's building deprived his neighbors of their sunshine, in violation of their constitutional rights, and that the guidelines were a legitimate means of protecting those rights. The court agreed that the building complied with all applicable regulations. It also held that the guidelines were unauthorized and without force of law. Nevertheless, the judge put great pressure on the parties to settle the case.

On December 20, 1975, after all-night talks in the judge's chambers, Kensetsu agreed to pay 10 neighbors about $1,000 each and about $3,500 to the city. The city agreed to supply water and sewer service, and the case was settled.

When word of the ruling in the Musashino case reached Atami, it confirmed a suspicion that development guidelines had no force of law. Two days later, a judge in Atami ruled that Fujima's project was in accord with the zoning code and could proceed. The judge suggested that the parties reach agreement on the amount of damages to be paid to Baba, without specifically ruling that Baba had any legal right to receive damages.

Fujima offered $17,000 compensation. Baba's lawyer advised him to accept the offer. Baba, however, wanted well over $100,000. He hired a new lawyer. And the battle continued.

Concord and Discord

The dispute between Baba and Fujima was handled in a way that seems strange to Western observers. Some light can be shed on the process by an understanding of how disputes were resolved in ancient Japan.*

Japanese society traditionally attached great significance to concord, and great opprobrium to discord. The document considered to be the first Japanese constitution, promulgated by Prince Shotoku in the year 604, stressed the importance of harmonious relationships.

> Above all else esteem concord; make it your first duty to avoid discord. People are prone to form partisanships, for few persons are really enlightened. Hence, there are those who do not obey their lords and parents, and who come in conflict with their neighbors. But, when those above are harmonious, and those below are friendly, there is concord in the discussion of affairs, and right views of things spontaneously gain acceptance.[7]

As this quotation indicates, concord meant knowing one's place in a hierarchical feudal society—but one in which a spirit of *noblesse oblige* would prevail. The upper classes were expected not to inflict injuries arbitrarily. The person causing injury was to apologize and exhibit an attitude of benevolence, no matter how rich or powerful he was.[8] On the other hand, an injured person had an equally strong obligation to accept a proffered apology, if offered with the proper attitude and accompanied by reasonable compensation.

Reasonable compensation in ancient Japan was quite different from what we would consider appropriate today. Money or property offered to the injured party was known as *mimiakin*, and was more a gift—a symbol demonstrating the benevolent thoughts of the giver—than an attempt to compensate for a loss. Because the compensation was moral rather than economic, gifts of small value often redressed great losses.

A person who failed to offer mimiakin, no matter how rich and powerful he might be, would likely become the target of public outrage. If ancient Japanese rulers neglected their duty, social norms recognized the subjects' right to revolution.[9]

On the other hand, if mimiakin were offered, the obligation to accept it was equally strong. A person who chose to seek relief through the courts risked ostracism. Moreover, few people could bring suit because laws were secret. A maxim declared: "The people must not know the law, they must obey it."[10] Public understanding of the law might interfere with their arbitrary powers, the rulers feared.[11]

Traditional Japanese society disappeared a century ago. The story of the overthrow of the Tokugawa rulers and the Meiji restoration is a familiar one. Still, though the Meiji government adopted Western-style laws, patterned after

---

*The term "ancient" is used here to refer to Japan prior to about 1870, when the Meiji restoration opened the country to significant Western influence. Obviously, this attempt to generalize centuries of history ignores many variations.

the civil codes of continental Europe, old traditions persist, influencing modern methods of resolving disputes.

Makers of Compromises

To understand the modern Japanese system of resolving disputes, one must forget the Western notion of deciding who is right and who is wrong.[12] In Japan, the parties avoid discussing fault and try to reach a compromise.

> The settlement of a dispute aims to maintain, restore or create a harmonious relationship, and . . . should not make any clear-cut decision on who is right or wrong or inquire into the existence or scope of the rights of the parties.[13]

The persistence of traditional attitudes is obvious. A familiar Japanese proverb says: "In a quarrel, both parties are to blame." In such settlement negotiations the personal relationship of parties is as important as any universal principles or "rights." Thus, the attitude of disputants toward each other becomes an integral element in the settlement.

In his book *Japan: The Fragile Superpower*, Frank Gibney gives a current example:

> If a driver injures someone in a traffic accident, one of the principal factors in determining his sentence, if not his innocence or guilt, is the alacrity with which he visits the victim in the hospital to offer gifts and apologies. Japanese judges set great store by such things. The rite of apology is almost as important in the late 20th century as it was in the early 12th.[14]

Japanese dispute-resolving systems are designed to produce compromise rather than justice. The traditional name for such systems is *chotei*. Although many variations of chotei exist, in general all bear some resemblance to American arbitration proceedings. A mediator, traditionally a person of higher social status than the disputants, is selected. His decision is not formally binding, but his prestige and authority ordinarily are sufficient to persuade the parties to settle the dispute.[15]

The mediator's role is to help the parties reach consensus. The settlements have the appearance of a "compromise." The element of coercion, however, is not far beneath the surface.[16] In fact, Japanese bill collectors who rely on threats of violence are known as *jidanya*, or "makers of compromises."

GNPism and Its Aftermath

As applied to disputes rising out of the land development process, the chotei system was reinforced by the "informal ideology" of postwar Japan—"GNPism," as Zbigniew Brzezinski has called it.[17] The success of Japanese industrial expansion, and the concomitant rise in economic prosperity, carried with it a national patriotic psychology in support of growth and development. Injuries resulting from industrial pollution or the construction of new facilities were considered inescapable by-products of Japanese modernization. Traditional apologies and *mimiakin* were still obligatory; however, the patriotic nature of the developers' cause deterred hard bargaining by injured parties.[18]

To appreciate fully the extent to which mimiakin was symbolic, rather than compensatory, one can consider the infamous Minimata case. During the height of GNPism, a chemical company was found to have poisoned the waters of Minimata bay with mercury. Hundreds of fishermen and other people who regularly ate seafood from the bay developed serious symptoms of mercury poisoning, a painful and disabling disease. In 1959, a group of victims accepted, in settlement of their complaints, the company's offer to make annual mimiakin payments of $280 to each adult sufferer and $83 to each child.[19]

During the 1960s, it gradually became apparent that Japan's rapid industrial development was creating problems more serious than first realized. Disabling illnesses caused by mercury and chromium poisoning received worldwide attention. Apparent attempts by government and industry to cover up some of the problems shocked the Japanese public deeply.[20] Water pollution threatened fish—the keystone of the Japanese diet. Air pollution, too, became a growing problem. To fumes from rapidly proliferating oil refineries and chemical plants was added the exhaust of millions of automobiles. Tokyo's smog began to rival that of Los Angeles and Mexico City.

Within a few years, the national unity behind rapid economic development collapsed. Complaints mounted, not only from people suffering disabling injuries, but from those living next to noisy bullet trains or in the shadow of high-rise buildings. Japanese newspapers and television regularly reported stories of protests arising out of pollution incidents.

Foreign observers had long noted that chotei and mimiakin seemed to favor the powerful over the weak by dulling the citizen's sense of having "rights."[21] Now, the Japanese themselves began to criticize the system. One commentator argued that the supposedly impartial chotei mediators invariably favored the "victimizers" from whom they had received benefits in the past, and thus tried to induce injured parties to settle for nominal damages.[22]

Increasing numbers of Japanese citizens felt inadequately compensated by traditional mimiakin. As the case of Fujima and Baba illustrates, the traditional system of reaching compromises has begun to break down. "As the protests of victim and citizen groups increased," says Professor Julian Gresser, the leading American expert on Japanese environmental law, "the fragile accommodation purchased through mimiakin collapsed."[23]

New Battleground

With the chotei system weakening, injured parties sought other forums for their grievances. Aided by militant young activists influenced by Ralph Nader, victims of pollution asked courts for relief. Available to the courts was a significant body of sparsely explored law designed to support individual rights—the so-called MacArthur Constitution, adopted by the Japanese after World War II. The constitution and accompanying laws contained many democratic-sounding clauses, but the laws had never been fully tested, because social pressures discouraged litigation.

To young activists seeking peaceful change, the courts appeared to be the soft spot in the system known colloquially as "Japan Inc."—the close alliance of business and government. The courts had the reputation of being the most democratic institution in Japan. They had never been highly prestigious in the eyes of the Establishment. Drafting, counseling, and negotiating, which occupies the time of most American lawyers, requires no license in Japan. Although a law degree is one of the most common in that country, people holding law degrees usually become bureaucrats, "salarymen," or academics, pursuing careers that promise job security, social status, and stable income. Of the 5 percent or less of law graduates who choose to become trial lawyers and judges, many are children of poorer families without good Establishment connections.

Litigation appealed to activists seeking social change for the very reason it was repellent to traditional Japanese mores: it would "assign a moral fault" to the party causing the injury.[24] In response to the activists, the courts began to take an increasingly aggressive role in environmental litigation.

The Yokkaichi Case

A damage suit by residents of Yokkaichi who had contracted a peculiar asthmalike disease brought the issues to a head.* Yokkaichi, which lies on Japan's Pacific coast, had been a peaceful farming and fishing village. Law professor Yoshihiro Nomura can remember "going on excursions and swimming at the Yokkaichi seashore when a primary school pupil about 1949 or 1950 . . . [and] . . . being greatly moved by the beauty of the flowers in rape fields, stretching away as far as the eye could see."[26]

In the 1950s, Yokkaichi, like most small towns in Japan, worked to attract industry. It was especially successful. The area's extensive rape fields and wetlands were transformed into a huge *kombinat* (industrial park). Tanker terminals were built, and Yokkaichi became one of Japan's leading producers of petrochemicals—a source of pride to local residents.

For residents downwind of the plants, breathing became difficult. Many developed lasting symptoms of pulmonary disease. They brought suit against six of the largest industries, seeking damages for jointly caused injuries.

Japanese environmental legislation had always sought "harmony" between environmental and economic objectives through a "balancing test." Compensation was to be awarded only if the injury exceeded "the limits of reasonable endurance." Moreover, the benefits created by development were to be balanced against the injury.[27] As national attitudes changed from postwar GNPism, when the courts found few plaintiffs, these flexible legal standards became subject to a new interpretation.

In reaching its decision in the Yokkaichi case, the court balanced the petitioners' injury against the public benefits and delivered a precedent-making ruling. It held that a project had *no* public benefits unless the developer had sought to ascertain the environmental impact of the project prior to construction. To demonstrate public benefits, said the court, "overall studies and surveys must be carried out beforehand on the types and amounts of substances emitted" and there must be "studies to determine the effect on local residents." The court imposed what amounted to a duty of environmental impact analysis, for breach of which absolute liability is imposed for environmental damage caused by the project. The Yokkaichi decision, says Professor Nomura, "led to a shaking of industrial land policy to its foundations."[28]

Thus, as public views toward growth and the environment changed, development interests that had benefited from the balancing test found that its vague standards could be turned to their disadvantage. The traditional test balanced

---

*The Yokkaichi suit was one of a series of well-publicized cases, known as the "big four," in which the courts ruled in favor of the plaintiffs against polluting industries. Of the three other cases, two involved mercury poisoning and one chromium poisoning.[25]

the victim's limits of reasonable endurance against the benefits to society created by the developer. The benefits of growth have become more dubious, and the limits of endurance have become narrower.

Some Japanese lawyers and activist groups, however, believe that even greatly augmented damages, such as promised under cases like the Yokkaichi decision, are inadequate. They seek to stop the harmful activity itself.[29] Many suits now seek injunctive relief, and Japanese courts are venturing into this field as well. For example, by court order the Osaka airport no longer permits takeoffs and landings at night.*

In other cases, citizens have stopped public works projects by refusing to accept any price as compensation for their injuries. Narita airport is the most famous of many examples. Located in rural Chiba Prefecture, it was built over the opposition of many local farmers. Those who objected to the airport's construction refused to sell the government right-of-way for an oil pipeline, thereby stalling the airport's opening for years. (Although the MacArthur Constitution gave the government the authority to condemn land, that power is not used because it is inconsistent with the goal of trying to reach agreement.)

Elsewhere in Japan highways lead nowhere and public buildings stand half completed. One Japanese official pointed out that a large share of the public works budget was spent on tunnels for highways, subways, and railways. "No one has figured out how to lie down in front of a tunnel," he said.

Brzezinski has described Japanese society as "characterized by a kind of metastability, that is to say, a stability that appears to be extremely solid until all of a sudden a highly destabilizing chain reaction is set in motion by an unexpected input."[32] The new Japanese environmental activism has clearly been such an "unexpected input."

Compromise Reinforced

The virtual impasse created by opposition to many development projects led the Japanese government to reexamine its development policies.[33] Not surprisingly, the government response has emphasized new variations of the traditional system of seeking compromise through payment of modest compensation.

For sufferers of the most serious environmental diseases, the government has established special procedures for identifying and compensating victims. In the Minimata area over 1,000 victims of mercury poisoning have been identified, though hundreds died before receiving compensation. The government's efforts have not been universally lauded. A court recently ruled that 362 victims had been wrongfully excluded from the program.[34]

---

*The legal basis for injunctive relief has not been settled clearly in sunshine and noise cases, although a number of injunctions have been granted in Tokyo and elsewhere since 1972. Plaintiffs' lawyers claim that Article 29 of the postwar Japanese constitution, which says that "the right to own or to hold property is inviolable," requires that neighbors' property rights be considered before any construction is commenced. Plaintiffs also cite Article 25, which states that "all people shall have the right to maintain the minimum standards of wholesome and cultured living," which has been interpreted as providing a right to a decent environment by a committee of the Japan Federal Bar Association.[30] The bar association committee argues that because a healthy environment is a resource that all people share, no development activities should be permitted without agreement of the affected people, no one should be required to endure damage caused by pollution, and all people should have standing to institute litigation demanding injunctive relief. Not surprisingly, this view is highly controversial.[31]

For more generalized environmental injuries, the government has established a major program in which over 3,500 pollution-grievance counsellors have been appointed to serve as mediators.[35] A tax on polluters has been established to fund the program.[36] In today's Japan, however, reaching agreement on the amount of damages is not as easy as it once was. As the case of Baba and Fujima illustrates, people place high value on a wide variety of amenities. The value of these amenities is not easily quantified by any recognized formula.

The prolific sunshine cases are a good example of the problem. Takayoshi Igarashi, a Tokyo attorney who has represented many plaintiffs in these cases, estimates that property deprived of sunshine will lose about 20 percent of its value, on average, but the extent of loss depends on how much time the sun is shadowed, and the cost of replacing the sunlight by heat, light, and dehumidification equipment in the particular house. Lack of insulation in Japanese houses makes the belated addition of central heating quite difficult. Thus, when most or all sunshine is lost, the house may be abandoned.

The courts' assertiveness has also spurred firmer legislative controls on the amount of sunshine that a new building may take from an old. The Buildings Standards Act now regulates the number of hours that a building's shadow at the winter solstice is permitted to fall on neighboring properties. Activist lawyers are not satisfied, however. They argue that the act provides inadequate compensation, and believe that neighbors' consent—not extent of shading—should be the determining factor in permitting new buildings.

For large construction projects, the impact on neighbors' sunshine may someday be incorporated into a more extensive system of impact analysis. Requirements for environmental impact assessment have been studied for years, but a workable consensus is hard to reach.

All of these efforts indicate that the powerful grip of tradition is weakening, taking with it the old ways of chotei and mimiakin. Conciliation and token compensation are no longer adequate. Environmental law in Japan has become a highly complex intermixture of various types of judicial litigation, government regulation, traditional mediation, and private negotiation. Nowhere in the world would an American environmental lawyer feel more at home.

A Question of Values

Traditionally, the Japanese emphasized nation, culture, people, place, rather than the individual. Thus, each person not only had a strong identification with Japan as a society but with Japan as a land.[37] Immersed in the landscape, the citizen of ancient Japan lacked the Western attitude that man must conquer the land. Like the Australian aborigine, he might have been hard pressed to say whether the land belonged to him or he belonged to it.

As recently as the 1950s, this willingness to submerge individual interests in the overall national interest fueled Japan's industrialization. GNPism became merely the latest in a series of national goals with which the individual could identify.

The traditional system may be breaking down, however. Postwar changes have carried the seeds of a different value system, one that places greater stress on the wants and needs of the individual. Some people are beginning to consider maximizing their own pleasure, and minimizing pain, as more important than abstract national goals. The result is an atmosphere of mixed and confusing values, in which the decision-making processes evolved under the earlier system of values do not adapt easily.

Nonetheless, in the midst of this ferment, in some parts of Japan people still clearly recognize that their immediate pains and pleasures are intertwined with a larger whole. In some of Japan's most famous places, people treat the place as having value beyond the perceived sum of values attached to it by currently living individuals. And observation suggests that in these places the development process works in a more sensitive and equitable fashion.

Can or should a place have value in itself? The concluding chapters will explore this question, beginning with a look at one of Japan's most magnificent places, Mt. Fuji.

V PLACEMAKING

Chapter 9
A Park Is a State of Mind

Attempts to apply development policies of general applicability to specific cases have proved difficult. Perhaps a major source of this difficulty is that not enough attention has been paid to the special qualities of places. Policies for dealing with high-rise hotels in London and campgrounds in Zeeland, for example, reflect similar conflicts between general principles and place-related specifics.

Most countries have some places that are recognized as special. This chapter examines areas in England and Japan where control of development has proceeded more successfully than it has in others. The areas are called parks— though the English and Japanese concept of park is probably quite alien to most Americans.

An Awesome Mountain

Mt. Fuji is, certainly, a special place. The tallest mountain in Japan, its 12,000-foot height appears especially impressive because Fuji is set apart from the main ridges of the Japanese Alps.

As recently as 1707, Fuji was an active volcano; it still has a symmetrical cone shape. At altitudes of 8,000 feet or so, strong winds and loose gravel preclude significant vegetation. The upper third is covered by snow most of the year.

Throughout much of Japanese history Fuji has had religious significance, attested to by its Shinto and Buddhist shrines, some of which date back to 800 A.D. An awe-inspiring expression of the splendor of nature, Fuji has never been worshipped simply from a distance. For the Japanese, appreciation of nature is not a sedentary, visual occupation, but something in which people participate actively.[1] Traditionally, a harmonious relationship with nature, a partnership with it, was seen as one of man's most important goals.[2]

Today, Western science dominates many aspects of Japanese life. Rapid industrialization has transformed the landscape. But to the urban Japanese, the bucolic features around Mt. Fuji still awaken a yearning for that amalgamation with nature that their ancestors cherished.[3] More and more people are leaving

---

Field research for this chapter was conducted by Christopher J. Duerksen and John G. Gissberg.

cities to vacation in the Fuji area. So many tourists, in fact, now visit the region that a young environmental reporter for the *Asahi Shimbun* has said that he feels Fuji has taken on a new symbolic significance. "It is a symbol of land-use problems in Japan."

Mansions and Villas

To appreciate Japanese land-use problems, it must be kept in mind that intensive urbanization has occurred on a relatively small area of Japan's developable land. "Living in Tokyo," comments one writer, "is like taking part in a marathon race which requires tremendous endurance, patience and stamina." It is like being at a "sample fair" of every type of environmental pollution.[4]

The problems are compounded by Japan's crowded conditions. About 32 percent of the population lives in the environs of Tokyo, Osaka, or Nagoya, on approximately 1 percent of the country's land.[5] One of the world's most highly urbanized areas, commonly known as the Tokkaido corridor, connects these cities, symbolizing for Paul Theroux the "pure horror" of the megalopolis: "Under a sky, which tawny fumes have given the texture of wool, are pylons secured by cables, buildings shaped like jumbo rheostats, and an unzoned clutter of houses, none larger than two stories, whose picture windows front onto factories."[6]

Adjacent to the Tokkaido corridor is Mt. Fuji, some 75 miles from downtown Tokyo. Spreading from the mountain's base are lovely forests, tea plantations,

Mt. Fuji. (Copyright National Geographic Society.)

rice paddies, cabbage fields, lakes with fishermen—the rustic, picturesque Japan that conveys a timeless beauty. But Fuji's magnetism has led to changes in this scene. In 1969, two major expressways were completed between Tokyo and Osaka, one along the Pacific coast and one in the interior. Fuji lies between them, and the lower slopes and surrounding lakes have become major tourist destinations. Located within a few hours of any part of the Tokyo metropolitan area, the region is popular with day trippers and is increasingly used for second homes and hotels.

The new development around Fuji reflects major shifts in the nature of Japanese tourism. During the industrial boom of the 1950s and 1960s, the average Japanese worked long hours. Vacations typically consisted of groups of peers traveling together—schoolchildren, professional associates, women's clubs.[7] Family vacations were rare. Increased automobile ownership, however, has hastened the outflow of population from older cities to surrounding suburbs, and this has resulted in Japanese men spending more time with their families, rather than with their coworkers.[8] In addition, many companies have switched from six- to five-day weeks, generating more spare time.

With more leisure time has come an interest in more active forms of tourism. No longer do Japanese simply want to soak in hot water at a traditional inn; increasingly, they want to be on the water as well as in it. The area around Fuji—with clear lakes and opportunities for boating—has seen a boom in automobile-oriented, self-catering tourism, accompanied by ever-greater num-

Another view of Mt. Fuji. (Photo by John G. Gissberg.)

Scars created by erosion resulting from road cuts. (Photo by Kazuma Anezaki.)

bers of condominiums and second homes. Most of these are owned by residents of Tokyo, Nagoya, and Osaka. Few are occupied full time—retired people usually cannot afford them—and few, if any, are rented in the owners' absence, as is common elsewhere in the world. The new dwellings are used only for vacations and occasional weekends.

In the Fuji region, an agricultural area that accommodated limited numbers of week-long vacationers at traditional inns has gradually been transformed over the past 15 years into a place of active recreation for thousands of self-catering weekenders. Many others come for the day to play golf, one of Japan's most popular sports. The new type of tourism development has had sharp social and economic effects in many traditional resort communities. In the rural countryside around Fuji, its impact on the natural environment is major.

Going Downhill

The physical characteristics of land in Japan pose problems for developers. Approximately 80 percent of the land is officially classified as mountainous, over three-quarters of it sloping more than 15 percent and much less than a fifth truly level.[9] Most Japanese soils tend to be loose, and susceptible to landslides during the heavy rains that are common in typhoon season. People must be constantly aware that anything not securely fastened may go downhill.

In an extensive road-building program during the 1950s and 1960s, Japanese engineers developed techniques for countering the threat of landslides. Many highway cuts on mountain roads have been covered with concrete from top to bottom. In other places, the hillsides above roads have been covered with wire mesh similar to chain-link fencing. A traveler driving through the Japanese mountains, his view alternating between green forests and sculpted concrete, might have the strange impression of riding through scenery on a gigantic model railroad, or possibly liken his experience to a trip down the Disneyland Matterhorn.

For years, engineers paid little attention to the effect of the highways on the physical environment of the mountains. Runoff from roads washed away thin forest topsoil, and the resulting erosion caused gaping scars, sometimes denuding the area between a series of switchbacks. Additional artificial soil stabilization is then required, portending the eventual establishment of a completely concrete mountain slope.

The ecological effects of logging for road construction were discussed in a 1975 report issued by the Nature Conservation Society of Japan. It cited the roads on the slopes of Mt. Fuji as particularly destructive examples of thoughtless highway engineering techniques. The study found that the growth of new trees was inhibited for a wide area below the roads and that many other forms of vegetation were affected as well.* The society recommended that alternative forms of access to the alpine regions be preferred over traditional highway construction.

The soil is not the only thing going downhill. Runoff from tourist-oriented

---

*There was also a reduction in the number and types of wildlife found in the area because feral dogs and cats and other animals that lived off tourists' garbage competed with native species.

Bungalows at Lake Seiko near Mt. Fuji. (Photo by John G. Gissberg.)

developments around the Fuji lakes has created serious water-quality deterioration.

The slopes above Lake Hakone are dotted with hotel-type facilities used by major Japanese corporations as retreats and conference centers and for employee vacations. Over 400 companies maintain such establishments in the Hakone area alone, accommodating more than 14,000 persons. Japanese corporations see the opportunity to provide for the recreational needs of their employees as a key to good labor relations, with the added potential benefit of a bit of long-range real estate speculation.

As tourism patterns in Japan changed, many family-oriented developments were constructed in the Fuji foothills. For the business executive, subdivisions of second homes emulate the styles of Switzerland or Colorado. The omnipresent "salary man" can choose among a wide variety of less-expensive accommodations, including campgrounds and mobile-home parks.

Almost no sewers exist in the region. Effluent is disposed of through septic tanks, and the soil allows it to sink rapidly into the groundwater supply.

Serious deformities and catastrophic illnesses caused by heavy metals and other industrial pollutants in Japan have attracted worldwide attention and made the Japanese particularly sensitive to water-pollution problems. Although this sensitivity has been largely restricted to pollution caused by industry, in the Fuji area people are showing increasing concern about the long-range quality of their water. The construction of sewage-treatment plants, promised by the Ministry of Construction, will, residents believe, alleviate problems in the once

Close-up of bungalows. (Photo by John G. Gissberg.)

crystal-clear lakes. Yet experience in places like Cancún (see chapter 1) indicates that, even if advanced sewage-treatment systems are used, care must also be taken to avoid pollution from surface-water runoff. Whether sewage treatment is enough to protect the Fuji lakes remains to be seen.

Teed Off

The environmental problems in the Fuji area have been compounded by another kind of tourism development, which, at least in its scope, may be unique to Japan. So many Japanese play golf seriously that "golfing has become a mania with the new middle class."[10] By the spring of 1975, Japan had some 900 golf courses, most of them built within the past few years. By the end of 1975, an additional 1,400 courses were planned or under construction.

Americans are accustomed to environmentalists trying to protect existing golf courses. In Japan, the construction of a new course is greeted by neighbors with about as much joy as high-rise public housing in Westchester County.

Because Japan contains so little flat land, and the demand for agricultural use of that land is great, almost all the golf courses were constructed by clear-cutting the forest along the slopes of foothills. Apparently due to the scarcity and high cost of land, few bands of trees remain between fairways. Landslides have occurred along the cleared slopes, resulting in injuries and even deaths.[11] In addition, since the grass used on fairways is not native to Japan, it requires heavy applications of fertilizers and pesticides. Areas downstream from golf courses have been adversely affected by increasing siltation and runoff which clogs the streams, and the fertilizers and pesticides have further reduced water quality.

Beyond the concerns raised by these problems, there is a social basis for opposition to golf. Residents of rural areas look upon the sport as a pastime that only Tokyo businessmen can afford, a complaint that is not without foundation. Golf in Japan is quite expensive by American standards. In 1975, a public course in the Tokyo area was likely to charge about a $20 greens fee on a weekday and $40 or more on weekends. The private clubs typically have initiation fees in the five-figure range. Much of this money pays for the cost of assembling many small tracts of land at high Japanese land prices.

Because of its proximity to metropolitan Tokyo, the Fuji foothill region has been particularly attractive for golf-course development. The courses are used by people who come for the day, as well as by the large number of summer-home residents.

The antagonism of rural residents to new golf courses was clearly evident in a 1975 controversy over the Minami Fuji Golf Club's plans to build an 18-hole course in the Fuji foothills. The course complied with all legal requirements and was consistent with existing zoning restrictions. So the club began construction. Considerable opposition developed at the local level, however, leading to the formation of the Citizens Group to Oppose the Construction of Minami Fuji Golf Links.

The citizens complained that stripping the forest in the hills above their homes would cause flash floods and landslides during the rainy season. The national government stepped in on their behalf and sought to stop the golf club, but the local district court ruled in the club's favor. Requests from both the municipal government of Fuji City and the prefectural authorities in Shizuoka to

Golf course on steep slopes near Lake Hakone. (Photo by author.)

halt construction were ignored. The course was built. When the club staged its official opening, enraged citizens massed in front of the gates and blocked cars trying to enter. The citizens marched down the fairways and sat on the greens until prospective golfers gave up and went home.

For the time being, at least, further controversies of this type may be rare. The golf boom seems to have reached its peak in Japan, and the threat from the construction of new golf courses has diminished. Some 16 clubs went bankrupt in the first five months of 1976, and many others are in shaky financial condition.[12] Problems generated by the hundreds of existing courses, however, will continue.

Sharing Control

The Japanese government has long recognized that areas where tourism has had a particularly heavy impact, as it has in the Fuji region, need national subsidies to cope with such problems as erosion, aesthetic degradation, crowding, and water-quality deterioration. The Natural Park Law is the vehicle for administering such subsidies. Under it, over two dozen areas have been designated as national parks, including part of the area around Mt. Fuji, which lies in the Fuji-Hakone-Izu National Park.[13]

The designation "national park" is used differently in Japan than in the

United States. The land in a Japanese national park is not acquired by the agency administering the Natural Parks Law (except for occasional small tracts), but remains in private ownership or under the administration of other agencies. The system involves not only the national government but two other levels: prefectures (which have independently elected governors and legislatures but receive most of their authority as delegated powers from the national government) and local governments (which perform traditional municipal services but have less regulatory authority than Americans are accustomed to).

Although the national parks were conceived primarily as a vehicle for funneling national government funds into local infrastructure and recreational facilities, since 1971 more attention has been paid to the regulation of development within the parks, and some park land has been brought under a special form of land-use regulation supervised by the national Environment Agency. This agency has the authority to impose detailed restrictions on building, site planning, and other land-use practices.

Of the roughly 62,000 hectares of land included within the serpentine boundaries of the Fuji-Hakone-Izu Park, about one-fourth is national forest. One-half is owned by prefectural or local governments, mostly for forest use, and one-fourth is privately owned. Some 40,000 of the 70,000 people in the Fuji region live within the boundaries of the national park.

In practice, the Environment Agency has applied land-use controls to only a portion of the park. Within that portion, the regulations vary considerably in their restrictiveness. Five different zones are used:

1. A special protection area for wilderness preservation, used in a very few locations in the Fuji area.

Lake Hakone. (Photo by John G. Gissberg.)

2. A conservation district in which individual houses might be permitted for farmers or other residents, but no second-home or hotel development.

3. A general-use district, which permits most types of second-home and recreational development subject to certain site planning standards, but does not permit clear-cutting of timber.

4. A zone similar to a general-use district, except that clear-cutting is permitted.

5. An "ordinary" zone, in which regulation is left to the discretion of local government authorities, except that prior to development the developer must give notice to the Environment Agency and wait a month before proceeding with the project. This enables the agency to negotiate with the developer, but the agency has no legal power to change the project.

In the more restrictive zones, the Environment Agency has established a series of general building standards governing height, lot size, and floor area. Development on slopes exceeding 30 percent is prohibited; new golf courses are "not to be approved."* Responsibility for implementing the standards lies with the prefectural governments (the prefectures are roughly equivalent to U.S. states, but with less constitutional autonomy) except in cases involving more than 1,000 square meters (about 10,760 square feet) of land, in which case the Environment Agency steps in directly. Although enforcement responsibility is held by the prefectures, park rangers must review every permit application and offer comments. In a 1975 study of the Japanese parks by David Bruns, the rangers surveyed complained of spending an average of 70 percent of their time on paperwork, largely relating to various types of permits.[15] The Environment Agency employs fewer than 100 rangers for the entire national park system.[16]

Most of the higher mountain regions and the heavily forested land owned by the national and prefectural forest agencies have been placed in the restrictive zones 1 and 2. In those few instances where privately owned land has been placed under these classifications, there have been claims for compensation. In response, the Japanese government has instituted a program in which landowners receive bonds issued by the prefectures, with some guarantees of principal and interest by the national government.

Much of the Fuji lakes region is in the "ordinary zone" and is being developed for second homes without interference by the Environment Agency. In some cases, however, the prefectures have imposed tight restrictions on development. In part of the Hakone section of the national park, for example, Kanagawa prefecture has imposed a two-story height limitation and 10-percent maximum lot coverage where the Environment Agency would permit three stories and 20-percent coverage. Meanwhile, the agency, recognizing the rapidly growing demand for outdoor recreation, is increasingly encouraging the development of recreational facilities at appropriate places in the park and is revising plans to provide more recreation opportunities.**

The balance of power over the use of land within the Fuji-Hakone-Izu park

---

*To compare the Japanese with the American national park system, it might be best to equate the zone 1 and 2 land with the land within the boundaries of our national parks, and zones 3, 4, and 5 as surrounding land. The Japanese exercise varying degrees of national control over this "surrounding land."[14]

**In winter, downhill skiing is popular on Fuji's lower slopes. Within the park, on the southern slopes, "Japanland" has been constructed with ski runs, a skating rink, and a large amusement park.

住友銀行箱根山荘
石川島播磨箱根クラブ

ヤクルト松園荘　日本酸素(株)山の家、別荘

箱根尚友荘　千代田区立箱根高原学校

第一勧業銀行仙石山荘　大日本印刷芦の湖山荘

三井物産健康保険組合保養所　長銀箱根山荘

日商岩井避雲荘　日本銀行箱根山荘

國學院大学業陽寮　千山荘

日産自動車仙石寮　宇都興産小石寮

新日本製鐵仙石寮　三井精機仙石原保養所

日本不動産銀行仙石山荘　いすゞ仙石原クラブ

三井物産仙石荘　姥子温泉秀明館

B&S　東亜燃料保養所

動火災健保箱根仙石寮　昭赫亭

リス化粧品山の家　飯野箱根温泉荘

日動箱根クラブ箱根阿弥荘　住友ベークライト健保らこ荘

竹友荘

ッシュクラブ

水建設事務所

Road sign directing visitors to corporate resorts. (Photo by John G. Gissberg.)

seems to be divided about equally among the Environment Agency, prefectural planning authorities, and local governmental officials. An attempt by any one group to exert too much muscle generally arouses a strong reaction. Regular meetings of officials from the various levels of government are held, and for the most part a genuine search for consensus seems to exist. On occasion, however, real conflicts have arisen, often over the construction of new roads—perhaps the thorniest issue in parks all over the world.[17]

One of the most significant current controversies in the Fuji region involves the proposed Fuji Expressway, a connector freeway that would be built on the lower eastern slopes of the mountain to connect the two major expressways that traverse the length of Japan.

At present, most local roads through this region run along the lakes and valleys, where second-home development has been growing rapidly. In summer and on weekends at any time of the year, traffic is extremely heavy. Local residents strongly support a by-pass, which they believe would take traffic off their streets. Many developers view the highway as potentially opening up large new areas for easy access and providing additional opportunities for recreational development.

As might be expected, environmental groups tend to look upon the proposed highway as undesirable. Past experiences with highways in the area have been bad, and the new highway would pass through some of the best remaining forest land. Moreover, the environmental groups express doubt that the new highway would reduce traffic congestion. Rather, they suggest, it would just bring more cars into the region and aggravate the problem.

Since the proposed road would go through a significant portion of the national park, it would need the approval of the Environment Agency. As of early 1978, no official application had been filed, and the agency had indicated informally that it was not pleased with the prospect of this particular road. There is strong local and prefectural pressure for construction, but to date neither side has tried to press for a definitive decision. The agency is in no rush to decide, exemplifying a patience characteristic of the Japanese decision-making process.

The fact that neither side is pressing for a quick decision reflects another aspect of the Japanese decision-making process discussed in the previous chapter. For the Japanese seek consensus not only on answers to questions, but in determining what questions need to be asked. As Peter Drucker has put it:

> To the Japanese, the important element in decision-making is defining the question. . . . It is, indeed, this step that, to the Japanese, is the essence of the decision. The answer to the question—that is, what the West considers the "decision"—follows.[18]

What are the questions that need to be asked about the Fuji highway? Analysts

Highway construction in Japanese mountains. (Photo by M. Kiuchi.)

can provide reams of data on the mountain's geological structure and the economic profile of its visitors, but the image of Fuji is at least as important.

Splendid Witness

Even people who have never visited Mt. Fuji are fascinated by the images of it created by the Japanese artist Hokusai. In the mid-19th century, his book *Thirty-Six Views of Mt. Fuji* was circulated widely in Europe, influencing the development of impressionism.

Hokusai's work, symbolizing the traditional Japanese view of man's relationship to nature, is neither landscape art nor portraiture, but a skillful fusion of the two:

> It is remarkable how this human element is incorporated with the landscape surrounding it without either dominating or being dominated. It is as though Hokusai achieved a perfect fusion of two aspects of his art that had been developing parallel to each other—the interest in the human figure and in humanity as such, and the fresh interest in nature for its own sake that was in part a product of the intellectual atmosphere of his period.[19]

Like the English, the Japanese occupy islands that have been heavily populated for centuries. Unexplored wilderness is a foreign concept, but a love of the natural world is deeply imbedded in the Japanese character. Hokusai captured

One of Hokusai's Thirty-six Views of Mt. Fuji.

that in his *Thirty-Six Views*. In this series of prints, he occasionally portrayed Fuji alone, but, more often, everyday activities of farmers and fishermen were also depicted, with Fuji in the background. The mountain was frequently seen from some oblique and unexpected angle, "a mutely splendid witness to the intense human beings who scramble in the foreground."[20]

Fuji's role as the mutely splendid witness is illustrated by Japan's famous summer tradition—the great climb.

Social Mountaineering

The Japanese enhance their intimate relationship with Fuji by traveling all around the lakes and forest at its base, enjoying the accent the mountain gives to the scenery. But perhaps the activity that best expresses the Japanese interrelationship with nature is the ascent to the top of the mountain.

A common Japanese proverb says a person is a fool if he doesn't climb Mt. Fuji—or if he climbs it more than once. The season when Fuji can be climbed without great difficulty is short, beginning when the snow melts, usually late in June, and ending with the autumn storms, generally in early September. During this two-month period, some two million people make the ascent each year, arriving by train and bus at way stations halfway up the mountain, then clambering to the top across rocky lava.

The middle of the night is the favorite time to begin, for it allows climbers to reach the summit with the first rays of the sun. In the predawn grayness, long

Climbers on Mt. Fuji at sunrise. (Photo by John G. Gissberg.)

files stride up the winding trails with purposeful tread. Japanese young and old make the climb, some trading banter as they go, others saving their breath. For though the climb is not difficult by mountaineering standards, to reach the peak by sunrise requires that a steady pace be maintained. On top of the mountain, climbers cheer the sunrise, offer toasts from Thermoses, stop briefly at one of the shrines, and then begin the bounding descent to buses and trains that will return them to their homes.

The ritual ascent characterizes the Japanese attitude toward the mountain and toward nature itself. In the days when Fuji frequently buried neighboring villages with volcanic eruptions, the Japanese lived in awe of the mountain and worshipped it in the hope of placating its anger. Today, they treat the mountain with a mixture of love, respect, pride, and neglect—not unlike their attitude toward their own children! Still the attitudes of the Japanese reflect a persistence of the values inherent in the artistic vision of Hokusai.

Art's Invisible Hand

Hokusai's view of the interrelation of man and nature was not unlike that of the English poet William Wordsworth. Like Hokusai, Wordsworth enjoyed natural areas enhanced by tasteful works of man. He urged builders: "Work, where you can, in the spirit of Nature, with an invisible hand of art."[21]

Thanks in part to Wordsworth, the British have devised a system for controlling development in some of their more popular natural areas that is similar to the Japanese system for controlling development around Fuji. The English version can be examined by looking at the area where it originated—that part of Cumbria known as "the Lake District," where the blue waters of Windermere, Ullswater, Grasmere, and dozens of other lakes provide the focus of one of England's favorite vacation areas.

The Lake District shows evidence of the last ice age. From its hills, U-shaped valleys extend down toward meandering lakes. The hills reach no higher than 3,000 feet and have the rounded contours and rocky soil typical of glaciated regions, though to the English they are mountains as picturesque as any alpine crag.

There are no historical records of a Lake District undisturbed by the works of man.[22] Traditionally, the Lake District has been sheep country. Heavy rainfall promotes lush growth of pasture despite the rocky soil. Even the steeper slopes of the valleys appear lawnlike, having been cropped by clambering flocks of Herwick sheep, the trademark of the region. In the valleys, ancient stone walls mark boundary lines between the holdings of herdsmen.

In his *Guide Through the District of the Lakes*, Wordsworth extolled the area's beauty in a way that served as a model for 19th-century guidebook writers. Wordsworth believed that man and nature should coexist in a "natural" fashion, and idealized the thatched-roof cottage:

> . . . these humble dwellings remind the contemplative spectator of a production of Nature, and may (using a strong expression) rather be said to have grown than to have been erected;—to have risen, by an instinct of their own, out of the native rock—so little is there in them of formality, such is their wildness and beauty.[23]

The roofs and walls of such cottages "have furnished places of rest for the seeds

Ullswater, the Lake District. (Photo by David L. Callies.)

of lichens, mosses, ferns and flowers."* Like trees clothed in mistletoe, buildings "clothed in part with a vegetable garb, appear to be received into the bosom
of the living principle of things" and "direct the thoughts to that tranquil course
of Nature and simplicity."[24] Indeed, as Aldous Huxley observed, in the
Wordsworthian view "a walk in the country is the equivalent of going to
church."[25]

For over a century the railroads, and then the highways, have brought
tourists to the Lake District. Only recently, however, has the government taken
steps to control the impact of development on the area.

---

*The English occasionally go to great lengths to maintain this image. According to a story in the
Guardian (September 11, 1974), a rural community had recently granted permission for the erection
of a series of bus shelters, but only on condition that manure be spread on top of the shelters so that
grass and moss would be encouraged to grow.

A Sort of National Property

Wordsworth called the Lake District "a sort of national property in which every
man has a right and an interest who has an eye to perceive and a heart to enjoy."[26]
In the mid-19th century, admirers of the Lake District formed the National Trust,
a nonprofit organization dedicated to preserving some of the region's more
beautiful property. The Trust, which has become a powerful national institution
with property throughout England, now owns some 90,000 acres of the most
sensitive land in the Lake District, particularly along the lake shores and at the
heads of valleys.[27]

For almost a century and a half, there was no official support for
Wordworth's gentle suggestion that the Lake District deserved to be a "national
property." Nor, for that matter, did the government designate any other parts of
the country as having particular national status. In 1945, however, a study
undertaken by John Dower recommended the creation of a system of national
parks. In Dower's words, these parks should consist of "beautiful and relatively
wild country" in which "(a) the characteristic landscape beauty is strictly preserved, (b) access and facilities for public open-air enjoyment are amply provided, (c) wildlife and buildings and places of architectural and historic interest
are suitably protected, while (d) established farming use is effectively maintained."[28] In 1949, Parliament created a National Parks Commission (now called
the Countryside Commission), authorized to designate national parks. In 1951,
the Lake District was one of the first to be designated; it remains the largest and
most popular of Britain's 10 national parks.[29]

Designation of a national park does not require government acquisition of
land within the park. In fact, Dower's report suggested that such acquisition was

*Great Langdale, from the side of Tarn Crag, The Langdales, the Lake District. (Photo by
David L. Callies.)*

undesirable: "The available funds, whatever their scale, would go many times further on a procedure that relies mainly on control, reinforced when necessary by assistance, compensation or purchase, than on a procedure that takes outright purchase as its normal rule. For the broad purposes of planning and agriculture, public ownership is no more and no less desirable in National Parks than in the rest of the country."[30]

Thus, most land in the English national parks is in private ownership. Development is controlled through a special system of planning controls, distinct from but integrated with the overall system of planning in England.

Balancing Man and Nature

The administration of the national park system puts strong emphasis on local control, and this usually means the involvement of citizens oriented toward conservation. Residents of areas such as the Lake District, according to Peter Hall, chose quality of life over economic growth nearly a quarter century before the trade-off became fashionable.[31] The Lake District National Park is managed by a park planning board, two-thirds of its members appointed by the local government and one-third by the national Department of the Environment. The national government pays 75 percent of the board's administrative costs.

The planning board adopts an overall plan establishing guidelines for park management, and exercises control through the power to grant or deny planning permission for any development within the parks. The board often attaches conditions designed to avoid "intrusiveness." The goal is to give the appearance that the landscape is "the joint product of nature and of human use over many generations."[32]

Since the English concept of scenic beauty ranks pastoral scenes as high as it does untamed nature, the English see no anomaly in permitting traditional agricultural land uses in the national parks, and park management makes every effort to encourage this. One American observer finds in these parks "a human element" often lacking in their North American counterparts—"a harmony in the way that the natural environment is infused with the works of man, especially in the way that the old villages and farms fit into the landscape."[33] The sheep, says one commentator, are "the architect[s] of the scenery of the Lakes," keeping the grass short and easy to walk on, and preventing scrub from growing up to obscure the view.[34]

Preserving traditional agriculture has not been easy. In England, as in many other parts of the world, the operation of small farms grows less economic over the years.[35] Substantial government subsidies for sheep production, however, enable small farmers to continue in the traditional manner, and there is strong local support for maintaining the national park as an example of traditional rural scenery.

Despite this, numerous disagreements arise over the various uses of park land. One of the more controversial issues in areas like the Lake District is the extent of afforestation to be permitted. Whereas in Japan the clearing of forests for golf courses arouses opposition, in England it is the planting of forests on pasture land that is controversial. The forests are looked upon as aesthetically destructive because the orderly rows of pine detract from the "natural" appearance. Wordsworth himself objected to the "stern regimentation" created by this type of "vegetable manufactury."[36]

A demand for second homes has also created controversies, particularly along the shores of major lakes. The spread of second homes has been substantial, though design controls are imposed to avoid intrusive developments. Probably the most common complaint against second homes is that they drive up land values, making it impossible for young people in the region to find reasonably priced housing.[37]

From time to time, disputes erupt over the extent to which outdoor recreation should be encouraged in the Lake District. City dwellers seeking to race motorboats or motorcycles get little sympathy, but the national government tries to see that reasonable recreational uses are accommodated.*

During the past two decades the English have instituted a number of variations on the national park concept, extending it to many smaller areas under a variety of programs.

The Countryside Commission now designates Areas of Outstanding Natural Beauty, which are smaller than national parks but eligible for grants for the protection of amenities and the construction of recreational facilities. Development in these areas requires prior consultation with the Countryside Commission, but unlike the National Parks no special local planning mechanism is

---

*The national government pays up to 80 percent of the cost of constructing recreational facilities in the national parks, but local residents are often reluctant to build such facilities because they fear an increased volume of tourists. For example, a recent inquiry into the continued use of portions of Dartmoor National Park for a military firing range found that the great majority of local residents preferred the spent ammunition left by the army to the litter left by tourists.[38] The Countryside Commission has sought powers to overrule local actions viewed as arbitrary, but the government still lacks clearly defined park management policies, having substantially rejected the suggestions of a 1974 policy review committee.[39] Consequently, development decisions are made on a pragmatic and *ad hoc* basis, with many points of view expressed on major decisions relating to the national parks.

Grasmere, the Lake District. (Photo by David L. Callies.)

required. As of the end of 1976, the commission had designated 33 Areas of Outstanding Natural Beauty covering over 5,000 square miles.

Since 1973, the commission has also been authorized to designate Heritage Coasts, segments of the coastline having scenic or historic value, which are then subjected to control by local authorities. In some cases, the commission pays local authorities to employ heritage-coast officers and rangers, who develop plans and enforce regulations to maintain the amenities in these coastal areas.[40]

Initially, most American conservationists are shocked by the amount of development permitted in the English and Japanese national parks. When one remembers, however, that these parks are not parks at all, in U.S. terms, but merely areas subject to special development controls, the system makes sense. While far from perfect, the British system, for example, seems to have achieved a balance of man and nature that is far better than typical for the British countryside.[41]

Virtue through Diversity

Within the last few years, Americans have begun looking closely at parks of the type established in England and Japan. Interest is gathering momentum, and it now seems likely that the United States soon will have a number of new parks consisting of a mixture of public land and publicly regulated private land.

The first step in this direction was the creation of National Seashores, beginning in the early 1960s during the Kennedy administration.[42] In places like Cape Cod and Fire Island, Congress recognized that proposed federal acquisition of all privately owned homes scattered through the area was not feasible. It agreed not to acquire these properties as long as they met federally approved local regulatory standards. Most people viewed this as a compromise necessary to obtain the legislation's passage rather than a policy to be emulated elsewhere.[43]

As the 1970s began, two significant developments took place: New York State created the Adirondack Park Agency, authorized to prepare plans and regulations for the region of mixed public (state) and private land known as Adirondack Park.[44] And the states of California and Nevada, with federal cooperation, adopted an interstate compact creating the Tahoe Regional Planning Agency.[45] The agency was directed to prepare plans and regulations for the private lands in the Lake Tahoe watershed, which contains a mixture of private and public (mostly national forest) lands.

In 1975, Charles E. Little of the Library of Congress authored a legislative report that stimulated interest in establishing public parks with an intentional mixture of public and private lands.[46] Other American scholars called attention to the English model,[47] and the idea attracted the active interest of a number of Senators, notably Bennett Johnston, Harrison Williams, and Clifford Case.

At the same time, local groups in more than a dozen areas of the country were independently petitioning Congress to protect quite diverse special places through a range of protective measures, including regulation of private land, rather than through public acquisition alone. These areas were thought to be too complex, too valuable, too big, or too interwoven with the fabric of existing communities to be protected by the traditional park protection measure: acquisition and management by a government agency.

Mt. Fuji. (Photo by John G. Gissberg.)

The Carter administration began to draw together some of the common threads of these proposals. In May 1978, Carter and Interior Secretary Cecil D. Andrus proposed the creation of an "area of national concern" (inevitably, the new category quickly became known as ANC) for the Santa Monica mountains, which would provide unified management for a recreation area of public and private land within the Los Angeles metropolitan area.[48]

The administration's interest coincided with strong congressional support for more innovative approaches toward parks. Under the leadership of Congressman Phil Burton of California, the House of Representatives in July 1978 passed the first omnibus "park barrel" bill authorizing many of these innovative proposals for protecting special places in various congressional districts.[49] The Senate, too, was considering different approaches to new parks.[50]

As of late summer 1978, Congress seemed likely to establish mixed public-private parks in the following areas: Jean Lafitte National Historical Park (Louisiana), Lowell National Cultural Park (Massachusetts), San Antonio Missions National Historical Park (Texas), and Upper Delaware National Scenic and Recreational River (Pennsylvania and New York). In addition, it appeared likely that Congress would approve federal funds for cooperative federal, local, and state planning for mixed public-private approaches to a proposed Pine Barrens National Ecological Reserve (New Jersey) and Jackson Hole Scenic Area (Wyoming), as well as for a Santa Monica Mountains National Recreational Area provided that state and local governments protectively regulate adjacent private lands.

A number of states are using "critical-area" legislation to accomplish similar objectives. And local communities all over the United States, without waiting for aid from higher levels of government, are putting into effect a wide variety of programs that direct development in a way complementary to the special qualities of the community and individual neighborhoods. These programs emphasize custom-tailoring for individual places.

There is no need to force all of these efforts into the same mold, to hold them up against a Yosemite model, for instance, and either cut them to fit or reject them. Diversity can be seen as a virtue rather than a vice. A *uniform* system for recognizing the special qualities of places might, in fact, lose sight of special qualities in a quagmire of bureaucratic analysis.

Not even the best system of generalized rules can stay perfectly attuned to the constantly changing and complex interrelationship of man and nature. Mt. Fuji epitomizes that interrelationship, as Hokusai perceived. Fuji standing alone is awesome; its partnership with man is intimate and subtle. It was so for the early Buddhist monks who climbed to the summit, and it is today for the millions of Japanese who climb Fuji as a communal rite. The rice farmer of Hokusai's day, having the mountain looking over his shoulder, probably thought of it as something special. The new summer-home resident may have a similar feeling. Hokusai perceived that the beauty of Fuji was in the way it participated with man in his daily life. As daily life changes, the participation must change as well.

If Hokusai could see Fuji today, he would surely be sad to see the lakes polluted and the mountain slopes scarred. But the great artist still would recognize his mountain, and one suspects that he might enjoy some of the changes. For Hokusai was enamoured of change, a restless man who moved constantly and said that his whole property consisted of an artist's tools and a teapot from the Shogun's palace. He claimed that only after he had moved a hundred times would he settle down in the house where he would like to die.[51] When he died in 1849, having achieved 93 of the 100 moves that he sought, his last words were: "Freedom, wonderful freedom."[52]

Chapter 10
A Lake in Galilee, and Other Special Places

A Lake in Galilee, and Other Special Places

The previous chapter pointed out that a park is not simply an institution or a demarcation on a map, but a state of mind. The word *park* is a shorthand way of saying that people have a particular attitude about a place: they have been attracted to it, and they want to preserve the qualities that make it attractive. It is this attitude that defines the special places of the world, whether they are called parks or not.

Like central Amsterdam, the island of Sylt, or the dunes of Aquitaine, most of the world's special places bear no common label. Americans' attitudes toward Nantucket, San Francisco's Russian Hill, and Greenwich Village are comparable to their attitudes toward Yosemite. Recognition of a place's particular amenities and a determination to maintain them is what shapes a state of mind that makes a place special.

The Quality of Specialness

What specific qualities create this attitude about one place and not another? Almost by definition, specialness is an elusive characteristic. The more we analyze and define, the more the special becomes routine. We murder, as Wordsworth said, to dissect. Some qualities, however, are *not* essential to specialness.

First, a special quality need not be static. Some places are special because they allow us to witness a fixed and unchanging beauty. In other places, specialness has a dynamic quality, and adaptability to change may be important. The aborigines did not intend their paintings to be permanent. They valued Ayers Rock as a place in which to paint rather than as a place to view the paintings of others. The appeal of an aboriginal cave painting, a nap on the Dam, or a fleeting glimpse of Mt. Fuji may depend in part on the ephemeral nature of the event.

Second, specialness need not be natural. Some places derive special qualities from their wild and untouched appearance. Other places, however, derive their special qualities from the complex interplay of nature and culture.[1] Mt.

Field research for this chapter was conducted by Abraham Rabinovitch and Shelly Rothschild.

Fuji's natural beauty is enhanced by juxtaposition with the farms and fishing villages depicted in Hokusai's prints. Indeed, it would be foreign to the traditional Japanese concept of the union of man and nature to make clear distinctions between natural and man-made attributes of a place. And Bayswater and central Amsterdam are special places where the attractions have almost no relation to the characteristics of the area before man arrived.

Third, special qualities need not be uniquely local. Frequently, each identifiable quality of a place also can be found elsewhere. The white sand beach of Cancún, though exceptional, is only one of the world's many spectacular beaches. Aquitaine's large dunes are similar to many others; so are its pine forests, its dynamic beach, and its wide-ranging tide. Its inland lakes are quite typical; even the great vineyards of the Medoc have rivals in the Moselle or Napa valleys. It is not particular features but the overall combination that makes a place like Aquitaine special.

This suggests a fourth, and perhaps most important, point. The special qualities of a place may not be understood, or may be understood only subconsciously. To René Dubos, the specialness of a place is often determined by "forces and structures hidden beneath the surface of things."[2] Lawrence Durrell makes a similar statement: to get the essential sense of a place, he says, "Just close your eyes and breathe softly through your nose; you will hear the whispered message, for all landscapes ask the same question in the same whisper, 'I am watching you—are you watching yourself in me?' "[3]

Certainly, in some cases, knowledge of a place's qualities comes only through study.[4] In Torquay, it was only as the Victorian style began to be appreciated in architectural history that the public became aware of the value of what had been seen as antiquated and commonplace buildings. When Languedoc was built, wetlands were usually thought of as useless swamps. More was learned about the function of wetlands, however; this knowledge was popularly disseminated; and people began to perceive wetlands as special places. The qualities were always there; public recognition was not.

Why Specialness Is Important

Most people would say intuitively that there is value in maintaining the special qualities of a place. Yet the more one tries to pin down just what the value is, the more it eludes one's grasp.

Some would argue that special places are valuable because they serve as symbols for important emotions and ideas.[5] Others would argue that such places are valuable even if they influence one's attitudes only subconsciously.[6] Wordsworth believed that experiences in special places continually brought back feelings "of unremembered pleasure."[7] Or perhaps the desirability of maintaining a diversity of special places can be justified on the same basis as the need to maintain a wide variety of biological species: to ensure the availability of a maximum number of "ingredients" for creative responses to unpredictable future conditions.[8]

One need not resolve such philosophic questions to observe that when people treat places as special, the development process generally seems to work out better. An exception that proves this rule was discussed in the prologue—Jerusalem, a very special place that has been abused. There, the Israelis allowed their eagerness for participation in the worldwide tourism boom to override their recognition of the city's unique qualities.

It is fitting, therefore, to end this book in another very special place, where the Israelis have not only rejected inappropriate tourism development, but are trying to encourage those types of tourism that will contribute to specialness.*

The Garden That Has No End

Lake Kinneret, known to many as the Sea of Galilee, has always had fresh, though brackish, water. The lake is familiar in the history, literature, and travels of Christians, Jews, and Moslems. Writers of pilgrim literature sometimes emphasized the Kinneret region's lush, tropical aspects: "Here in this 'garden that has no end,' flourished the vine, the olive, and the fig; the oak, the hardy walnut, the terebinth, and the hot-blooded palm; the cedar, cypress, and balsam; the fir-tree, the pine, and sycamore; the bay-tree, the myrtle, the almond, the pomegranate, the citron, and the beautiful oleander."[9]

In summer, temperatures regularly top 100°F; and except in irrigated areas the landscape is brown and shimmering. Thus, Mark Twain described his first view of the lake as follows: ". . . this cloudless, blistering sky; this solemn, sailless, tintless lake, reposing within its rim of yellow hills and low, steep banks, and looking just as expressionless and unpoetical (when we leave its sublime history out of the question) as any metropolitan-reservoir in Christendom—if these things are not food for 'Rock Me To Sleep, Mother,' none exist, I think."[10] Even for Twain, however, when the sun went down, Galilee was haunting:

> Night is the time to see Galilee . . . . Its history and its associations are its chiefest charm in any eyes, and the spells they weave are feeble in the searching light of the sun. . . . But when the day is done, even the most unimpressible must yield to the dreamy influences of this tranquil starlight. The old traditions of the place steal upon his memory and haunt his reveries, and then his fancy clothes all sights and sounds with the supernatural. In the lapping of the waves upon the beach he hears the dip of ghostly oars; in the secret noises of the night he hears spirit voices; in the soft sweep of the breeze, the rush of invisible wings. Phantom ships are on the sea, the dead of twenty centuries come forth from the tombs, and in the dirges of the night wind the songs of old forgotten ages find utterance again.[11]

For Jews, the area became a spiritual and cultural center after the Romans destroyed Jerusalem. It is the place where such learned men as Maimonides and Rabbi Meir resided and are buried. Archaeologists have found ancient Jewish temples around the lake, and some Jews believe that Tiberias—the largest settlement—is a holy city where the Messiah eventually will appear. In modern Israel, the first kibbutz was established at Deganya on the southern shore.

For Moslems as well, the lake plays a historical role. Nearby, in 634 A.D., the Byzantines were driven from Palestine. And in the hills overlooking the lake, on a hot July day in 1187, Saladin's army met and defeated the Crusaders at the Horns of Hittin, which was the critical battle in ending the Crusaders' occupa-

---

* It should be reemphasized that in Jerusalem, as well, many Israelis recognize past mistakes and seek to ensure that future development enhances the city's special qualities. Any substantial project proposed for Jerusalem is now the subject of thoughtful and often heated debate. The outcome may not please everyone, but the process is open and the right questions are being asked.

Roman ruins on edge of Lake Kinneret. (Photo by author.)

tion of the region. The ruins of winter palaces subsequently built by the caliphs may still be seen around the lake.

For Christians, this is the body of water on which Jesus walked—the place where Jesus healed the sick and preached a message of brotherly love. From these shores, after the resurrection, Jesus called to the disciples, who were fishing, telling them to cast their empty net on the opposite side of the boat, where "they were not able to haul it in, for the quantity of fish."[12]

Thus the lake has served as a symbol of rebirth and redemption. After its early prominence, it largely disappeared from the pages of history; its lightly populated basin was occupied by frequently warring tribes of herdsmen. A 19th-century traveler observed: "In the Roman period fishing boats . . . appear to have been numbered by the hundreds; now there are not many over a score."[13] With the founding of Israel in 1948, Lake Kinneret once again began to thrive.

Creating Facts

The Kinneret Basin today is the site of a fertile, flourishing agricultural community. Citrus, date, and banana groves give the region a semitropical air. Fish are raised commercially in artificial ponds. Cattle graze on the Golan slopes bordering the lake. Grain ripens under the winter rains. And Kinneret is alive with plans for new development, much of it for tourism.

For the most part, settlement of the basin is recent. In 1948, 77 percent of the Jewish population of Israel lived on 11 percent of the land—particularly on the flat and fertile coastal plain in and around Tel Aviv. From the outset, however,

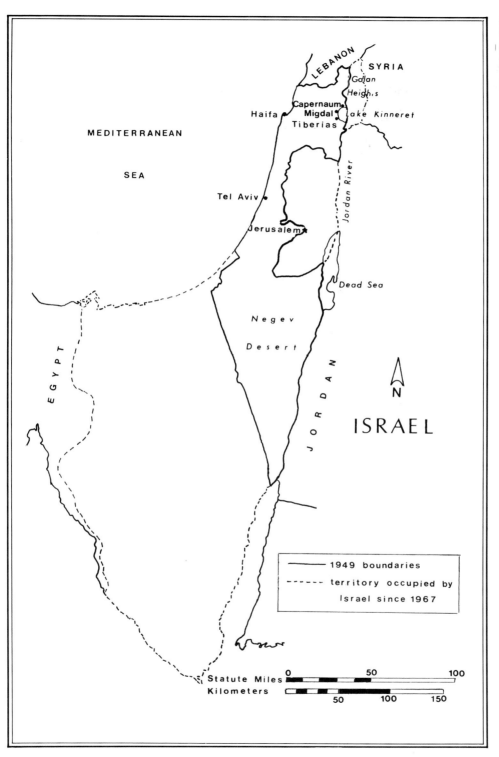

Israel has sought to prevent urbanization of the best agricultural areas, and to disperse the population to strengthen the nation's claim to all of the land within its boundaries.[14] In a part of the world where national boundaries historically have been tenuous, a nation's best guarantee of future sovereignty is to make sure its people actually occupy an area. "Creating facts" is the phrase Israelis use to describe this policy.

Even prior to creation of the State of Israel, pioneer Jewish settlers farmed the upper Jordan Valley, which lies north of and feeds into the Kinneret Basin.[15] In the 1950s the government drained the valley's wetlands to provide a fertile area of some 15,000 acres for orchards, dairying, and cotton and other crops.[16] Towns such as Kiryat Shemona, Hazor, and Zefat (Safad) were developed, and by 1955 more than 10 percent of Israel's Jewish population was living in this northern part of the country.[17]

After the 1967 war, the government redoubled its efforts to create new communities in northeast Israel to provide protection for the area. As the population grew, the demand for flood prevention grew. In the late 1960s and early 1970s, therefore, the Jordan was straightened and deepened, increasing runoff into Lake Kinneret.

The town of Kiryat Shemona and commercial fish ponds. (Photo by author.)

A New Tourist City

Second only to agriculture, tourism is the major contributor to the Kinneret area's economy. Many foreign tourists are attracted to religious sites, such as Capernaum. The lakeshore is also a traditional winter resort for Israelis. Lying about 200 meters below sea level, the lake is surrounded by hills that shield it from the coastal winds. As a result, the shores have a mild winter climate, unlike that of Israel's major cities. Hot springs for many years have attracted older people who seek relief from the cool dampness of the Israeli winter. Recently, younger Israelis, too, have visited the lake in increasing numbers year-round. Despite the summer's desertlike heat, in August 1976 all 5,000 beds in hotels and boarding houses near the lake were occupied, and another 5,000 tourists camped along the shore.[18]

Recognizing the Kinneret area's magnetism, Israel's Ministry of Tourism in 1973 proposed to build a major resort city, Aaqeb, on the lake's northeastern shore.[19] The new city was to be located southeast of Capernaum in territory formerly held by Syria. Fifteen hotels containing a total of almost 2,000 rooms were proposed. Beaches and marinas were to be built, and transportation provided to skiing facilities on the slopes of Mt. Hermon, also acquired in the 1967 war.

Capernaum. (Copyright National Geographic Society.)

The Tourism Ministry projected Aaqeb as one of Israel's major tourist attractions, believing it could help overcome the tendency of many tourists to concentrate on quick trips to historical sites. Aaqeb held potential for a different kind of tourism. The ministry hoped to provide winter tourists with both swimming and skiing facilities.[20] In addition, it proposed a major expansion of the city of Tiberias as a tourism destination, which would increase the existing 900 hotel rooms to 5,000 by 1985. Widening of the beaches and landfill projects would create a seven-mile beachfront to be backed with high-rise hotels. Long-term, low-interest loans would finance the project.[21]

The ministry believed that Aaqeb and Tiberias, as winter resorts, might prove as attractive to Europeans as Eilat, the very successful resort city that provides Israel access to the Red Sea. Moreover, the resorts on Lake Kinneret would be easily accessible to the rest of the country, and could serve as a base for tourists interested in historical and religious sites. Eilat, isolated from the rest of Israel by the Negev desert, tends to attract package tour groups who do not visit other parts of the country.

The Tourism Ministry's brochure soliciting developer interest in Aaqeb reads like those of a hundred other countries seeking to attract tourism. The same kinds of convention centers, golf courses, marinas, and shopping centers are proposed all over the world. If the "nearby historical sites" had Mayan names, Aaqeb would sound just like Cancún.

Aaqeb might have been the beginning of the end for Kinneret as a special place. Luckily, however, the proposed development encountered strong resistance, growing, in part, out of recognition that the lake's water quality was already endangered by existing projects. The threat was a national concern. For beyond its symbolic or historical importance, Lake Kinneret is Israel's primary source of fresh water for drinking and irrigation.

The Water Carrier

According to some Israelis, their country is described in the Bible as a land flowing with milk and honey for at least one very good reason: it has no water. Israel lives at the edge of water scarcity, having captured about 95 percent of available resources. The coastal plain gets from 10 to 30 inches of rain per year.[22] The rainy season, however, lasts only about two months, and over two-thirds of the rain is lost through runoff or evaporation. The rain also falls at the wrong time and place—in the winter in the north, while summer is the best growing season, and the best soils are in the south.

Only one river, the Jordan, brings fresh water into the country. Drawing from sources in Lebanon, Syria, and Israel, including Mt. Hermon's extensive snows, the Jordan's waters combine near Israel's northern boundary to form the river's main channel, which flows south through the Hula Valley into Lake Kinneret. From the southern end of the lake the Jordan flows southward to the Dead Sea.[23]

Under Israeli law, all water resources are state property, and annual quotas are set for all users. A water commissioner in the Ministry of Agriculture controls these resources.[24] A water planning commission known as TAHAL was created in the 1950s.

The early settlers of modern Israel realized that groundwater supplies were limited, and looked to the Jordan River as a potential means of irrigating land to

New hotel in Tiberias. (Photo by author.)

the south. Even before Israel's founding as a nation, W. C. Lowdermilk published a proposal for doing this by damming the waters of the Jordan near what is now Israel's northern boundary, and creating an extensive aqueduct system. But because of hostility between Israel and its northern neighbors, the government's water planners decided not to construct new reservoirs in the headwaters of the Jordan Valley. Instead, they began a project to use Lake Kinneret as the main reservoir for a national water supply system.

Now known as the National Water Carrier, the system was completed in 1964. Water is pumped from Lake Kinneret to a point near the northwestern shore, about 100 feet above sea level. From there, open canals and large pipes carry it to fertile agricultural lands throughout central Israel and into the southern Negev.

The government regulates the cost of water to influence the location and character of development. Rates in the water-scarce south are subsidized up to 90 percent, and agricultural consumers pay less than domestic or industrial consumers. By charging higher rates in areas where water is more abundant, the system has encouraged agriculture in dry southern Israel, "making the desert bloom."

The National Water Carrier system, which cost $120,000,000 to construct, is recognized as a major engineering achievement. (Pumping water, incidentally,

Until the 1967 war, occupation of the Golan Heights (pictured) by Syria posed a hazard to Kinneret region settlers. (Photo by author.)

requires almost one-quarter of all the electric power generated in Israel.[25]) The carrier meets about 40 percent of Israel's needs.

Dim Waters

Given Kinneret's importance to water supply, it is not surprising that new development proposals for its shores would raise questions about water-quality impact. The concern is reinforced by the fact that the quality of the lake's waters has never been excellent. At the beginning of the 12th century, Saewulf, a pilgrim who accompanied the Crusaders, noted that the "water of the Jordan is whiter and more of a milky colour than any other water, and it may be distinguished by its colour a long distance into the Dead Sea."[26] Mark Twain, comparing Kinneret to the lake by which he measured all others, also commented on its paleness: ". . . this sea is no more to be compared to Tahoe than a meridian of longitude is to a rainbow. The dim waters of this pool cannot suggest the limpid brilliancy of Tahoe. . . ."[27]

Mineral springs on Kinneret's bottom emit about 150,000 tons of chlorides into the lake each year. In 1964, the larger springs were capped and piped into the lower Jordan, reducing the lake's salinity. But Kinneret water still must be diluted with fresher water from a variety of local sources along the route of the National Water Carrier before it is usable for irrigation and drinking.

Beyond this problem, man-made pollution in recent years has further reduced the quality of the lake's water.* Peridinium algae, which feed on fertilizers and sewage, bloom intensely between January and April each year. They not only produce taste and odor problems in the nation's drinking water, but detract from the lake's beauty because of the ugly, coffee-colored patches they create on the lake's surface.

A major contributor to the deterioration of Kinneret has been increasing development around the lake and in the Jordan Valley to the north. About 110,000 people live in the Israeli portion of the Kinneret Basin, and another 80,000 in the Lebanese portion. The urban settlements in the region dump untreated sewage into the lake and the Jordan River. In addition to the pollution from settlements, moreover, nutrients supplied by agricultural uses are a major cause of eutrophication. The basin is heavily used for agricultural purposes. Runoff from cattle pastures, cropland, fishponds, and the rich Hula peat lands carries nutrients, bacteria, pesticides, and fertilizers into the lake.

All of this has led to increased public concern. In June 1976, environmentalists staged a demonstration outside Safad, protesting the dumping of sewage into a stream that flows into the lake.[28] There have also been widely publicized studies of Kinneret's water quality.

In the late 1960s Israel's Ministry of Agriculture retained a South African

---

*Water pollution is a chronic problem throughout Israel. Many rivers formerly used for fishing or recreation are now "dead"—black, mosquito-infested, and notable only for their stench. The Crocodile River, once a famous nature reserve, has become a dumping ground for sewage and industrial wastewater. The stench from the Yarkom River, which runs through Tel Aviv, is so overpowering that thousands of residents have complained. In a contemporary Israeli anecdote, a child and her father are riding from Tel Aviv to Haifa when the passengers in the car are suddenly overwhelmed by a noxious odor emanating from a nearby factory. The child jumps up excitedly and asks her father, "Daddy, daddy, where's the river?"

Banana plantation near Lake Kinneret. (Photo by author.)

sanitary engineer, R. J. Davis, to study Lake Kinneret. His report attracted widespread attention because it spoke of imminent catastrophe:

> There is ample evidence that the Kinneret is "sick." How "sick" we are still not sure, but it is "sick." Progressive eutrophic conditions have developed and unless urgent radical remedial measures are taken, the process will continue to develop. Unless this process is arrested and reversed, the Kinneret will "die." [29]

In a second report, Davis made even more specific predictions. He found declining oxygen concentrations showing "serious symptoms of mere-asphyxia" and suggested that this would reach a critical level "possibly as early as the end of 1975; most probably in 1976 and possibly not later than the end of 1977 or early 1978." This would trigger a chain reaction that would completely remove the oxygen from the lake within 24 hours. [30]

The Davis reports created widespread public concern, some of it spirited: "Soon we'll all be able to walk on the waters of the Sea of Galilee."

In response, the Israeli government declared a moratorium on building along the shores. An interministerial study committee was directed to examine the lake's future. It retained a planning team headed by Professor Yohanan Elon of the Technion to prepare master plans for the Kinneret Basin.

Planners and Pioneers

The planners encountered numerous bureaucratic obstacles because the drainage basin overlapped the jurisdictions of many local governments and special

Sprinklers in field near kibbutz on southern end of Lake Kinneret. (Copyright National Geographic society.)

agencies. Each of these guarded its turf jealously, but perhaps the most sensitive was TAHAL, the national water planning agency, a powerful political force akin to the U.S. Bureau of Reclamation. In an attempt to co-opt TAHAL, therefore, the task force asked it to prepare a water-quality plan covering the entire Kinneret drainage basin. A second plan, to be prepared by Professor Yigil Tsamir of the Technion, would propose specific uses of the land along the immediate shores of Lake Kinneret.

Working together, the planners completed their efforts in late 1975. They assigned primary importance to construction of a central sewage treatment plant to produce water of sufficient quality to be used for irrigation. (New government funds were necessary for this project because, although the World Bank had given Israel a loan in 1972 to construct a nationwide sewage system for urban areas, most communities in the Kinneret Basin were too small to qualify under this program.) The plan also recommended that agricultural uses on the shore be eliminated and that grazing cattle near the watercourses leading into the lake be prohibited, since the nutrients created by fertilizers and cattle wastes were a primary cause of eutrophication.

To replace agriculture, the planners recommended low-intensity recreational uses, such as campgrounds. These facilities would enable tourists to appreciate the historic amenities of the region in a pastoral setting, which would be more appropriate than a forest of high-rise hotels.

The planners also recommended that a modest number of hotels be permitted, but only in the existing city of Tiberias and in a second center to be created at the little community of Migdal, a short distance north of Tiberias. They emphasized that hotels must not proliferate along the entire lakeshore and strongly recommended *against* the Ministry of Tourism's proposal to develop a large hotel and tourism area at Aaqeb. The planners suggested that this area be placed in an extensive nature reserve. The remainder of the lakeshore would be devoted to outdoor recreation. A road would be constructed around the lake to provide access to picnic facilities and beaches as well as campgrounds.

The most controversial aspect of the plan was the proposed belt of low-intensity recreational land. At the time, only about 7 of the 35 miles of lakeshore were devoted to recreational use. The new plan was to triple this at the expense of agricultural land. Not unexpectedly, the farmers expressed strong opposition when the plan was presented at local public hearings which took place in the spring of 1976.

The land along much of the lakeshore belongs to various kibbutzim, many of whose members farmed the area when it was a dangerous frontier region. "These people haven't come here to be waiters," said Menahem Rol, chairman of the Jordan Valley Regional Council, which represents 21 farming settlements on the lake. He pointed out that the strip of land immediately adjoining the lake, on which bananas and dates are grown, is the most fertile in the area. Even Ein Gev, a kibbutz that operates a popular restaurant on the lakeshore and already makes 20 percent of its income from tourism, strongly objected to the plan. "The

Farmlands and settlements along shore of Lake Kinneret, across which boat is heading toward Tiberias. (Copyright National Geographic Society.)

planners want to make our land an open beach," said Uzi Keren, secretary of the kibbutz, "and we can't make any profit on that."

Promoters of more intensive tourism development along the lake were inclined to accept the plan, at least temporarily, but emphasized that they were merely biding their time. The Tourism Ministry put its plans for Aaqeb on the back burner. "We agreed to keeping it open," said Arye Efrat, chief planner for the ministry, but "this might or might not change in ten years."

The mayor of Tiberias also expressed reservations about the plan, particularly its proposals to develop neighboring Migdal as a rival tourist center. Nevertheless, he found it basically acceptable because it allows Tiberias as many hotels as it can reasonably expect in the near future. Migdal will not prove an attractive site for hotel builders, he believes, so when Tiberias reaches the level of hotel development proposed, the mayor will seek a revision of the plan to allow more.

The farmers may prove the most difficult to convince. Like most farmers, their attachment to land is strong—even stronger than in many other places, since the land of Israel has such religious and historical significance. Valerie Brachya of the Ministry of Interior's Environmental Protection Service has suggested that the plan's success depends on the farmers' becoming convinced they can turn a profit on tourism.

Making long-range plans has not been easy in Israel. Throughout the nation's existence, the Israelis have had to deal with major problems on short notice—wars, waves of immigrants, financial crises. Pragmatism is a way of life.

Tourist water-skiing in Lake Kinneret near Tiberias. (Photo courtesy Israel Government Tourist Office.)

Moreover, the Israelis cherish their image as pioneers. The development ethic is very strong. Heroism is associated with the original settlers. The environmental ethic, on the other hand, is new and strange to many older politicians. Even the most profit-oriented kibbutzim will acknowledge that Lake Kinneret is a very special place. But this is not by itself sufficient to ensure that the impact of development will be carefully evaluated. In Israel, as elsewhere in the world, there are factors prevalent today that detract from the special qualities of places.

The Specter of Placelessness

Throughout the world, places increasingly resemble one another. Technology that was once confined to the West can now be found everywhere. International communications media spread ideas, fashions, and fads rapidly, so that each of the world's places may seek to imitate the places deemed most beautiful, efficient, or modern.

When an individual is made to seem more like a number than a person, the process is described as "dehumanization." Much concern has been expressed about the tendencies of modern society to dehumanize people. Less concern has been expressed about an analogous tendency in the treatment of *places*, but the problem is equally real.

In a recent book, *Place and Placelessness*, Canadian geographer Edward Relph views with foreboding the rapid acceleration of the trend toward placelessness:

> Cultural and geographic uniformity is not, of course, an entirely new phenomenon. The spread of Greek civilisation, the Roman Empire, Christianity, or even the diffusion of the idea of the city, all involved the imposition of a homogeneity on formerly varied cultures and landscapes. What is new appears to be the grand scale and virtual absence of adaptation to local conditions of the present placelessness, and everywhere the shallowness of experience which it engenders and with which it is associated.[31]

Will an increasingly placeless society deprive life of some of its richness? Will commonplace and mediocre experiences replace the stimulation that results from an authentic sense of the special qualities of a place? For reasons implanted deep in their human and physical nature, says René Dubos, people search for distinctiveness in their surroundings.[32] What will happen as their quest is increasingly stymied by a society heavy with pressures toward uniformity?

Relph classifies these pressures into two basic categories: self-conscious techniques based on desires to achieve efficiency, and unselfconscious techniques resulting from an uncritical acceptance of mass values.[33]

The English system of regional planning discussed in chapter 5 is a good example of a worldwide trend toward placeless planning, cited by Relph as an example of his first category:

> Much physical and social planning is founded on an implicit assumption that space is uniform and objects and activities can be manipulated and freely located within it; differentiation by significance is of little importance and places are reduced to simple locations with their greatest quality being development potential. . . . [I]t is but a short jump from this to the idea that a major

aim of planning is to overcome spatial incongruities and inefficiencies. . . . This is indeed *technique*-dominated planning, divorced from places as we know and experience them in our daily lives, and quite casually ignoring or obliterating them.[34]

It is against this type of technique-dominated planning that the French, in their planning for Aquitaine (discussed in chapter 2), are rebelling. Yet to a realistic observer it must appear that Biasini and his compatriots are swimming against a powerful tide.

Relph's second category—the worldwide spread of mass concepts of status or beauty—is equally hard to combat. Western intellectuals decry the willingness of exotic cultures to destroy their authenticity by accepting modernization, but to the intended audience these warnings often seem patronizing. Aren't we good enough for high-rise buildings, ask the citizens of Jerusalem?

As peoples of the world become more aware of each other's fashions, skills, and conveniences, they increasingly ask why they can't have the same. World travel has increased this awareness, and many commentators have criticized tourism as contributing to the trend toward placelessness.

Seeing Ourselves

It is mass tourism, not the selective traveling of more sophisticated tourists, that has been accused of contributing to placelessness. The mass tourist is depicted as one for whom the act of going has become more important than the place to which he goes.[35] He can find uniform lodgings, uniform conveyances; precooked food, prearranged entertainment; tea as mum makes it in Palma, beer from Frankfurt on the Zeeland coast. The mass tourist, says Daniel Boorstin, prefers to be "no place in particular—in limbo . . . [T]ravel itself has become a pseudo event. . . . [W]e look into a mirror instead of out a window, and we see only ourselves."[36]

People in the tourism business suggest that this tendency toward uniformity is a result of an unprecedented increase in the numbers of new tourists, who are typically nervous about unfamiliar places. The travel explosion resulting from the jet plane, automobile, economic prosperity, and increased leisure has created millions of inexperienced travelers. Working-class Englishmen, whose parents thought a week in Blackpool a luxury, now visit Spain and Yugoslavia. Japanese, whose grandparents never left their village, now circle the globe.

The number of experienced travelers has also increased, though they form so small a percentage of the total that the mass tourist has become the stereotype. As today's mass tourists become tomorrow's seasoned travelers, however, they will likely be more inclined to seek out the unfamiliar and exotic.[37] In the process, they may develop greater respect and appreciation for the places they visit, and thereby become more welcome tourists.[38]

The traveler can often perceive and define the special qualities of a place better than those who live there.[39] He sees it with a fresh eye, while the resident may be so familiar with his surroundings that he overlooks what others find attractive. An old proverb of the Ruanda says succinctly: "Much traveling teaches how to see."[40]

Hokusai was one of many artists whose travels were a fundamental part of his creativity. To Gertrude Stein, the creative force was a "romance" born from the land and air of one's birthplace, but not nurtured until combined with recollections of experiences in other places and cultures. So, she said, "America is my country and Paris is my home town. . . ."[41] Creativity, according to René Dubos, is a consequence of the desire for adventure.[42]

Ordinary tourists can learn the lore of the aborigines at Ayers Rock, or the legacy of the Mayans at Cancún, or discover something about new life-styles in Amsterdam. And in some places, tourists can become part of the solution to problems: by camping on the shores of Lake Kinneret; joining in the drive to prevent overcrowding at Westerland; petitioning to preserve Bayswater's bed-and-breakfast hotels. Tourists have many opportunities to be creative.

How will the placelessness of modern tourism affect these opportunities? Are Boorstin's tourists, who look out the window and see themselves, deprived of the creative experience? That tourists see many familiar things in far away places is not without benefit. The "ugly American" who comes home expressing surprise that hotels in a developing country have elevators and flush toilets has at least learned which qualities of American life are not special.

Material progress is bringing common features to many parts of the globe. Although a tourist may criticize the proliferation of the commonplace, a resident may well view "commonplace" items as "progress," allowing him to catch up with people in more economically advanced areas. The benefits of modern international culture need not be rejected, but must be integrated carefully with the special qualities of places. And if, in the end, the tourist is impressed with the similarities as well as the differences; if he recognizes that many places in the world share qualities with his own; if he experiences the common thread of humanity in the world's people, isn't this a useful lesson?

To "see ourselves" in other places is to learn something about ourselves and the places in which we live. Indeed, perhaps the most creative aspect of travel is not what one finds out about the places visited, but what one finds out about home. The traveler may realize that some qualities he once thought were special are not actually so special after all, while once familiar qualities assume a new significance.

The Sojourner's Home

For the Israelis, of all the world's peoples, the image of the traveler returning to his homeland and seeing it with a new eye is most appropriate. Although the Israelis may be pragmatic pioneers, one can be optimistic about Lake Kinneret because of an even more basic aspect of the Israeli character—their attitude toward the land in which they live.

The land of Israel is more than just a place the Jewish people happen to be. It has a deeper significance, for it is the land that has called the Jewish people back again and again. Lake Kinneret's historical associations, and its present significance as a water source, give it unique qualities that should temper the desire for immediate self-interest. Throughout the world, it is the recognition that places are special that seems most likely to augur a successful development process, and gives hope for the future of the "garden that has no end."

The Israelis, because of their history, realize that sensible development decisions cannot be made by weighing only today's pleasures and sorrows. Israel as a *place* transcends individual Jews or generations of Jews. "We are strangers

Headwaters of Jordan River, with Golan Heights in background. (Photo by author.)

before thee, and sojourners, as all our fathers were," said David in his final prayer. "Our days on earth are like a shadow, and there is no abiding."[43]

Everyone is a sojourner, a traveler, a tourist—for whom there is no abiding. The land a person visits, and the land in which he lives, is the heritage of generations yet unborn. Can the tourist contribute to the quality of that heritage?

People who become aware of the special qualities of one place can easily broaden their consciousness of land in general. Those who recognize that their neighborhood has an individual character will see qualities in other neighborhoods that they might not have noticed before. They may begin to look upon a larger community as a special place. And they should, in turn, be more concerned about the qualities of their region and state and even their nation. Concern for special places is a stepping stone—a consciousness raising. Defining a geographic area and emphasizing its intrinsic merits helps people sharpen their perceptions, reorient their values, and take a new look at the world.

The recognition that areas have special qualities should not encourage petty factionalism or a chauvinistic sense of superiority. Rather, it must lead to the realization that the whole world is a "special place." Barbara Ward phrased it eloquently. "We can hope to survive in all our prized diversity" only if "we can achieve an ultimate loyalty to our single, beautiful and vulnerable planet Earth."[44] This "enlargement of allegiance" must be achieved without wiping out respect for the smaller places that can be more easily comprehended. It is respect for the special qualities of specific places, in fact, that underlies a broader allegiance toward the world at large.

By broadening horizons, the same attitudes can be applied to small and large areas. Technicians can control the environmental impact of development if the consumer demands it. If the public would view the whole world as a special place having amenities that need to be carefully maintained, then the technology could be found, the laws written, the plans prepared to maintain these amenities. If tourism is used to enhance these attitudes, then future generations can be left a better world in the wake of the tourist.

REFERENCES

1. Jacques Ellul, *The Meaning of the City* (Grand Rapids, Mich.: William B. Eerdmans, 1970), p. 144.

2. Mark Twain, *The Innocents Abroad* (New York: Harper & Brothers, 1869), vol. 2, p. 326.

3. I. W. J. Hopkins, *Jerusalem: The Land Where East Meets West* (London: John Lane, 1907), p. 30.

4. Herman Melville, *Clarel* (New York: Hendricks House, 1960), p. 408, pp. 6-7.

5. David Amiran, Arie Shacher, and Israel Kimhi, *Urban Georgraphy of Jerusalem* (New York: Walter DeGruyter, 1973), pp. 33 and 25.

6. Myron Goldfinger, *Villages in the Sun: Mediterranean Community Architecture* (New York: Praeger, 1969), p. 9.

7. Mark Twain, *The Innocents Abroad*, vol. 2, p. 220.

8. Louis Turner and John Ash, *The Golden Hordes: International Tourism and the Pleasure Periphery* (London: Constable, 1975), p. 290. See also Dennison Nash, "Tourism As a Form of Imperialism," in Valene L. Smith, ed., *Hosts and Guests: The Anthropology of Tourism* (Philadelphia: University of Pennsylvania Press, 1977), p. 33.

9. Daniel J. Boorstin, *The Image, or What Happened to the American Dream* (New York: Atheneum, 1962), p. 103.

10. E. J. Mishan, *Making The World Safe For Pornography, And Other Intellectual Fashions* (London: Alcove Press, 1973), pp. 242-43.

11. E. J. Mishan, *Growth: The Price We Pay* (London: Staples Press, 1969), p. 83.

12. Aldo Leopold, *A Sand County Almanac* (New York: Oxford University Press, 1949), p. 173.

13. Gerardo Budowski, "Tourism and Environmental Conservation: Conflict, Coexistence, or Symbiosis," *Environmental Conservation*, vol. 3 (Spring 1976), p. 31.

14. Yoram Blizovsky, "The Role of Tourism in the Economy," in Chaim H. Klein, ed., *The Second Million: Israel Tourist Industry, Past, Present, Future* (Tel Aviv: Amir Publishing, 1973), pp. 117-28.

15. Ibid.

16. Michael Peters, *International Tourism* (London: Hutchinson & Company, 1969), p. 88.

17. George Young, *Tourism: Blessing or Blight?* (London: Penguin, 1973), p. 137.

18. Samuel Federmann, "The Hotel Sector," in Chaim H. Klein, ed., *The Second Million: Israel Tourist Industry, Past, President, Future* (Tel Aviv: Amir Publishing, 1973), pp. 194, 196.

19. Yoram Blizovsky, "The Role of Tourism in the Economy," p. 111.

20. Ministry of Tourism (Israel), *A Survey of Tourism in Israel* (Jerusalem: 1973).

21. *Jerusalem Post*, January 8, 1976.

22. Moshe Kol, "Introduction," in Chaim H. Klein, ed., *The Second Million: Israel Tourist Industry, Past, Present, Future* (Tel Aviv: Amir Publishing, 1973), p. 12.

23. *Jerusalem Post*, January 8, 1976.

24. *International Herald Tribune*, July 9, 1975.

25. Arthur Kutcher, *The New Jerusalem: Planning and Politics* (Cambridge, Mass.: M.I.T. Press, 1975), p. 71.

26. *International Herald Tribune*, July 9, 1975.

27. *Jerusalem Post*, August 12, 1976.

28. Charles E. Gearing, William W. Swart, and Turgut Var, *Planning for Tourism Development: Quantitative Approaches* (New York: Praeger, 1976), p. 151.

29. Arthur Kutcher, *The New Jerusalem: Planning and Politics*, pp. 93-94, 97.

30. Teddy Kollek with Amos Kollek, *For Jerusalem* (New York: Random House, 1978), p. 226.

31. John M. Bryden, *Tourism and Development: A Case Study of the Commonwealth Caribbean*

(Cambridge: Cambridge University Press, 1973), pp. 135-36.

32. National Tourism Review Commission, *Destination USA* (Washington, D.C.: Government Printing Office, 1973), vol. 2, p. 9.

33. Organisation for Economic Co-operation and Development, *Tourism Policy and International Tourism in OECD Member Countries* (Paris: OECD, 1977), p. 173.

34. Organisation for Economic Co-operation and Development, *Tourism Policy and International Tourism in OECD Member Countries* (Paris: OECD, 1974), p. 77.

35. Organisation for Economic Co-operation and Development, *Tourism Policy and International Tourism in OECD Member Countries* (Paris: OECD, 1977), p. 61.

36. H. Robinson, *A Geography of Tourism* (London: Macdonald & Evans, 1976), p. xxii.

37. English Tourist Board, *Tourism and Conservation: Report of a One-Day Conference* (London: English Tourist Board, 1974), p. 21.

38. A. J. Burkart and S. Medlik, *Tourism: Past, Present, and Future* (London: Heinemann, 1974), pp. 193-94.

39. Vojislav Popovic, *Tourism in Eastern Africa* (Munich: Weltflorum Verlag, 1972), p. 161.

40. English Tourist Board, *Tourism and Conservation: Report of a One-Day Conference*, p. 34.

41. George Young, *Tourism: Blessing or Blight?*, pp. 151-52.

42. Raymond F. Dasmann, John P. Milton, and Peter H. Freeman, *Ecological Principles for Economic Development* (New York: John Wiley & Sons, 1973), p. 9.

43. See Garrett Hardin, "The Tragedy of the Commons," *Science*, vol. 162 (December 13, 1968), pp. 1243-48; Fred Hirsch, *Social Limits to Growth* (Cambridge, Mass.: Harvard University Press, 1976), p. 5.

44. Jacques Ellul, *The Meaning of the City*, p. 146.

CHAPTER 1 Mexico Reaches for the Moon (pp. 37-57)

1. Andrew Hepburn, *Great Resorts of North America* (New York: Doubleday & Company, 1965), p. 214; Louis Turner and John Ash, *The Golden Hordes: International Tourism and the Pleasure Periphery* (London: Constable, 1975), p. 94.

2. FONATUR *(Fondo Nacional de Fomento al Turismo), Estudio Sobre la Actividad Turistica en Acapulco* (Mexico City: FONATUR, 1973), p. 16.

3. Ibid., pp. 20-21.

4. John L. Stephens, *Incidents of Travel in Yucatan* (New York: Dover, 1963), vol. 2, p. 244.

5. Mario Schjetnam, "The Cancun Strip: Mexico's Bid for Touristic Dollars," *Landscape Architecture*, November 1977, p. 491.

6. *Travel Weekly*, May 10, 1976, p. 51.

7. Frans Blom, *The Conquest of Yucatan* (Boston: Houghton Mifflin Company, 1936), p. 84.

8. *New York Times*, February 20, 1977.

9. *New York Times*, March 13, 1977.

10. Felix Sanchez, "Cancun: Superb Site, Blue Water, But an 'Absence of Good Urban Design Principles' " *Landscape Architecture*, November 1977, p. 500.

11. T. Patrick Culbert, *The Lost Civilization: The Story of the Classic Maya* (New York: Harper & Row, 1974), p. 117. Culbert's thesis has recently been supported by scientists from the University of Florida. See *Ft. Lauderdale News*, May 17, 1978.

12. J. Eric S. Thompson, *The Rise and Fall of Maya Civilization*, 2nd ed. (Norman, Okla.: University of Oklahoma Press, 1966), pp. 135, 263.

CHAPTER 2 France Creates New Rivieras (pp. 59-75)

1. Alec Waugh, "Return to the Riviera," *Illustrated London News*, April 1975, p. 58.

2. French Embassy Press and Information Division, *France,* October-November 1975, p. 3.

3. Arthur Haulot, *Tourisme et Environnement: La Recherche d'un Equilibre* (Marabout, France: Verviers, 1974), pp. 289-90.

4. Ann Louise Strong, *Planned Urban Environments* (Baltimore: The Johns Hopkins Press, 1971), p. 367.

5. Délégation à l'Amènagement du Territoire et à l'Action Régionale, *France: Real Estate Market* (Paris: La Documentation Française, 1975), pp. 49-50.

6. Ann Louise Strong, *Planned Urban Environments,* p. 367.

7. Lloyd Rodwin, *Nations and Cities: A Comparison of Strategies for Urban Growth* (Boston: Houghton Mifflin Company, 1970), p. 203.

8. Délégation à l'Amènagement du Territoire et à l'Action Régionale, *France: Real Estate Market,* p. 47.

9. P. Florenson, *Over-all Strategies and Policy Measures for the Implementation of Tourism Development Plans,* a paper prepared for the Symposium on the Planning and Development of the Tourist Industry in the ECE Region, Dubrovnik, October 13-18, 1875, p. 4.

10. Melvin Benarde and Anita Benarde, *Beach Holidays from Portugal to Israel* (New York: Dodd, Mead & Company, 1974), pp. 91-92.

11. Organisation for Economic Co-operation and Development, *Tourism Policy and International Tourism in OECD Member Countries* (Paris: OECD, 1976), p. 137. See also Sophie Lannes, "The French and their Holidays," *New Society,* July 31, 1975, p. 239.

12. Michel Schifres, "A Place in the Country," *The Guardian Weekly* (London), July 26, 1974, p. 13.

13. George Perkins Marsh, *Man and Nature* (Cambridge, Mass.: Harvard University Press, Belknap Press, 1965), pp. 417-20.

14. *Le Monde,* February 1967.

15. Délégation à l'Amènagement du Territoire et à l'Action Regionale, *France: Real Estate Market,* p. 59.

16. Mission Interministerielle pour l'Amènagement de la Côte Aquitaine, *La Mi-Parcours: Printemps 1976* (Bordeaux: 1976), pp. 28-29.

17. *Le Monde,* February 2, 1974, p. 13.

18. Mission Interministerielle pour l'Amènagement de la Côte Aquitaine, *Nouvelles de la Côte Aquitaine,* March 1978, p. 8.

19. Mission Interministerielle pour l'Amènagement de la Côte Aquitaine, *La Mi-Parcours: Printemps 1976,* p. 57.

20. Ibid.

21. See, generally, John Clark, *Coastal Ecosystems: Ecological Considerations for Management of the Coastal Zone* (Washington: The Conservation Foundation, 1974).

22. Délégation à l'Amènagement du Territoire et à l'Action Regionale, *France: Real Estate Market,* p. 62.

23. Ibid.

24. Mission Interministerielle pour l'Amènagement de la Côte Aquitaine, *Nouvelles de la Côte Aquitaine,* June 1978, p. 1.

25. William K. Reilly, ed., *The Use of Land: A Citizens' Policy Guide to Urban Growth* (New York: Thomas Y. Crowell, 1973), pp. 219, 223. See also George Lefcoe, "When Governments Become Land Developers: Notes on the Public-Sector Experience in the Netherlands and California," *Southern California Law Review,* vol. 51 (1978), p. 196. See, generally, Neal Alison Roberts, ed., *The Government Land Developers: Studies of Public Land-Ownership in Seven Countries* (Lexington, Mass.: Lexington Books, D.C. Heath & Company, 1977).

26. H. C. Coombs, "Matching Ecological and Economic Realities," Australian Conserva-

tion Foundation Occasional Publication No. 9 (Melbourne: June 1972), pp. 8, 12.

27. See Max Nicholson, *The Environmental Revolution* (London: Hodder & Stoughton, 1970), p. 282.

CHAPTER 3   **Dreamtime at Ayers Rock**   (pp. 79-98)

1. John Nance, *The Gentle Tasaday: A Stone Age People in the Philippine Rain Forest* (New York: Harcourt Brace Jovanovich, 1975), p. ix.
2. John Derek Mulvaney, *The Prehistory of Australia* (London: Thames and Hudson, 1969), p. 164.
3. Douglass Baglin and David R. Moore, *People of the Dreamtime: The Australian Aborigines* (New York: John Weatherhill, 1970), p. 51.
4. Frederick D. McCarthy, *Australia's Aborigines: Their Life and Culture* (Melbourne: Colorgravure, 1957), p. 60; Geoffrey Blainey, *Triumph of the Nomads: A History of Aboriginal Australia* (Woodstock, N.Y.: The Overlook Press, 1976), p. 153.
5. Aboriginal Land Rights Commission, *Second Report* (Canberra: Australian Government Publishing Service, 1974), p. 138; Allen Keast, *Australia and the Pacific Islands: A Natural History* (New York: Random House, 1966), p. 178.
6. Ronald M. Berndt and Catherine H. Berndt, *The First Australians,* 3rd ed. (Sydney: Ure Smith, 1974), p. 39.
7. Frederick D. McCarthy, *Australia's Aborigines: Their Life and Culture,* p. 34.
8. Ronald M. Berndt and Catherine H. Berndt, *The First Australians,* p. 43.
9. David R. Harris, ''Land of Plenty on Cape York Peninsula,'' *The Geographical Magazine,* vol. 48, no. 11 (August 1976), p. 657. See also John C. Taylor, ''Mapping Techniques and the Reconstruction of Traditional Aboriginal Culture,'' *Australian Institute of Aboriginal Studies Newsletter,* New Series, no. 5 (January 1976), p. 34.
13. Kenneth Maddock, *The Australian Aborigines: A Portrait of Their Society* (Sydney: Allen Lane, 1971), p. 27.
14. Aboriginal Land Rights Commission, *Second Report,* p. 138; E. P. Milliken, ''Northern Territory Protection and Preservation of Aboriginal Sites,'' in Robert Edwards, ed., *The Preservation of Australia's Aboriginal Heritage,* Australian Aboriginal Studies, no. 54 (Canberra: Australian Institute of Aboriginal Studies, 1975), p. 21.
15. Aboriginal Land Rights Commission, *Second Report,* p. 138. See Claude Levi-Strauss, *The Savage Mind,* trans. George Weidenfeld (Chicago: University of Chicago Press, 1966), p. 85.
16. Frederick G. G. Rose. *The Wind of Change in Central Australia* (Berlin: Akademie Verlag, 1965), p. 27.
17. Elspeth Huxley, *Their Shining Eldorado: A Journey Through Australia* (London: Chatto & Windus, 1967), p. 267.
18. Charles P. Mountfort, *Ayers Rock: Its People, Their Beliefs and Their Art* (Sydney: Angus & Robertson, 1965), p. 144.
19. Ibid, p. 198.
20. Baldwin Spencer, *Wanderings in Wild Australia* (London: Macmillan & Co., 1928), vol. 1, pp. 169-172.
21. See, generally, F. D. McCarthy, ed., *Aboriginal Antiquities in Australia: Their Nature and Preservation,* Australian Aboriginal Studies, no. 22 (Canberra: Australian Institute of Aboriginal Studies, 1970).
22. John Derek Mulvaney, *The Prehistory of Australia,* p. 175.
23. Ronald M. Berndt and Catherine H. Berndt, *The Barbarians: An Anthropoligical View* (London: C. A. Watts, 1971), p. 74.
24. Charles P. Mountfort, *Ayers Rock: Its People, Their Beliefs and Their Art,* p. 74.

25. Bill Harney, *The Significance of Ayers Rock for Aborigines* (Canberra: Northern Territory Reserves Board, 1970), p. 160.

26. Charles Darwin, *The Voyage of the Beagle* (New York: Bantam Books, 1958), p. 375.

27. *The Australian* (Canberra), August 27, 1976, p. 4.

28. *The Age* (Melbourne), July 14, 1977. Brian Beedham, "Second to None: Survey of Australia," *The Economist*, March 27, 1976, p. 8. See also H. H. Finlayson, *The Red Centre: Man and Beast in the Heart of Australia*, 3rd ed. (Sydney: Angus & Robertson, 1936), pp. 93-95.

29. Ronald M. Berndt and Catherine H. Berndt, *The First Australians*, p. 125. See, generally, John W. Bennett, "Anticipation, Adaptation and the Concept of Culture in Anthropology," *Science*, vol. 192 (May 28, 1976), p. 847.

30. Australian Information Service, *Australia Handbook: 1974* (Canberra: Australian Government Publishing Service, 1974), p. 158.

31. Australian Information Service, *Australia's Uranium Policy* (Canberra: Australian Government Publishing Service, 1977), p. 3.

32. David R. Anderson, "A Black Sees His Problems," *The Bulletin* (Australia), April 24, 1976, p. 35. For a comparison of the land rights of the Australian aborigines and the Canadian Eskimos, see Peter F. Rhodes, "The Report of the Australian Aboriginal Land Rights Commission—A Comment," *Saskatchewan Law Review*, vol. 39 (1974-75), p. 199.

33. Committee of Inquiry into the National Estate, *Report of the National Estate* (Canberra: Australian Government Publishing Service, 1974), p. 169. See Ronald M. Berndt and Catherine H. Berndt, *The First Australians*, p. 146.

34. Raymond F. Dasmann, John P. Milton, and Peter H. Freeman, *Ecological Principles for Economic Development* (New York: John Wiley & Sons, 1973), p. 127.

35. R. D. Piesse, "Tourism, Aboriginal Antiquities, and Public Education," in F. D. McCarthy, ed., *Aboriginal Antiquities in Australia: Their Nature and Preservation*, p. 180.

36. Geoffrey Sawer, "Conservation and the Law," in A. B. Costin and H. J. Frith, eds., *Conservation*, rev. ed. (Ringwood, Victoria, Aus.: Penguin Books, 1974), p. 270.

37. Phyl Wallace and Noel Wallace, *Children of the Desert* (Melbourne: Thomas Nelson, 1968), p. 59.

38. Ibid., p. 61. See also Noel M. Wallace, "Pitjantjatjara Wiltja or White Man's House?" *Australian Institute of Aboriginal Studies Newsletter*, New Series, no. 6 (June 1976).

39. Australia House of Representatives, Standing Committee on Environment and Conservation, *Report on Ayers Rock-Mount Olga National Park*, Parliamentary Paper no. 215 (Canberra: 1973), p. 9.

40. Dean MacCannell, *The Tourist: A New Theory of the Leisure Class* (New York: Schocken, 1976), p. 42.

41. Dartington Amenity Research Trust, *Amenity and Tourism in Remote Rural Areas* (Exeter, Eng.: 1969), p. 15.

42. P. Stanev, "Harmful Ecological Consequences of the Development of the Tourist Industry and Their Prevention," a paper presented at the ECE symposium on the Planning and Development of the Tourist Industry in the ECE Region, Dubrovnik, October 13-18, 1975, p. 3.

43. *The Economist*, January 29, 1977, p. 27.

44. Quoted in A. J. Goldman, "The Adequacy of Management Science Technology for Nonmilitary Applications in the Federal Government," in Michael J. White, Michael Radnor, and David A. Tansik, eds., *Management and Policy Science in American Government* (Lexington, Mass.: Lexington Books, D.C. Heath & Company, 1975), p. 135.

45. Theodore Roszak, *Where the Wasteland Ends* (New York: Doubleday, 1972), p. 252.

46. David Halberstam, *The Best and the Brightest* (New York: Random House, 1972), p. 247.

47. Laurence H. Tribe, "Policy Science: Analysis or Ideology," *Philosophy and Public*

Affairs, vol. 2 (1972), p. 96.

48. Stuart Hampshire, *Morality and Pessimism* (Cambridge: Cambridge University Press, 1972), p. 7.
49. Laurence H. Tribe, "Policy Science: Analysis or Ideology," p. 75.
50. William H. Matthews, "Objective and Subjective Judgments in Environmental Impact Analysis," *Environmental Conservation,* vol. 2 (Summer 1975), p. 122.
51. Peter Hall, "Manpower and Education," in Peter Cowan, ed., *The Future of Planning* (London: Heinemann, 1973), p. 53.
52. Kenneth E. Boulding, "A Ballad of Ecological Awareness," in M. Taghi Farvar and John P. Milton, eds., *The Careless Technology: Ecology and International Development* (Garden City, N.Y.: The Natural History Press, 1972), p. 157.
53. Kath Walker, *We Are Going: Poems* (Brisbane: The Jacaranda Press, 1964), pp. 40-41.
54. Robert Goodman, *After the Planners* (New York: Simon & Schuster, 1971), p. 172.
55. See Harvey Brooks, "Environmental Decision Making: Analysis and Values," in Laurence H. Tribe, Corinne S. Schelling, and John Voss, eds., *When Values Conflict: Essays on Environmental Analysis, Discourse and Decision* (Cambridge, Mass.: Ballinger Publishing Company, 1976), pp. 115, 127-28.
56. E. J. Mishan, *Cost-Benefit Analysis: An Introduction* (New York: Praeger, 1971), p. 175.
57. Yehezkel Dror, *Design for Policy Sciences* (New York: American Elsevier, 1971), pp. 52-53.
58. See Peter Self, *Econocrats and the Policy Process: The Politics and Philosophy of Cost-Benefit Analysis* (London: Macmillan, 1975), p. 202; Kevin Lynch, *Managing the Sense of a Region* (Cambridge, Mass.: MIT Press, 1976), p. 78.
59. Laurence H. Tribe, "Ways Not to Think About Plastic Trees: New Foundations for Environmental Law," *Yale Law Journal,* vol. 83 (1974), p. 1340.

CHAPTER 4 Drifting through Amsterdam (pp. 99-112)

1. Selwyn Gurney Champion, *Racial Proverbs* (New York: Barnes & Noble, 1964), p. 344.
2. Daniel J. Boorstin, *The Image, or What Happened to the American Dream* (New York: Atheneum, 1972), p. 84.
3. Robert W. McIntosh, *Tourism Principles, Practices, and Philosophies* (Columbus, Ohio: Grid, Inc., 1972), p. 63.
4. Dean MacCannell, *The Tourist: A New Theory of the Leisure Class* (New York: Schocken, 1976), pp. 10, 177.
5. Ibid., p. 155.
6. Erik Cohen, "Toward a Sociology of International Tourism," *Social Research,* vol. 39 (1972), pp. 167-68.
7. Ibid., pp. 177-78.
8. Erik Cohen, "Nomads from Affluence: Notes on the Phenomenon of Drifter-Tourism," *International Journal of Comparative Sociology,* vol. 14 (1973), p. 95.
9. Barbara Beck, "Too Good to Be True: Survey of Holland," *The Economist,* May 29, 1976, p. 23.
10. See William Z. Shetter, *The Pillars of Society: Six Centuries of Civilization in the Netherlands* (The Hague: Martinus Nijhoff, 1971).
11. Frederick A. Pottle, ed., *Boswell in Holland 1763-64* (New York: McGraw-Hill, 1952), p. 289.
12. Thomas Nugent, *The Grand Tour,* 2nd ed. (London: D. Browne, 1956), vol. 1, p. 79.
13. Geoffrey Cotterell, *Amsterdam: The Life of a City* (Boston: Little, Brown & Company 1972), p. 327.
14. For a discussion of other examples of this phenomenon, see Dean MacCannell, *The*

15. Geoffrey Cotterell, *Amsterdam: The Life of a City,* p. 335.

16. Ibid., p. 339.

17. Frank E. Huggett, *The Modern Netherlands* (New York: Praeger, 1971), p. 221.

18. Louis Turner and John Ash, *The Golden Hordes: International Tourism and the Pleasure Periphery* (London: Constable, 1975), p. 276.

19. See Dean MacCannell, *The Tourist: A New Theory of the Leisure Class,* pp. 86-87.

20. George Young, *Tourism: Blessing or Blight?* (London: Penguin, 1973), p. 141; Louis Turner and John Ash, *The Golden Hordes,* p. 245.

21. R. G. Scott, *The Development of Tourism in Fiji Since 1923* (Suva: Fiji Visitors Bureau, 1970), p. 1.

22. Daniel Boorstin, *The Image,* p. 103. See also Ann Crittendon "Tourism's Terrible Toll," *International Wildlife,* March-April 1975, p. 4.

23. Erik Cohen, "Toward a Sociology of International Tourism," p. 170. See Dean Mac-Cannell, *The Tourist: A New Theory of the Leisure Class,* p. 178.

24. Claude Levi-Strauss, *Tristes Tropiques* (New York: Atheneum, 1974), p. 27 See also Theron Nuñez, "Touristic Studies in Anthropological Perspective," in Valene L. Smith, ed., *Hosts and Guests: The Anthropology of Tourism* (Philadelphia: University of Pennsylvania Press, 1977), p. 207.

25. Garrett Eckbo, "The Landscape of Tourism," *Landscape,* vol. 18, no. 2, (Spring-Summer 1969), p. 29.

26. Quoted in Louis Turner and John Ash, *The Golden Hordes,* p. 141.

27. V. E. Ritchie, "The Honest Broker in the Cultural Marketplace," a paper delivered at the Conference on the Impact of Tourism on Development of Pacific Island Countries, East-West Center, Honolulu, May 1974, pp. 12, 22; also see, René Dubos, *A God Within* (New York: Charles Scribner's Sons, 1972), pp. 185-86; Arthur Haulot, *Tourisme et Environnement: La Recherche d'un Equilibre* (Marabout: Verviers, 1974), p. 89.

28. Margaret Mead, *World Enough: Rethinking the Future* (Boston: Little, Brown & Company, 1975), p. 107.

29. Russell Baker, "Jet-set Fret," *New York Times Magazine,* April 11, 1976, p. 6.

30. *St. Petersburg Times,* June 20, 1976.

31. W. H. Auden, *Van Gogh: A Self-Portrait* (Greenwich, Conn.: New York Graphic Society, 1961), p. 333.

CHAPTER 5   Sprawl Is Beautiful?   (pp. 115-149)

1. Organisation for Economic Co-operation and Development, *Tourism Policy and International Tourism in OECD Member Countries* (Paris: OECD, 1977), appendices.

2. Jost Krippendorf, *Die Landschaftsfresser* (Bern: Hallwag Press, 1975), pp. 38-39.

3. Ella Odmann and Gun-Britt Dahlberg, *Urbanization in Sweden: Means and Methods for the Planning* (Stockholm: Allmanna Forlaget, 1970), pp. 40-42. See also Fred Hirsch, *Social Limits to Growth* (Cambridge, Mass.: Harvard University Press, 1976), pp. 28, 32-36.

4. *The Economist,* May 20, 1978, p. 95.

5. Karel Capek, *Letters from Holland* (New York: G. P. Putnam's Sons, 1933), p. 99.

6. Edmondo DeAmicis, *Holland,* trans. Helen Zimmern (Philadelphia: Porter & Coates, 1894), vol. 1, p. 31.

7. Frank E. Huggett, *The Modern Netherlands* (New York: Praeger, 1971), p. 179.

8. Jost Krippendorf, *Die Landschaftsfresser,* p. 42.

9. A. A. H. C. van Onzenoort, "Outdoor Recreation Planning in the Netherlands," *Planning and Development in the Netherlands,* vol. 7 (The Hague: Government Printing, 1973), p. 51.

10. For a more detailed exposition of Dutch planning law, see René Crince LeRoy, "The Netherlands: The Dutch Physical Planning Act," in J. F. Garner, ed., *Planning Law in Western Europe* (Amsterdam: North-Holland Publishing Company, 1975).

11. Netherlands, Ministry of Housing and Physical Planning, *Report on Physical Planning in the Netherlands* (The Hague: 1971), p. 28.

12. Urban Development Study Group, Technical University of Delft, *Second Homes: Policy Research in Westerschouwen* (Delft: 1974), sec. 3.4.

13. Ibid., sec. 5.3. For a description of analogous American experience, see George Lefcoe, "When Governments Become Land Developers: Notes on the Public-sector Experience in the Netherlands and California," *Southern California Law Review*, vol. 51 (1978), pp. 204-5.

14. Ann Louise Strong, *Planned Urban Environments* (Baltimore: The Johns Hopkins Press, 1971), p. 258.

15. Max G. Neutze, *The Price of Land and Land Use Planning: Policy Instruments in the Urban Land Market* (Paris: OECD, 1973), pp. 53-60; George Lefcoe, "When Governments Become Land Developers: Notes on the Public-sector Experience in the Netherlands and California," *Southern California Law Review*, vol. 51 (1978), pp. 208-45.

16. S. J. Simon, *Why You Lose at Bridge* (New York: Simon & Schuster, 1946), p. 81.

17. Washington Irving, *The Sketch Book* (New York: Dodd, Mead & Co., 1954), pp. 90-91, 95.

18. John Betjeman, "The Newest Bath Guide," in *A Nip in the Air* (New York: W. W. Norton, 1974), pp. 17-18.

19. William Wordsworth, "The Tables Turned," in Thomas Hutchinson, ed., *The Poetical Works of Wordsworth* (London: Oxford University Press, 1936), p. 377.

20. Inigo Jones, *The Most Notable Antiquity of Britain Vulgarly Called Stone-Henge, on Salisbury Plain Restored,* 2d ed. (London: D. Browne, Jr., 1725), p. 7.

21. A. L. Owen, *The Famous Druids: A Survey of Three Centuries of English Literature on the Druids* (Oxford: Clarendon Press, 1962), p. 24; Nora K. Chadwick, *The Druids* (Cardiff: University of Wales Press, 1966), p. 34.

22. William Butler Yeats, "To Ireland in The Coming Times," *The Collected Poems of W. B. Yeats* (New York: Macmillan, 1963), pp. 49-50.

23. Lewis Keeble, *Town Planning at the Crossroads* (London: The Estates Gazette, 1961), p. 8.

24. Gordon E. Cherry, *The Evolution of British Town Planning* (London: Leonard Hill, 1974), p. 39.

25. Lewis Keeble, *Town Planning at the Crossroads*, p. 7.

26. Peter Hall, Harry Gracey, Roy Drewelt, and Ray Thomas, *The Containment of Urban England* (London: George Allen & Unwin, 1973), p. 107.

27. Ebenezer Howard, *Garden Cities of Tomorrow*, F. J. Osborn, ed. (Cambridge, Mass.: The MIT Press, 1965), p. 3.

28. H. Robinson, *A Geography of Tourism* (London: Macdonald & Evans, 1976), p. 234.

29. J. Allan Patmore, *Land and Leisure* (London: Penguin, 1972), p. 134.

30. *Torbay Times*, May 14, 1976.

31. K. J. Gregory, "Face of the Southwest Is Its Fortune," *Geographical Magazine*, vol. 48 (1976), p. 544.

32. South West Economic Planning Council, *Second Homes in the South West* (London: Her Majesty's Stationery Office, 1975).

33. David Mahon, *No Place in the Country: A Report on Second Homes in England and Wales* (London: Shelter—National Campaign for the Homeless, 1973), p. 9.

34. Devon Conservation Forum, *Urbanization in Devon* (Exeter: Devon Conservation Forum, 1976), p. 10.

35. Ewan Clarkson, "Drought," *Audubon*, vol. 78, no. 6 (November 1976), p. 20.

36. James L. Sundquist, *Dispersing Population: What America Can Learn from Europe* (Washington: The Brookings Institution, 1975), p. 57.

37. J. D. McCallum, "U.K. Regional Policy 1964-72.," in Gordon Cameron and Lowdon Wingo, eds., *Cities, Regions, and Public Policy* (Edinburgh: Oliver & Boyd, 1973), pp. 271-74.

38. Peter Hall, *The Theory and Practice of Regional Planning* (London: Pemberton Books, 1970), p. 64.

39. David Eversley, address to conference at the Lincoln Institute of Land Use Policy, Cambridge, Mass., June 30, 1976.

40. J. D. McCallum, "U.K. Regional Policy 1964-72," p. 296.

41. David Eversley, address to conference of the Lincoln Institute of Land Use Policy, Cambridge, Mass., June 30, 1976.

42. Anne Lapping, "London's Burning! London's Burning! A Survey," *The Economist,* January 1, 1977, pp. 17, 20.

43. *Sunday Times* (London), January 11, 1976.

44. Peter Self, *The Econocrats and the Policy Process: The Politics and Philosophy of Cost-Benefit Analysis* (London: Macmillan, 1975), p. 191.

45. Devon Conservation Forum, *Urbanization in Devon,* pp. 30-31.

46. Patrick McAuslan, *Land, Law and Planning* (London: Weidenfeld and Nicholson, 1975), p. 233.

47. *Planning Bulletin* (London), September 23, 1977.

48. George Dobry, *Review of the Development Control System* (London: Her Majesty's Stationery Office, February 1975), p. 94.

49. English Tourist Board, *Tourism and Conservation: Report of a One-Day Conference* (London: English Tourist Board, 1974), p. 25.

50. *Planning Bulletin,* September 23, 1977. See George Dobry, "Testimony Before the Expenditure Committee, Environmental Subcommittee, House of Commons, June 9, 1976" (London: Her Majesty's Stationery Office, 1976), p. 26.

51. Neal Allison Roberts, *The Reform of Planning Law* (London: Macmillan, 1976), p. 191.

52. J. Brian McLoughlin, *Control and Urban Planning* (London: Faber & Faber, 1973), p. 155.

53. Lutz Luithlen, "Structure and Local Plans," *Built Environment Quarterly* (London), vol. 2 (June 1976), p. 163.

54. Patrick McAuslan, *Land, Law and Planning,* pp. 361-62.

55. Alice Coleman, "Land Use Planning, Success or Failure," *Architects' Journal,* vol. 165 (January 19, 1977), p. 109.

56. Gordon E. Cherry, *The Evolution of British Town Planning,* p. 183.

57. Patrick McAuslan, *Land, Law and Planning,* p. 243.

58. George Dobry, "Testimony Before the Expenditure Committee, Environmental Subcommittee, House of Commons, June 6, 1976," p. 38.

59. Allen V. Kneese and Charles L. Schultze, *Pollution, Prices, and Public Policy* (Washington: The Brookings Institution, 1975), p. 2.

60. William J. Baumol and Wallace E. Oates, "The Use of Standards and Prices for the Protection of the Environment," *Swedish Journal of Economics,* vol. 73 (March 1971). See Ralph W. Johnson and Gardner M. Brown, Jr., *Cleaning Up Europe's Waters: Economics, Management and Policies* (New York: Praeger, 1976).

61. Fred P. Bosselman, *Alternatives to Urban Sprawl* (Washington: Government Printing Office, 1968), p. 7.

62. John H. Noble, *A Proposed System for Regulating Land Use in Urbanizing Counties* (Chicago: American Society of Planning Officials, 1967), p. 26.

63. William K. Reilly, ed., *The Use of Land: A Citizens' Policy Guide to Urban Growth* (New York: Thomas Y. Crowell, 1973), p. 248. See also Donald Priest, ed., *Large Scale Development* (Washington: Urban Land Institute, 1977).

64. E. F. Schumacher, *Small Is Beautiful: Economics As If People Mattered* (New York: Harper & Row, 1973), p. 33.
65. Ann Louise Strong, *Planned Urban Environments*, p. 241.
66. Norman Taylor, ed., *Taylor's Encyclopedia of Gardening, Horticulture and Landscape Design*, 4th ed. (Boston: Houghton Mifflin Company, 1961), p. 759.
67. M. E. Pufendorff, *A Dissertation Upon the Druids*, trans. Edmund Goldsmith (Edinburgh: Bibliotheca Curiosa, 1887), p. 41.

Bavaria: Mad Ludwig's Backyard

1. *Newsweek* (European Edition), June 30, 1975, p. 36. Germans were the largest block of tourists in such far-flung countries as Turkey, Iceland, and Yugoslavia. See Organisation for Economic Co-operation and Development, *Tourism Policy and International Tourism in OECD Member Countries* (Paris: OECD, 1977), appendices.
2. Bayerische Staatsregierung, *Program Freizeit und Erholung* (Munich: 1973).
3. Wilfrid Blunt, *The Dream King: Ludwig II of Bavaria* (New York: Viking Press, 1970), p. 167.
4. Jost Krippendorf, *Die Landschaftsfresser* (Bern: Hallwag Press, 1975), p. 136.
5. Ibid., pp. 67-68.

Australia: Rediscovering the Bush

1. Clair Wagner, *Rural Retreats: Urban Investments in Rural Land For Residential Purposes* (Canberra: Department of Urban and Regional Development, 1975), p. 45.
2. A. S. Fogg, *Australia Town Planning Law, Uniformity and Change* (Brisbane: University of Queensland Press, 1974), p. 11.
3. A. J. Brown and H. M. Sherrard, *An Introduction to Town and Country Planning*, rev. ed., with J. H. Shaw (Sydney: Angus & Robertson, 1969), pp. 29-30.
4. A commission of inquiry established by the national government made similar complaints about the slow processing of, as well as lack of public participation in, planning decisions, not only in New South Wales but in other states. See Commission of Inquiry into Land Tenures, *Final Report* (Canberra: Australian Government Publishing Service, 1974), pp. 39-41.
6. A. S. Fogg, *Australian Town Planning Law, Uniformity and Change*, p. 66.

CHAPTER 6   The Coast in Sickness and in Health (pp. 151-180)

1. Colin Bell and Rose Bell, *City Fathers: The Early History of Town Planning in Britain* (London: Penguin, 1972), p. 109.
2. Donald E. Lundberg, "A New Look in Social Tourism," *The Cornell Hotel and Restaurant Administration Quarterly*, vol. 13, no. 3 (November 1972), p. 65.
3. Elizabeth Stone, *Chronicles of Fashion* (London: Richard Bentley, 1845), vol. 2, p. 27.
4. H. Robinson, *A Geography of Tourism* (London: Macdonald & Evans, 1976), p. 161.
5. R. Klopper, "Physical Planning and Tourism in the Federal Republic of Germany," a paper prepared for the Symposium on the Planning and Development of the Tourist Industry in the ECE Region, Dubrovnik, October 13-18, 1975, p. 2.
6. Gutachtergruppe Sylt, *Gutachten zur Struktur und Entwicklung der Insel Sylt* (Kiel: 1974), sec. I, 1.3.
7. Ibid.
8. Ibid., Sec. II.1.
9. *Die Zeit*, July 30, 1971.

10. *Der Spiegel,* August 23, 1971.

11. Ministry of the Interior, State of Schleswig-Holstein, *Regional Plan for the North Sea Islands* (Kiel: 1967). English translation by Eastern Tin.

12. See H. Bruns, *Sylt: Natur, Erholung, Forschung, Lehre, Umweltbelastung, Inselplanning und Bürgerinitiative* (Wiesbaden: Biologie-Verlag, 1977).

13. Gutachtergruppe Sylt, *Gutachten zur Struktur und Entwicklung der Insel Sylt,* Sec. I, 91.

14. Ministry of the Interior, State of Schleswig-Holstein, *Regional Plan for Planning Area 5 of the State of Schleswig-Holstein* (Kiel: 1975), secs. 9, 2.1 and 10.6. English translation by Eastern Tin.

15. Ibid., sec. 10.6.

16. Norman Wengert, "Land Use Planning and Control in the German Federal Republic," *Natural Resources Journal,* vol. 15 (1975), p. 511.

17. R. A. J. Walling, *The West Country* (New York: William Morrow & Company, 1935), p. 129.

18. J. T. White, *The History of Torquay* (Torquay: Directory Company, 1878), p. 226.

19. John R. Pike, *Brixham, Torbay: A Bibliographic Guide* (Borough of Torbay: 1973), p. 5.

20. In his recently published diaries Richard Crossman, who headed the planning ministry when the consolidation took place, describes his motive as "trying to end the miserable parochialism and incompetence of the three little local councils. . . ." Richard Crossman, *The Diaries of a Cabinet Minister* (London: Hamish Hamilton and Jonathan Cape, 1975), vol. 1, p. 429. Other commentators have suggested that the consolidation of local governments was primarily motivated by the desire to make life administratively simpler for the central government. Peter Self, *The Econocrats and the Policy Process: The Politics and Philosophy of Cost-Benefit Analysis* (London: Macmillan, 1975), p. 191.

21. *Torbay Times* (England), May 14, 1976.

22. Ibid.

23. William George Hoskins, *Devon* (London: Collins, 1954), p. 6.

24. John Betjeman, *Collected Poems,* 3rd ed. (London: John Murray, 1970), p. 180.

25. *Torbay News* (England), November 26, 1976.

26. Sheila Hardaway, *The Charm of Torquay* (Torbay: Meadfoot-Wellsworth Area Residents Association, 1973), p. 1.

27. Neal Alison Roberts, *The Reform of Planning Law* (London: Macmillan, 1976), p. 188.

28. See Richard Crossman, *The Diaries of a Cabinet Minister,* vol. 1, pp. 430, 622.

29. *Torbay News* (England), June 18, 1976.

30. William Tucker, "Environmentalism and the Leisure Class," *Harper's* (December 1977), pp. 49, 79.

31. Neal Alison Roberts, *The Reform of Planning Law,* p. 232.

32. George Young, *Tourism: Blessing or Blight?* (London: Penguin, 1973), p. 120.

33. Theodore Roszak, *Where the Wasteland Ends* (New York: Anchor Books, 1969), p. 243.

34. Anthony James Catanese, *Planners and Local Politics: Impossible Dreams* (Beverly Hills: Sage Publications, 1974), p. 161.

35. Patrick McAuslan, *Land, Law and Planning* (London: Weidenfeld and Nicolson, 1975), p. 402.

36. René Dubos, *So Human an Animal* (New York: Charles Scribner's Sons, 1968), p. vii.

CHAPTER 7   The Ancient Lights of London   (pp. 183-198)

1. See George Lefcoe, "The Neighborhood Defenders," *U.C.L.A. Law Review,* vol. 23 (1976), p. 823.

2. Robert Ellickson, "Alternatives to Zoning: Covenants, Nuisance Rules, and Fines as

Land Use Controls," *University of Chicago Law Review,* vol. 40 (1973), p. 681.

3. Warren Burger, "The Direction of the Administration of Justice," *American Bar Association Journal,* vol. 62 (1976), p. 727.

4. James Kent, *Commentaries of American Law,* O. W. Holmes, Jr., ed., 12th ed. (Boston: Little, Brown & Co., 1873), vol. 3, p. 448.

5. William Blackstone, *Commentaries on the Laws of England,* W. D. Jones, ed. (San Francisco: Bancroft-Whitney Co., 1916), vol. 2, pp. 216-17. For a modern commentary see Daniel P. Moskowitz, "Legal Access to Light: The Solar Energy Imperative," *Natural Resources Lawyer,* vol. 9 (1976), p. 185.

6. James Kent, *Commentaries on American Law,* p. 448.

7. *Cherry* v. *Stein,* 11 Md. 1, 21 (1858).

8. Morton Horwitz, *The Transformation of American Law, 1780-1860* (Cambridge, Mass.: Harvard University Press, 1977), p. 31.

9. A. Dan Tarlock, "A Comment on Meyers' Introduction to Environmental Thought," *Indiana Law Journal,* vol. 50 (1975), p. 463.

10. Morton Horwitz, *The Transformation of American Law, 1780-1860,* p. 31. See also Paul M. Kurtz, "Nineteenth Century Anti-Entrepreneurial Nuisance Injunctions—Avoiding the Chancellor," *William and Mary Law Review,* vol. 17 (1976), p. 621.

11. Geoffrey Little, "Some Facets of the Amenity Concept," *Journal of Planning and Environmental Law* (May 1976), p. 277.

12. "Cashing In On The Golden Horde," *The Economist,* September 3, 1977, p. 90.

13. British Tourist Authority, *Survey Among Visitors to London* (London: British Tourist Authority, 1974).

14. London Tourist Board, *London Tourist Statistics 1973* (London: London Tourist Board, 1974), p. 9. See also David Eversley, "The Ganglion of Tourism: An Unreasonable Problem for London?" *The London Journal,* vol. 3 (1977), p. 186.

15. English Tourist Board, *The Hotel Development Incentives Scheme in England* (London: English Tourist Board, 1977).

16. "Hotels: Inquest on a Defeat," *Architectural Review,* vol. 152 (September 1972), p. 132.

17. Greater London Council, *Tourism and Hotels in London* (London: Greater London Council, 1971), p. 1.

18. William Blake, "Jerusalem," *Poems and Prophecies* (London: J. M. Dent & Sons, 1975), p. 173.

19. Anthony Haden-Guest, *The Paradise Program* (New York: William Morrow & Company, 1973), p. 142. See also Ada Louise Huxtable, *Will They Ever Finish Bruckner Boulevard?* (New York: Macmillan, 1970), p. 135.

20. Donald G. Hagman, "The Greater London Development Plan Inquiry," *Journal of the American Institute of Planners,* vol. 37 (September 1971), pp. 290-97.

21. See Nerina Shute, *London Villages* (London: R. Hale, 1977).

22. Central London Planning Conference, *An Advisory Plan for Central London* (London: Her Majesty's Stationery Office, 1976) para. 6.4.

23. See James L. Sundquist, *Dispersing Population: What America Can Learn From Europe* (Washington: The Brookings Institution, 1975), pp. 37-90.

24. David Eversley, "Comment: The Inner Area Studies," *Built Environment Quarterly,* vol. 3 (September 1977), p. 172. The population of greater London is now below 7,000,000 for the first time in 70 years. *The Times* (London), August 3, 1978.

25. *Municipal Journal,* October 28, 1977. See, generally, Department of the Environment, *Policy for the Inner Cities* (London: Her Majesty's Stationery Office, June 1977); Graeme Shankland, Peter Wilmott, and David Jordan, *Inner London: Policies for Dispersal and Balance: Final Report of the Lambeth Inner Area Study* (London: Her Majesty's Stationery Office, 1977).

26. Richard Crossman, *Diaries of a Cabinet Minister* (London: Hamish Hamilton and

Jonathan Cape, 1975), vol. 1, p. 623.

27. Quoted in Philip Rahv, *Discovery of Europe, The Story of American Experience in the Old World* (Boston: Houghton Mifflin Company, 1947), p. 276.

CHAPTER 8   The Ancient Lights of Japan   (pp. 199-213)

1. Warren Burger, "The Direction of the Administration of Justice," *American Bar Association Journal*, vol. 62 (1976), p. 727.
2. Isaiah Ben-Dasan, *The Japanese and the Jews* (New York: Weatherhill, 1972), p. 43.
3. Takematsu Okada, "The Climate of Japan and Its Influences on the Japanese People," in Kokusai-Bunka-Shinkokai, ed., *Readings In Japanese Culture* (Tokyo: Sanseido Company, 1937), pp. 171, 183.
4. Jichi Kenshu Kyoka, *Local Government System in Japan* (Tokyo: Ministry of Home Affairs, 1973), p. 44.
5. Ikumi Hoshino, "Housing and Urban Design in Tokyo," a paper delivered at a conference on New York and Tokyo, November 24, 1975 (New York: Japan Society, 1975), p. 9.
6. Kazuo Hayakawa, "Housing and the Quality of Life," *Built Environment Quarterly*, vol. 4 (March 1978), pp. 23-24.
7. Nakamura Hajime, "Basic Features of the Legal, Political and Economic Thoughts of Japan," in Charles A. Moore, ed., *The Japanese Mind: Essentials of Japanese Policy and Culture* (Honolulu: East-West Center Press, 1973), pp. 143, 145. See also Ezra F. Vogel, *Japan's New Middle Class: The Salary Man and His Family in a Tokyo Suburb* (Berkeley: University of California Press, 1963), p. 97.
8. Takeyoshi Kawashima, "The Status of the Individual in the Notion of Law, Right and Social Order in Japan," in Charles A. Moore, ed., *The Japanese Mind: Essentials of Japanese Policy and Culture* (Honolulu: East-West Center Press, 1973), p. 263.
9. F. G. Notehelfer, "Japan's First Pollution Incident," *Journal of Japanese Studies*, vol. 2 (1975), p. 382.
10. George B. Sansom, *The Western World and Japan* (New York: Alfred A. Knopf, 1951), p. 447.
11. K. Asakawa, "Notes on Village Government in Japan After 1600," *Journal of the American Oriental Society*, vol. 13 (1910), p. 266.
12. Melvin Aron Eisenberg, "Private Ordering Through Negotiation: Dispute-settlement and Rulemaking," *Harvard Law Review*, vol. 89 (1976), p. 646.
13. Takeyoshi Kawashima, "Dispute Resolution in Contemporary Japan," in Arthur T. Von Mehren, ed., *Law In Japan: The Legal Order In A Changing Society* (Cambridge, Mass.: Harvard University Press, 1963), p. 51.
14. Frank Gibney, *Japan: The Fragile Superpower* (New York: W. W. Norton & Company, 1975), p. 92.
15. Takeyoshi Kawashima, "Dispute Resolution in Contemporary Japan," p. 50.
16. See Dan Fenno Henderson, *Conciliation and Japanese Law: Tokugawa and Modern* (Seattle: University of Washington Press, 1965), p. 241.
17. Zbigniew Brzezinski, *The Fragile Blossom: Crisis and Change in Japan* (New York: Harper & Row, 1972), p. 9.
18. Tadashi Fukutake, *Japanese Society Today* (Tokyo: University of Tokyo Press, 1974), p. 116.
19. Norie Huddle and Michael Reich, with Nahum Stiskin, *Island of Dreams: Environmental Crisis in Japan* (Tokyo: Autumn Press, 1975), p. 117. See also F. G. Notehelfer, "Japan's First Pollution Incident," p. 366. A recent American visitor to Japan expressed surprise that, after settling into an apartment next to a new bank under construction, he was

visited by a bank officer with a gift of a case of Pepsi-Cola. Wilbur M. Fridell, "Tokyo Pollution Firsthand: Present Reality and Future Prospects," *The East* (Tokyo), vol. 12, no. 6 (August 1976), p. 89.

20. See Norie Huddle, Michael Reich, with Nahum Stiskin, *Island of Dreams*, p. 143.
21. Jun Ui, "The Singularities of Japanese Pollution," *Japan Quarterly*, vol. 19 (July-September 1972), pp. 286-87.
22. See Dan Fenno Henderson, *Conciliation and Japanese Law: Tokugawa and Modern*, p. 241.
23. Julian Gresser, "The 1973 Japanese Law for the Compensation of Pollution-related Health Damage: An Introductory Assessment," *Environmental Law Reporter*, vol. 5 (December 1975), pp. 502-3.
24. Takeyoshi Kawashima, "Dispute Resolution in Contemporary Japan," p. 43.
25. See Frank K. Upham, "Litigation and Moral Consciousness in Japan: An Interpretive Analysis of Four Japanese Pollution Suits," *Law and Society Review*, vol. 10 (1976), p. 579.
26. Yoshihiro Nomura, "Japan's Pollution Litigations," a paper prepared for the International Congress of Scientists on the Human Environment, Kyoto, November 1975, p. 16.
27. Yoshihiro Nomura, "The Place of Environmental Assessment Duty in Environmental Litigation in Japan," a paper prepared for the International Congress of Scientists on the Human Environment, Kyoto, November 1975, p. 5. Litigation was also discouraged by the traditional unwillingness of the courts to consider anything equivalent to a class action. See Hajime Nito, "A Legal Right to Environmental Quality," a paper prepared for the International Congress of Scientists on the Human Environment, Kyoto, November 1975, p. 7.
28. Ibid., p. 17.
29. Julian Gresser, "A Japan Center on Human Environmental Problems," *Ecology Law Quarterly*, vol. 3 (1973), p. 764.
30. Japan Federal Bar Association, *Environmental Protection and the Role of Lawyers* (Tokyo: 1975), p. 16.
31. See Kazuaki Sono and Yasuhiro Fujioka, "The Role of the Abuse of Right Doctrine in Japan," *Louisiana Law Review*, vol. 35 (1975), p. 1,037.
32. Zbigniew Brzezinski, *The Fragile Blossom: Crisis and Change in Japan*, p. 16.
33. See Mitchio Nishihara, "The Relationship Between Judicial and Administration Techniques in the Control of Pollution," unpublished paper, (Kobe, Japan, 1975), p. 3.
34. Environment Agency (Japan), *The Quality of Environment in Japan, 1977* (Tokyo: 1977), pp. 189-90.
35. Ibid, p. 223. See also Organisation for Economic Cooperation and Development, *Environmental Policies in Japan* (Paris: OECD, 1977), pp. 42-49.
36. Julian Gresser, "The 1973 Japanese Law for the Compensation of Pollution-related Health Damages," p. 504-5.
37. See John Frisch, "Japan's Contribution to Modern Anthropology," in Joseph Roggendorf, ed., *Studies In Japanese Culture* (Tokyo: Sophia University, 1963), p. 225; Masao Watanabe, "The Conception of Nature in Japanese Culture," *Science*, vol. 182 (January 25, 1974), p. 279.

CHAPTER 9 A Park Is a State of Mind   (pp. 217-238)

1. Edwin O. Reischauer, *The Japanese* (Cambridge, Mass.: Harvard University Press, Belknap Press, 1977), p. 148.
2. John Frisch, "Japan's Contribution to Modern Anthropology," in Joseph Roggendorf, ed., *Studies In Japanese Culture* (Tokyo: Sophia University, 1963), p. 225.

3. Masao Watanabe, "The Conception of Nature in Japanese Culture," *Science*, vol. 182 (January 25, 1974), p. 279.

4. Kazuyuki Hibino, "Tokyo: The Overcrowded Megalopolis," *Japan Quarterly*, vol. 20 (April-June 1973), pp. 206-7. "Oriental civilizations give lip service to the holiness of nature," says René Dubos, "but in practice they . . . pollute their environments at least as ruthlessly as do Western civilizations." René Dubos, *A God Within* (New York: Charles Scribner's Sons, 1972), p. 204.

5. Yoshiro Hoshino, "Remodeling the Archipelago," *Japan Quarterly*, vol. 20 (January-March 1973), p. 39. The size and population of the Tokkaido corridor are approximately equal to the Boston-Washington corridor. John W. Bennett and Solomon B. Levine, "Industrialization and Social Deprivation: Welfare, Environment, and the Postindustrial Society in Japan," in Hugh Patrick, ed., *Japanese Industrialization and Its Social Consequences* (Berkeley: University of California Press, 1976), p. 468.

6. Paul Theroux, *The Great Railway Bazaar: By Train Through Asia* (New York: Ballantine Books, 1975), p. 289.

7. David W. Plath, *The After Hours: Modern Japan and the Search for Enlightenment* (Berkeley, University of California Press, 1964), p. 134.

8. The idea that parents and children should vacation together is beginning to catch on. A 1968 survey found that some 45 percent of Japanese men preferred vacationing with their families, while 44 percent still preferred the traditional vacation with fellow workers. Since then, the ratio of family vacations has undoubtedly increased. Takeshi Ishida, *Japanese Society* (New York: Random House, 1971), p. 104.

9. Pierre Pfeffer, *Asia: A Natural History* (New York: Random House, 1968), p. 60.

10. Donald R. Kelley, Kenneth R. Stunkel, and Richard R. Wescott, *The Economic Superpowers and the Environment* (San Francisco: W. H. Freeman & Co., 1976), p. 252.

11. *Mainichi Times*, July 30, 1976.

12. *Mainichi Times*, July 6, 1976.

13. The national parks are complemented by "quasi-national" and "prefectural natural" parks, all administered as part of the national park system. In total these occupy 13.6 percent of the country's land area. Environment Agency (Japan), *The Quality of Environment in Japan, 1977* (Tokyo: 1977), p. 198.

14. Although the extent of the constitutional authority of the U.S. federal government to control land adjacent to national parks is unclear, some commentators have urged that similar powers be exercised. The Conservation Foundation, *National Parks for the Future* (Washington, D.C.: The Conservation Foundation, 1972), p. 21. See also Joseph L. Sax, "National Parks: Sleeping Giants," *Michigan Law Review*, vol. 75 (1976), p. 239. Cf., Donald Hagman, "Planning and Regulatory Acquisition," in Donald Hagman and Dean J. Misczynski, eds., *Windfalls for Wipeouts: Land Value Capture and Compensation* (Chicago: American Society of Planning Officials, 1978), pp. 246-47, 249-50.

15. David R. Bruns, "The National Parks System of Japan," a paper prepared for the U.S. National Park Service, July 1975, p. 9.

16. Environment Agency (Japan), *The Quality of the Environment in Japan, 1977* (Tokyo: 1977), p. 200.

17. F. Fraser Darling and Noel D. Eichhorn, *Man and Nature in the National Parks: Reflections on Policy* (Washington, D.C.: The Conservation Foundation, 1967), p. 49.

18. Peter F. Drucker, *Men, Ideas, and Politics* (New York: Harper & Row, 1971), p. 205.

19. Muneshige Narazaki, *Hokusai: The Thirty-Six Views of Mt. Fuji*, trans. John Bester, Masterworks of Ukiyo-E Series, vol. 3 (New York: Kodansha International, 1968), p. 26.

20. Russell Connor, *Hokusai* (New York: Crown Publishers, 1962), p. 15.

21. William Wordsworth, *A Guide Through the District of the Lakes* (New York: Greenwood Press, 1968), p. 109.

22. Roger Bush, *The National Parks of England and Wales* (London: J. M. Dent & Sons, 1973), pp. 56-57.

23. William Wordsworth, *A Guide Through The District of the Lakes,* p. 96. For an interesting discussion of the writing of the guide, see Norman Nicholson, *The Lakers: The Adventures of the First Tourists* (London: Robert Hale, 1955).

24. William Wordsworth, *A Guide Through the District of the Lakes,* p. 97.

25. Aldous Huxley, "Wordsworth in the Tropics," *Yale Review,* vol. 18, (Summer 1929), p. 672.

26. William Wordsworth, *A Guide Through The District of the Lakes,* p. 127.

27. Robin Fedden, *The National Trust: Past and Present,* rev. ed. (London: Jonathan Cape, 1974), p. 102.

28. John Dower, *National Parks in England and Wales* (London: Her Majesty's Stationery Office, 1945), p. 6.

29. See Mervyn Bell, ed., *Britain's National Parks* (London: David & Charles, 1975), pp. 8-10; Roger Bush, *The National Parks of England and Wales,* pp. 55-67.

30. John Dower, *National Parks in England and Wales,* p. 45.

31. Peter Hall, Harry Gracey, Roy Drewett, and Ray Thomas, *The Containment of Urban England* (London: George Allen & Unwin, 1973), vol. 2, p. 374.

32. John Dower, *National Parks in England and Wales,* p. 19.

33. Warren A. Johnson, *Public Parks on Private Land in England and Wales* (Baltimore: Johns Hopkins Press, 1971), p. 102. See also John T. Starr, "The Green and Pleasant Land," *American Forests,* January 1978, pp. 38, 52.

34. C. H. D. Acland, "Lake District," in Mervyn Bell, ed., *Britain's National Parks,* p. 98.

35. See Exmoor National Park Committee, *Exmoor National Park Plan* (Somerset: Exmoor House, 1977), ch. 3. Economic pressures to modernize and expand agricultural operations have created conflicts with conservationists. See Christopher Hall, "More Public Discussion Wanted for Farm Grants," *Council for the Protection of Rural England Quarterly Bulletin,* vol. 10, no. 2 (1978), p. 2.

36. Quoted in William Rollinson, *A History of Man in the Lake District* (London: J. M. Dent & Sons, 1967), p. 149. See also Council for the Protection of Rural England, *Annual Report 1977,* 1978, pp. 13, 16.

37. C. H. D. Acland, "Lake District," p. 102.

38. "Dartmoor, A Report by Lady Sharp, C. B. E., to the Secretary of State for the Environment and the Secretary of State for Defense, of a public local inquiry held in December, 1975, and May, 1976, into the continued use of Dartmoor for training purposes" (London: Her Majesty's Stationery Office, 1977), p. 80.

39. Michael Dower, "National Parks, Three Paces Forward, March!" *Town and Country Planning,* vol. 44 (March 1976), p. 152.

40. Countryside Commission, *Ninth Report of the Countryside Commission, 1975-76* (London: Her Majesty's Stationery Office, 1977).

41. See Christopher Hall, "Is Compromise the Cure-all for Britain's Park System," *Planning* (U.S.), vol. 44, no. 3 (March 1978), p. 27.

42. See Jon A. Kusler and William Duddleson, "Alternative Federal Strategies for Strengthening State and Local Urban Outdoor Recreation and Open Space Programs Including the Establishment of Greenline Parks," National Urban Recreation Study Technical Reports, vol. 1, pt. B (Washington, D.C.: U.S. Department of the Interior, 1978), p. 62.

43. Jon A. Kusler, *Public/Private Parks and Management of Private Lands for Park Protection* (Madison, Wis.: University of Wisconsin Institute of Environmental Studies, 1974), p. 68. In addition, 1968 saw the inauguration of a system of Wild and Scenic Rivers, some of which also combine fee acquisition and regulatory techniques. See 16 U.S.C.A. Ch. 28 (1974).

44. Article 27, secs. 800-810, McKinney's Revised Statutes of New York (1971).

45. Public Law 91-148, 83 Stat. 360 (1969).

46. Charles E. Little, *Green-line Parks: An Approach to Preserving Recreational Landscapes In Urban Areas* (Washington, D.C.: Congressional Research Service, Library of Congress, 1975). See also J. William Futrell, "Parks to the People: New Directions for the National Park System," *Emory Law Journal,* vol. 25 (1976), p. 255.

47. See Warren A. Johnson, *Public Parks on Private Land In England and Wales;* Jon A. Kusler, *Public/Private Parks and Management of Private Lands for Park Protection.*

48. Department of the Interior, news release, May 5, 1978.

49. H.R. 12536, 95th Congress, 2nd session (1978).

50. Among other bills under consideration is a generic bill to create mixed public-private parks, introduced by Senators Williams and Case of New Jersey. S. 2306, 95th Congress, 1st session (1977).

51. Joe Hloucha, *Hokusai: The Man Mad-on-Drawing* (Prague: Artia, 1955), p. 37.

52. Ibid., p. 43.

CHAPTER 10   A Lake in Galilee, and Other Special Places   (pp. 239-258)

1. See René Dubos, *A God Within* (New York: Charles Scribner's Sons, 1972), pp. 132-33. See also Ian L. McHarg, *Design With Nature* (Garden City, N.Y.: Natural History Press, 1969), p. 196, and Kenneth Boulding, "Economics and Ecology," in F. Fraser Darling and John P. Milton, eds., *Future Environments of North America* (Garden City, N.Y.: Natural History Press, 1966), p. 232. For an even stronger position see John Passmore, *Man's Responsibility for Nature* (New York: Charles Scribner's Sons, 1974), p. 179.

2. René Dubos, *A God Within,* pp. 22-23.

3. Lawrence Durrell, *Spirit of Place: Letters and Essays on Travel,* Alan G. Thomas, ed. (New York: E. P. Dutton, 1969), p. 158.

4. See Kevin Lynch, *Managing the Sense of a Region* (Cambridge, Mass.: MIT Press, 1976), p. 71; Clare A. Gunn, *Vacationscape: Designing Tourist Regions* (Austin, Texas: University of Texas, Bureau of Business Research, 1972), p. 142.

5. Mark Sagoff, "On Preserving the Natural Environment," *Yale Law Journal,* vol. 84 (1974), p. 205.

6. René Dubos, *A God Within,* pp. 22-23.

7. "Lines Composed Above Tintern Abbey," in Thomas Hutchinson, ed., *The Poetical Works of Wordsorth* (London: Oxford University Press, 1936), p. 164. See also Christopher Salvesen, *The Landscape of Memory: A Study of Wordsworth's Poetry* (Lincoln: University of Nebraska Press, 1965), pp. 158-60.

8. See Robert Allen, "Sustainable Development and Cultural Diversity—Two Sides of the Same Coin," *IUCN Bulletin,* New Series, vol. 6, no. 4 (April 1975), p. 13.

9. Sarah Merrill, *Galilee in the Time of Christ* (Oxford: The Religious Tract Society, 1898), p. 26.

10. Mark Twain, *The Innocents Abroad* (New York: Harper & Brothers, 1869), vol. 2, p. 267.

11. Ibid., pp. 272-73.

12. John 21: 6

13. Ernest W. G. Masterman, *Studies in Galilee* (Chicago: University of Chicago Press, 1909), p. 37.

14. Ann Louise Strong, *Planned Urban Environments* (Baltimore: The John Hopkins Press, 1971), p. 161; Jacob Dash, "Physical Planning in the State of Israel," a paper presented at the Third World Congress of Engineers and Architects in Israel, Tel Aviv, 1973, p. 13.

15. Robin Dower and Adrian Stungo, *Regional Planning and Housing in Israel* (London: Anglo-Israel Association, 1965), p. 16.

16. Efriam Orni and Elisha Efrat, *Geography of Israel,* 3rd ed. (Jerusalem: Israel Universities

Press, 1971), p. 88.

17. Haim Drabkin-Darin, *Housing in Israel: Economic and Social Aspects* (Tel Aviv: Gadish Books, 1957), p. 76.

18. *Jerusalem Post*, August 15, 1976.

19. Israel Ministry of Tourism, *Kinneret Tourism Development Project* (Jerusalem: 1973).

20. Ibid.

21. Ibid.

22. Efriam Orni and Elisha Efrat, *Geography in Israel*, p. 88.

23. Yehuda Karmon, *Israel: A Regional Geography* (London: Wiley-Interscience, 1971), p. 163.

24. Ibid., p. 122.

25. Valerie Brachya and Paulette Mandelbaum, *Settlement in Israel* (Jerusalem: Environmental Protection Service, 1976), p. 31.

26. Thomas Wright, ed., *Early Travels in Palestine* (London: Henry G. Bohn, 1848), p. 47.

27. Mark Twain, *The Innocents Abroad*, vol. 2, pp. 264-65.

28. *Jerusalem Post*, June 6, 1976.

29. R. J. Davis, *Investigation of the Pollution Problem of the Lake Kinneret*, Report to the Water Commissioner, State of Israel (Jerusalem: 1971), vol. 1, p. 9.

30. Ibid., vol. 2, p. 11; vol. 3, pp. 35-36.

31. Edward Relph, *Place and Placelessness* (London: Pion Ltd., 1976), p. 79.

32. René Dubos, *A God Within*, p. 134.

33. Edward Relph, *Place and Placelessness*, pp. 82, 121.

34. *Ibid.*, pp. 87-89. See also George Lefcoe, "When Governments Become Land Developers: Notes on the Public-sector Experience in the Netherlands and California," *Southern California Law Review*, vol. 51 (1978), pp. 165, 233, 240-41.

35. Edward Relph, *Place and Placelessness*, p. 87. See also Garrett Eckbo, "The Landscape of Tourism" *Landscape*, vol. 18, no. 2 (Spring-Summer 1969), pp. 29-31.

36. Daniel Boorstin, *The Image, Or What Happened To The American Dream* (New York: Atheneum, 1962), pp. 114-17. See also Susan Sontag, *On Photography* (New York: Farrar, Straus & Giroux, 1977), p. 9; Earl Pomeroy, *In Search of the Golden West: The Tourist in Western America* (New York: Alfred A. Knopf, 1957), pp. 222-25.

37. Erik Cohen, "Toward a Sociology of International Tourism," *Social Research*, vol. 39 (1972), p. 164.

38. See Dean MacCannell, *The Tourist: A New Theory of the Leisure Class* (New York: Schocken Books, 1976), pp. 175-77.

39. See George Young, *Tourism: Blessing or Blight?* (London: Penguin, 1973), p. 141; Arthur Haulot, *Tourisme et Environnement: La Recherche d'un Equilibre* (Marabout: Verviers, 1974), pp. 208-9; Gerardo Budowski, "Tourism and Environmental Conservation: Conflict, Coexistence or Symbiosis," *Environmental Conservation*, vol. 3 (Spring 1976), p. 27; Paul Shepard, *Man In the Landscape: A Historic View of the Esthetics of Nature* (New York: Alfred A. Knopf, 1967), pp. 154-56.

40. Selwyn Gurney Champion, *Racial Proverbs* (New York: Barnes & Nóble, 1964), p. 470.

41. Gertrude Stein, *What Are Masterpieces?* (New York: Pitman, 1940), pp. 61-62.

42. René Dubos, *Beast or Angel: Choices That Make Us Human* (New York: Charles Scribner's Sons, 1974), p. 191. Charles Darwin is a classic example of a person whose most creative work grew out of his travels. See Jacques Barzun, *Darwin, Marx, Wagner: Critique of a Heritage*, rev. ed. (New York: Doubleday, 1958). For another long-ignored but very perceptive example see Herman Melville, *Clarel* (New York: Hendricks House, 1960).

43. I Chronicles 29:15.

44. Barbara Ward and René Dubos, *Only One Earth* (New York: W. W. Norton and Company, 1972), p. 220.

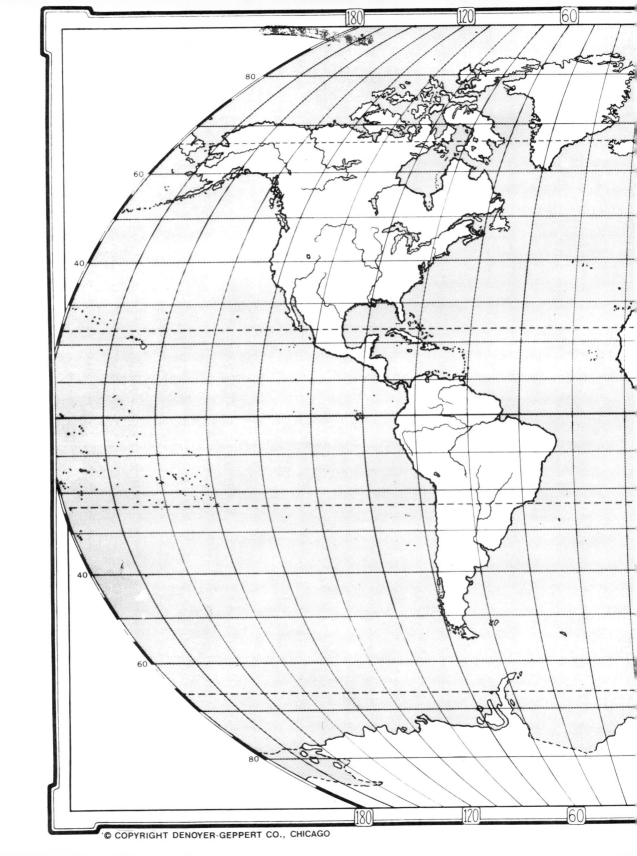

© COPYRIGHT DENOYER-GEPPERT CO., CHICAGO